The Nature of Law

European Studies in Law

Volume 9

General Editor

A. G. Chloros

M. A. (Oxon), LL. D. (London)
Professor of Comparative Law
Director, Centre of European Law
King's College
University of London

NORTH-HOLLAND PUBLISHING COMPANY
AMSTERDAM • NEW YORK • OXFORD

The Nature of Law

by

Thomas Glyn Watkin

B.C.L., M.A. (Oxon) of the Middle Temple

Barrister-at-Law

Lecturer in Law

University College, Cardiff

1980

NORTH-HOLLAND PUBLISHING COMPANY
AMSTERDAM • NEW YORK • OXFORD

ISBN: 0 444 85422 3

Publishers:
NORTH-HOLLAND PUBLISHING COMPANY
AMSTERDAM • NEW YORK • OXFORD

Sole distributors for the U.S.A. and Canada:
ELSEVIER NORTH-HOLLAND, INC.
52 VANDERBILT AVENUE, NEW YORK, N.Y. 10017

Cover design:
The illustration of Europa, "the wide-eyed one", running behind Zeus (her husband) transfigured as a bull, is taken from a bell-crater in Corneto (Tarquinia), Italy.

PRINTED IN THE NETHERLANDS

For
my mother
and
my father

PREFACE

The ideas presented in this volume first came to me shortly before the start of my last session as an undergraduate at Pembroke College, Oxford, where I was privileged to be tutored by Mr. J.M. Eekelaar. They developed slowly during the course of that session and the following year when I was studying for the degree of Bachelor of Civil Law. I did not, however, have the opportunity to bring them to fruition until I became a lecturer in the Department of Law at University College, Cardiff, since when I have been able to devote two entire summers to research into them and a third to committing them to paper. I wish to thank Professors L.A. Sheridan and H.G. Calvert for the faith and trust which allowed me to disappear from the college during those summers and pursue my own course of study with no questions asked. I hope the results justify their enlightened policy.

When the draft was complete, my father, Mr. T.G. Watkin, read it in holograph and saved me from numerous errors of style. For that help, and for his assistance in compiling the index, I am deeply grateful. My thanks are also due to Mrs. Elizabeth Riley who typed both the original manuscript and the final camera-ready copy, as well as to North-Holland Publishing for the assistance given in preparing the final draft.

Over the years, I have received much encouragement from friends and colleagues who have shown interest in my work; I cannot mention them all by name but I wish to acknowledge my debt to them here. My greatest debt, however, is without doubt to my parents, who provided the home in which virtually the whole of my work was done and without the support of which it could not possibly have been done. Any achievement is as much theirs as mine - although any faults are entirely my own - and to them, therefore, this volume is rightfully and respectfully dedicated.

Cwmparc,
September 20th, 1979 T.G.W.

TABLE OF CONTENTS

TABLE OF CASES CITED

TABLE OF ENGLISH STATUTES CITED

TABLE OF ABBREVIATIONS

CLH I	Continental Legal History Vol. I: General Survey.
CLH VI	Continental Legal History Vol. VI: History of Continental Criminal Law (Von Bar et al.).
D'Entrèves, NL	A.P. d'Entrèves, Natural Law.
Devlin	Sir Patrick Devlin, The Enforcement of Morals.
ELO	A.S. Diamond, The Evolution of Law and Order.
Freud, CW	S. Freud, Collected Works.*
Fuller, ML	Lon L. Fuller, The Morality of Law.
Hart, CL	H.L.A. Hart, The Concept of Law.
Hart, LLM	H.L.A. Hart, Law, Liberty and Morality.
Hoebel	E.A. Hoebel, The Law of Primitive Man.
ILS	J.D.M. Derrett (Ed.) An Introduction to Legal Systems.
Jung, CW	C.G. Jung, Collected Works.
Kenny	Anthony Kenny, Wittgenstein.
Leach, LS	E. Leach, Levi-Strauss.
Levi-Strauss, SSM	C. Levi-Strauss, "The Structural Study of Myth" in Structural Anthropology.
LMS	P.M.S. Hacker and J. Raz (Ed.) Law, Morality and Society: Essays in honour of H.L.A. Hart.
LQR	Law Quarterly Review.
Lucas, PP	J.R. Lucas, The Principles of Politics.
Maine, AL	Sir Henry S. Maine, Ancient Law.
Maine, ELC	Sir Henry S. Maine, Early Law and Custom.
Mill	J.S. Mill, On Liberty (Everyman Edition).
MLR	Modern Law Review.
Oxford Essays	A.W. Guest (Ed.), Oxford Essays in Jurisprudence.
Oxford Essays (2)	A.W.B. Simpson (Ed.), Oxford Essays in Jurisprudence Second Series.

PFL	Pelican Freud Library.*
PI	L. Wittgenstein, Philosophical Investigations.
PL	A.S. Diamond, Primitive Law. Past and Present.
TLP	L. Wittgenstein, Tractatus Logico - Philosophicus.
Wittgenstein, BBB	L. Wittgenstein, The Blue and Brown Books.

* In the footnotes, quotations from and references to the writings of Sigmund Freud are given to the Pelican Freud Library when the work has appeared there and to the Collected Works where it has not.

INTRODUCTION

The classical Roman jurist, Gaius, described in his _Institutes_ what has been called the "mode _par excellence_"[1] of transferring ownership (_dominium_) under the civil law (_ius civile_) of Rome, namely _mancipatio_. The transfer he described was that of a slave.

> "... in the presence of not less than 5 Roman citizens of full age and also of a sixth person, having the same qualifications, known as the _libripens_ (scale-holder), to hold a bronze scale, the party who is taking by the mancipation, holding a bronze ingot, says: 'I declare that this slave is mine by Quiritary right, and be he purchased to me with this bronze ingot and bronze scale.' He then strikes the scale with the ingot and gives it as a symbolic price to him from whom he is receiving by the mancipation."[2]

The ceremony of _mancipatio_ transferred _dominium_ in the slave from one person to another. Before the declaration, the slave was the property of the former; after the declaration and striking, he was the property of the latter.

A more familiar example to the modern reader would be that of a man entering a grocer's shop to purchase an apple. Having waited his turn, he approaches the counter and asks the grocer if he has any apples. The grocer replies in the affirmative and states the price. The customer hands over the purchase price, the grocer hands over the apple and the customer leaves the shop. Different legal systems will analyse this transaction in different ways, but all would agree that a sale has occurred and that ownership of the apple passed at some moment during the transaction from the grocer to the customer. Before the customer entered the shop, the apple was the property of the grocer; when the customer left, ownership of the apple had passed to him.

In England and Wales, young men and young women

come of age when they attain the age of eighteen years. Thus, when a young man goes to bed on the eve of his eighteenth birthday, he is a minor, but when he gets up on the morning of his eighteenth birthday, he has attained the age of majority and is looked upon, by the law at least, as an adult. During the night, at the stroke of midnight, he ceased being a minor and became an adult.

Likewise, if a man and a woman enter a church to marry one another, before the matrimony is solemnized by the priest, they are respectively a bachelor and a spinster, as indeed they will have been described when the banns were called. However, when having taken their vows, they leave the church, they are no longer respectively bachelor and spinster, but husband and wife, both married persons. When they entered the church, they both had capacity to contract a valid marriage; when they left, they had both lost this capacity and had acquired instead a number of obligations towards one another which they did not have on entering the building.

On the same day, a less fortunate couple find themselves in the law courts. Their marriage has irretrievably broken down and they both require a divorce. Before the judge pronounces the decree, they are husband and wife and have certain obligations towards one another; after the decree has been pronounced, they are once more a bachelor and a spinster, each having capacity to contract a valid marriage once the decree becomes absolute, and with the obligations between them at an end or at least substantially altered.

In each of the five examples given above, a transformation has taken place: the slave ceased to be the property of one person and became that of another; the apple ceased to be the property of the grocer and became that of the customer; the teenager ceased to be a minor and became an adult; the man and woman ceased to be a bachelor and a spinster respectively and became married persons, and, in the last example, the couple ceased to be married persons and became a bachelor and a spinster respectively. However, even though most people would ratify the fact that a change has taken place in at least some of these examples, it is difficult to explain how that change has occurred and to state its nature. The slave in the first example is not a different individual after the _mancipatio_ even though he follows a different master home; the apple is no different on inspection after the sale although it is in a different person's possession; the teenager is recognizably the same person before and after midnight; the man and woman the same people before and after the ceremony or hearing. The change, therefore, is not a physical change in the appearance or structure of the slave, the apple, the teenager, or the man and woman, but a change in the way in which they are classified by others and, where sensible, by themselves. The change, in other words, has not occurred in the external world perceived by the senses but is a change in the way these people think or are thought of by themselves, where sensible, and by others. In other words, the changes have occurred in the mind or minds of the people concerned.[3] The question of whether a particular slave, apple, teenager, man or woman exists is one which can be answered by examining the situation in the external world; whether the slave belongs to one master or another, the apple to the grocer or the customer, whether the teenager is an adult or a minor, whether the man and woman are married or single, are questions which cannot be answered by such an examination but require reference to mental concepts in the respective societies involved, an examination of how they are classified or thought of in their respective social groups.

Thus, the transformation described in the examples did not occur in the external world of physical facts perceptible to the senses, but this is not to say that they did not therefore occur at all or that they were unreal. The changes did occur, but they occurred in the minds of the people concerned and not in the external world of facts. Many changes occur in this way but are nevertheless accounted real. Thus, a senior member of the Bar may be appointed a judge, and from that moment will regard himself and will be regarded by others as being a judge. Indeed, that is what being a judge actually means.[4] Some such transformations require ceremonies, as did the *mancipatio* and the marriage; thus, law students when they qualify are called to the Bar and cease to be students and become, that is, are regarded as and regard themselves as, barristers; university students have degrees conferred upon them and become Bachelors of Arts; thus, also, are bishops consecrated, kings crowned, and so on.[5]

The significance of mental phenomena is not, however, confined to changes of this sort. Many things exist only in the mind but are nevertheless accounted real enough despite the fact that they have no existence in the perceptible, external world. Thus, a man may fall asleep and dream. When he wakes up, at least, he will realise that what he has been experiencing while asleep was only a dream. In one sense, therefore, the dream was not real, that is, it did not exist anywhere other than in his mind, but, in another and very real way to the dreamer, it did exist because he was experiencing it. In the same way, although a past event may actually have occurred in the external world, the memory of it has no existence in the external world but only exists in the mind of one who recalls the event. An imagining, on the other hand, never existed at all, but is nevertheless in existence in the mind of him who imagines.

However, whereas the dream, the memory and the imagining only existed in one person's mind, the fact that the senior member of the Bar has become a judge, that the eminent ecclesiastic is a consecrated bishop or that the teenager has come of age, is not so limited, but will be ratified by more than one person. These mental phenomena exist in more than one mind, that is, they are shared by several people, possibly all or a majority of a social group. Many such mental phenomena are shared.[6] Thus, the boundaries of a particular parish may be well known. For some of its length, the boundary may coincide with some perceptible physical feature on the landscape, for example, a river, but despite the fact that the river exists in the external world, its significance as a boundary does not and is still mental. For some of its length, however, the boundary may be totally arbitrary and, thus, clearly has only a shared mental existence. Likewise, whereas only one person has a dream, a community may share a myth, each member knowing its ingredients and outcome. Although the events never occurred, the myth nevertheless exists even though its existence is confined to the minds of the members of the community in question.

Some such shared mental phenomena form systems.[7] Two obvious examples are money and language. Taking money first, almost every member of a social group possesses small bits of metal and pieces of paper which are regarded as being valuable. The bit of metal which is a coin may be regarded as of greater value than another bit of metal, such as a shoe horn, although lacking the latter's practical utility. Similarly, a piece of paper called a pound note or a dollar bill is somehow more valuable in the popular estimation than a similar piece of writing paper, and while the latter may be idly doodled upon or fashioned into a paper aeroplane, to adopt such a course of action with the former would never seriously be contemplated. Yet, externally, money is no more than bits of metal and pieces of paper.[8] Its value exists in the minds of those members of the community who utilise it, and is, therefore, a shared mental phenomenon.[9]

Language is another system that consists of shared mental phenomena.[10] People who speak English refer to the four-legged domestic animal which barks as a dog. Clearly, the word dog has no obvious connection with the four-legged domestic animal; the connection is arbitrary and exists only in the minds of those persons who speak English. This much is obvious from the fact that to a Frenchman who speaks no English the word dog has no significance; the animal in question is to his mind not called dog but chien. The connection between the word and the object is, thus, arbitrary and without significance to persons who do not speak the language in question; the significance is limited to those who share the mental phenomenon of the language. The linguistic scholar, Ferdinand de Saussure, laid stress on the arbitrary nature both of the sign and the connection between the signifier and the signified. He also used a memorable phrase, the compass of which can easily be extended to all such mental phenomena: "the mind" he said "breathes life into a substance which is given".[11] What is true of the spoken word is also true of the written word; there is no connection between the sound which makes the spoken word dog and the lines and curves which compose the written word dog. Again, the connection is arbitrary but very real to all who can read or write the language.

Thus, a whole host of things, commonplaces of everyday life, when considered can be seen to exist only in the minds of men and not in the external world, although they greatly influence the ways in which men relate to and interpret the world in which they live. Sounds and signs are interpreted as meaningful words to make language, metal and paper as of value to make money, rivers and lines on paper as boundaries, and, so in our original examples, events are given a significance so that sales, marriages, divorces and comings of age occur. All these things are mental phenomena only, but their significance is shared by members of the social groups involved. The psychiatrist, R.D. Laing, has referred to such systems of shared mental phenomena as social phantasy systems[12]; social in that they are shared, and phantastic in that they exist in the mind and not in the external world. However, they are definitely regarded as real by those who share the phantasy.[13] Those who share the phantasy seldom realise that what they are doing is phantastic; there is a collusion to pretend that it is real, and to that extent it is real as far as the participants are concerned.[14] Thus, the slave has a new master, the apple a new owner, the teenager has come of age and the couple are married or divorced both in their own eyes and in those of the other members of the social group with whom they collude in the community's shared phantasies, although to an outsider who does not collude the effect is invisible and unreal.

To those who participate in the collusion, therefore, such social phantasy systems are a form of reality, so that money has value, language has meaning and laws have validity. All of the five original examples deal with legal situations. Thus, the fact that an article of property belongs to one person, that a particular act is illegal or that a particular person has a certain status are all matters which have to be determined according to the law of the social group in question, and that law is a social phantasy system of that group existing only in the minds of the group's members. Thus, whereas the question of whether an object exists is one concerned with external reality, the question of who owns it relates not to observable fact but to psychological fact, or, to give it another name, phantasy. Similarly, whether an event occurred is a question of fact, whether it was a crime a question of law and, thus, of phantasy. It is a fact that a particular person exists, a phantasy that he is a slave, a minor or a married man. In other words, laws are social phantasies and legal systems are social phantasy systems, like languages, currencies, latitude and longitude and a host of other phenomena familiar enough in everyday life.

An important concomitant of this may, however, have escaped attention and, thus, have misled legal theorists. If laws do not exist in the same way as mountains, rivers, people or planets, it is clearly fallacious to suppose that they can be accounted for according to the same sorts of theories. Planets move, mountains form and rivers flow in accordance with certain causes, and their respective motion, formation and flow can be described according to the causation involved, the respective descriptions forming the bases of various disciplines, such as astronomy or geomorphology.[15] Such has been the appeal of certain ascendant disciplines that attempts have been made to interpret legal reasoning as on a par with first the processes of mathematics and later the methods of the physical sciences, so that legal reasoning has sometimes been presented as being deductive, at other times as inductive, and sometimes even as a combination of both.[16] However, such theories lose sight of the fact that whereas the subject matter of the physical sciences exists in the external world, the subject-matter of legal reasoning does not, but is rather a phantasy, albeit a shared one. It should not be expected, therefore, that legal reasoning should be a sort of mathematical, logical or scientific process, because laws do not belong to the same category of existence as do the subject-matter described by those disciplines. Whereas a legal theory ought to be rational, it is not to be lightly expected that legal reasoning itself must be, unless the word rational is to be given a wider meaning than that normally attributed to it.[17] As the subject-matter of legal reasoning is a phantasy, as a process it is more likely to be similar in structure and function to other mental phenomena than to external phenomena. In other words, laws may be better explained according to the criteria used to explain other phantasies to which it bears family resemblances, phantasies such as meaning, myth, and, on a different level, dreams and memories.[18]

It is submitted that to attempt to explain law according to the criteria used for physical objects and events is a false step, for law is akin to, and bears family resemblances to, other social phantasy systems. It is the purpose of this book, therefore, to explore the phenomenon of law according to this method, and to see whether the structure and function of other phantasies when applied to the social phantasy of law can throw new light upon its nature. Thus, whereas the most persuasive modern theories of law attempt to explain it as a system of rules or norms,[19] the nature of legal rules is nowhere expounded, and this, it is submitted, prevents a deeper understanding of the subject being achieved. It is proposed, therefore, to commence the present study by examining the nature of legal rules according to the criteria set out above, and then to do the same for the validity of legal rules, and then legal concepts. After that, a speculative account will be given of the development of a hypothetical legal system according to what one would expect from the findings about the nature of legal rules, their validity and legal concepts which will have been presented. Although this account will be speculative in nature, it will be seen that it is supported by the historical evidence concerning the development of actual legal systems, and is, as a result, highly persuasive. A new theory of the nature of law will, therefore, have emerged, and this theory, unlike many previously advanced, will be seen to fit the facts concerning the phantasy. In the last part of the work, this new theory will be used in an attempt to answer traditional questions concerning law, namely must law be moral, should the law enforce morality, and what is the nature of civil disobedience and should it be tolerated or not. Again, it will be seen that the new theory throws new light on these questions and provides a framework in which better answers to them can be given, because it accepts the nature of law as a social phantasy system, and is a theory supported by the historical evidence.

****

1. J.A.C. Thomas, Textbook of Roman Law p. 152.
2. Gaius, Institutes I. 119.
3. Cf. H. Kelsen, Pure Theory of Law p. 2,3-4.
4. Cf. R.D. Laing, Self and Others p. 116-7; Thomas S. Szasz, The Myth of Mental Illness p. 223; Gilbert Ryle, The Concept of Mind p. 241; S.T. Coleridge, "that willing suspension of disbelief for the moment that constitutes poetic faith".
5. Vide Freud, PFL I, 41; II 200-1; cf. K. Olivecrona, Law as Fact, pp. 4-5, 22, 217-39, 245-50.
6. K. Olivecrona, op.cit., p. 4-5.
7. C. Levi-Strauss, SSM 208-9.
8. K. Olivecrona, op.cit., p. 247-9.
9. Thomas S. Szasz, op.cit., p. 263.
10. L. Wittgenstein, BBB, 19; Kenny, 174-7.
11. F. de Saussure, Course in General Linguistics (trans. Wade Baskin) (London, 1960), p. 85; vide J. Culler, Saussure, p. 44.
12. R.D. Laing, op.cit., pp. 38, 39-40.
13. A. Storr, Jung, pp. 33-4.

14. R.D. Laing, *op.cit.*, pp. 108, 142.
15. Lucas, *PP*, p. ix.
16. Vide G. Gottlieb, *The Logic of Choice*, pp. 33, 35-7.
17. Vide G. Gottlieb, *op.cit.*, *passim*.
18. Vide J. Culler, *Saussure*, p. 55.
19. Vide the works of H.L.A. Hart and H. Kelsen respectively.

CHAPTER 1

THE NATURE OF LEGAL RULES

I

The person who for his own purpose brings on his lands and collects and keeps there anything likely to do mischief if it escapes, must keep it in at his peril, and, if he does not do so, is *prima facie* answerable for all the damage which is the natural consequence of its escape.

The above is probably one of the best-known rules of English law, the rule in *Rylands* v. *Fletcher*. In form and expression, it may well appear to be a rule taken from a statute, but it is not. The rule in *Rylands* v. *Fletcher* is a rule of law developed in and through the courts, based on decided cases and not statutory enactment. It was first enunciated in the Court of Exchequer Chamber in 1866.[1]

The facts of the case were that the defendants owned a mill near Ainsworth in Lancashire, but were dissatisfied with the water supply to the mill and wished to improve it. To effect this improvement, they obtained permission from Lord Wilton to construct a reservoir on his land and employed reputable engineers to carry out the construction. The plaintiff, who had a mineral lease from Lord Wilton, had, all unknown to the defendants, worked his mine to a point not very far from where the reservoir was to be constructed, although separated from the construction area by land owned by third parties. While constructing the reservoir, the engineers came across some disused mine shafts and did not seal them properly. These shafts connected with the plaintiff's coal mine. The end result was that, when the construction was complete and the reservoir filled, water flowed down the shafts and into the plaintiff's coal mine, where it caused damage, the agreed value of which was £937. The Court of Exchequer Chamber decided that the plaintiff was entitled to recover this sum from the defendants, and the House of Lords affirmed this decision.

In the case, it was found that the events which had occurred entitled the plaintiff to a remedy. In discussing the case, Blackburn J. in the Court of Exchequer Chamber enunciated the rule for which the case stands as authority. The question which is now posed is how does the rule come to be formulated from the facts, how is the general proposition embodied in the rule obtained from the specific facts which gave rise to the decision. The answer may seem obvious - until an attempt is made to give it. There are no common factors in the facts and the rule, for the rule does not speak of mills, reservoirs, mine-shafts and flooding, but of purposes, collecting, mischief and escape. The problem is how did the court arrive at the abstract rule from the concrete decision.[2] This problem is referred to by lawyers as that of finding the <u>ratio decidendi</u> of a case, and it is one which has much exercised the minds of legal theorists.

It is at this point that various, honoured models of reasoning in other disciplines, such as logic or the physical sciences, are called upon to assist. Thus, some thinkers have thought that deciding cases involves deductive reasoning along the lines of a syllogism. Thus, the two premises, "All men are mortal" and "Socrates is a man", allow the conclusion to be drawn that "Socrates is mortal". Applying this model to a case, the first premiss, called the major premiss, would be the rule; the second, called the minor premiss, would be the facts of the case, and the conclusion would be the decision of the court. This model, the temptations of which are immediately apparent, does not, however, help to solve the problem for two reasons. Firstly, it requires that the rule antedate the case, and this is not so with all cases. Indeed, it is not true of <u>Rylands</u> v. <u>Fletcher</u>, although, and this point is very interesting, Blackburn J. emphasised that earlier examples of the application of the rule could be found, but that in them the rule was never actually enunciated. The learned judge thought that the rule was not new; only its actual enunciation was novel. He clearly regarded himself as giving content to an already existing form.[3] Sir Henry Maine drew attention to this facet of the development of the common law when he wrote:
"With respect to that great portion of our legal system which is enshrined in cases and recorded in law

reports, we habitually employ a double language, and entertain, as it would appear, a double and inconsistent set of ideas. When a group of facts comes before an English court for adjudication, the whole course of the discussion between the judge and the advocates assumes that no question is, or can be, raised which will call for the application of any principles but old ones, or of any distinctions but such as have long since been allowed. It is taken absolutely for granted that there is somewhere a rule of known law which will cover the facts of the dispute now litigated, and that, if such a rule be not discovered, it is only that the necessary patience, knowledge, or acumen is not forthcoming to detect it. Yet the moment the judgment has been rendered or reported, we slide unconsciously or unavowedly into a new language and a new train of thought. We now admit that the new decision *has* modified the law."[4]
The judge, according to this theory, merely discovers or enunciates the "rule of known law" so that it becomes a known rule of law;[5] in Professor Derrett's phrase - an "articulation of dumb knowledge".[6] Although this theory would always grant a rule chronological priority over the facts of the case in which it was utilised, it would not, however, solve the second difficulty. This difficulty is how the concrete facts are to be related to the abstract rule, because unlike the syllogism, there is no common factor or term. The problem of how the abstract relates to the concrete is not answered by the deductive model.

This second problem also confronts those who view legal reasoning as a sort of induction. The inductive model is based on the way hypotheses are formed in the physical sciences. A crude example would be the fact that as the sun has risen every day so far, then it is permissible to state that the sun rises every morning and to predict that it will rise tomorrow morning. Induction is based on framing hypotheses from empirical evidence; the more evidence there is, the stronger the hypothesis is likely to be. The legal rule is not so based. The rule in *Rylands* v. *Fletcher* was based initially on one decision but was no less a rule of law for this fact than if it had been based on ten. This model will not fit because whereas induction is descriptive, legal rules are prescriptive. However, even if this objection were overlooked, what has been termed the second problem concerning the deductive model still arises for there are no common factors in the rule and the facts, so that the inductive model fails to fit on this ground also.[7]

The problem of the transition from concrete facts to abstract rule is the problem of accounting for the generality of the rule, or the ratio decidendi, which has preoccupied many recent theorists. Professor Goodhart thought that the ratio could be determined from the facts treated as material by the judge, as opposed to the facts of the case, and his decision as based on them.[8] This reduction from facts to material facts is important to the view taken here and will be returned to. However, both Professor Stone and Professor Simpson have objected to his formulation on the basis that it fails to take account of the level of generality between facts and rule.[9] Stone illustrated the problem by reference to the case of Donoghue v. Stevenson[10], which is the basis of the common law concerning the tort of negligence, the facts of which were that a manufacturer of ginger beer was held liable for the harm caused to a consumer by supplying a bottle which contained a dead snail. Stone asked what was the correct level of generality:
"Dead snails or any snails or any noxious physical foreign body, or any noxious foreign element, physical or not, or any noxious element, ... Any opaque bottle of ginger beer, or any opaque bottle of beverage, or any bottle of beverage, or any container of commodities for human consumption, or any containers or any chattels for human use, or any chattel whatsoever, or any thing (including land or buildings)..."[11]
Clearly, unless there is a definite method of finding the correct level of generality, legal rules are only approximate and not firm guidelines of how the courts decide concrete cases. Such classification of particulars is the heart of a judicial decision, but logic is silent as to the method. However, even though the process cannot be satisfactorily explained, it is satisfactorily executed daily, so that its being done clearly antedates knowledge of how it is done, or in Professor Gilbert Ryle's telling phrase: "Efficient practice precedes the theory of it".[12]

A little later in The Concept of Mind, Ryle made another significant remark: "Overt intelligent performances", he wrote, "are not clues to the working of minds; they are those workings".[13] Applying this as a maxim to the present problem, it could be said that judgements, therefore, should not be treated as clues or evidence as to how an abstract rule is obtained from concrete facts, they are themselves the process.

The full impact of this will become clearer as the discussion proceeds.

The rule in Rylands v. Fletcher is not, if one looks at the textbooks, merely the rule in the case called Rylands v. Fletcher, but rather a rule which began its career in that case. The case called Rylands v. Fletcher is only the first stage in the career of the rule which bears that name. Even if the rule was not developed in previous cases, as Blackburn J. insisted, it certainly developed into its final, or at least current, state through subsequent decisions. These subsequent decisions are not all concerned with reservoirs, mines and floods, but have diverse facts so that any purported relationship among them stands in need of explanation. A few of these subsequent decisions will now be examined in an attempt to establish the nature of that relationship and thus of the rule for which they are authority. In two of them, a remedy under the rule was granted; in the other three, it was not.

In Shiffman v. Order of St. John,[14] the plaintiff, while out in Hyde Park, was struck and injured by a falling flag-pole which was under the control of the defendants. The defendants were held liable.

In Crowhurst v. Amersham Burial Board,[15] the defendants had on their land a yew tree which they had planted, and which had grown to project over the plaintiff's close where he grazed his cattle. The leaves of the yew tree are poisonous to cattle. A horse belonging to the plaintiff ate a portion of this growing yew and died. The defendants were held liable.

In Ponting v. Noakes,[16] the defendant had planted a poisonous tree near the boundary between his and the plaintiff's land. The plaintiff's horse reached over the boundary, ate some of the poisonous foliage and died. The defendants were not liable as there had been no escape of the dangerous thing but rather the horse had intruded.

In Giles v. Walker,[17] thistles grew abundantly on the defendant's land and thistle-seed was blown in large quantities by the wind onto the plaintiff's land. As the thistles were a natural growth, and had not been cultivated by the defendant, he was not liable for the escape.

In Read v. Lyons,[18] the plaintiff was an inspector of munitions at a munitions factory. She was injured by a shell which exploded while in the process of being manufactured. It was held that the rule did not apply as there was no escape from the premises of the dangerous thing.

It is now proposed to take each of the cases so far mentioned, beginning with Rylands v. Fletcher, and to construct a table to show how the facts of the cases correspond to the elements which make up the abstract rule. In the last five examples, the unnecessary facts, those not regarded by the court as material, have already been eliminated from the picture. Thus, the geographical location of the events, the exact interests of the parties in the respective parcels of land, and the mental state of the parties (whether they acted deliberately, recklessly, negligently or not) are all immaterial. So, in Rylands v. Fletcher itself, the fact that the defendants were mill-owners, that the mill was near Ainsworth, that the plaintiff was a lessee, that competent engineers were employed, are all treated as irrelevant to the decision. The significant facts are that the defendants to improve their own business, constructed a reservoir for water which if it escaped was likely to cause damage, and the water did escape and flooded the plaintiff's mine. On these facts the plaintiff was given a remedy. From the facts a general rule was abstracted, namely a person who for his own purposes brings on his lands and collects and keeps there anything likely to do mischief if it escapes, must keep it in at his peril, and, if he does not do so, is prima facie answerable for all the damage which is the natural consequence of its escape. This rule can be divided into elements so that one element corresponds to one material fact in the case itself. Thus, the defendants "for their own purpose" - to improve the water supply, "brought upon their lands and collected and kept there" - constructed a reservoir to retain the water, "something likely to do mischief if it escaped" - large quantities of water which could flood neighbouring land, "and failed to keep it in at their peril" - it escaped into the plaintiff's mine. This can be set out in the form of a table, with the rule-elements forming the horizontal axis and the cases the vertical, so that one material fact is placed under each rule element to see if the case can be subsumed under the rule. The same can be done with the subsequent cases of Shiffman v. Order of St. John and Crowhurst v. Amersham Burial Board where again a material fact will be found in each to correspond with a material fact in the original case, and

APPROXIMATION OF THE RULE	A person or persons	who, for their own purposes	brought onto their land and collected or kept there	something likely to do mischief if it escaped	and failed to keep it in at their peril	are liable for all the damage which is the normal consequence of the escape
Rylands v. Fletcher	Mill-owners	who, to improve the water-supply	constructed a reservoir to retain water	in large quantities which could flood neighbouring land	which water did escape and flooded a neighbour's mine-shafts	are liable
Shiffman v. Order of St. John	A St.John Ambulance brigade	who, as part of a display,	erected a flagpole	which could injure passers-by if it fell	and which did fall and hit a pedestrian	is liable
Crowhurst v. Amersham Burial Board	A burial board	who, to decorate their cemetery,	planted a yew tree	which was poisonous to cattle	which grew to extend into a neighbour's close where he grazed cattle and which a horse of his ate and was poisoned	is liable

Figure 1 : TABULAR Representation of the Rule in Rylands v. Fletcher thus with a rule element. In the remaining three, this cannot be done so that either a material fact is superfluous or the rule does not apply. The latter was held to be the case in all three instances: in Ponting v. Noakes because there was no escape; in Giles v. Walker because the thistles were not brought upon the land and collected and kept; in Read v. Lyons because, again, there was no escape. Just as what has hitherto been regarded as a material fact may later be discounted as superfluous, so a new material fact, and thus rule-element, may later be recognized. This actually occurs with the rule in Rylands v. Fletcher with the recognition that the bringing, collecting and keeping upon the land of what is likely to do mischief if it escapes, must be a non-natural user of the land.[19]

This table is to serve as the basis of the view to be given here of the nature of a legal rule developed in the courts. When the courts are seised of a case, a novel fact-situation is before them, and they wish to know whether they can apply the rule in question. To find the rule, they examine earlier cases which are cited to them as precedents, that is, cases having corresponding material facts or the same rule-elements. From the cases, they discover the relevant rule. This they do by seeing which corresponding facts are material in the sense that they must be present if a remedy is to be given. They, therefore, read the decisions, as it were, together, like an orchestral score to see which material facts correspond to form a rule-element as notes of different instruments harmonise to make a chord. The facts of the different cases are like melodic lines which when taken together form the chords of rule-elements. The overall impression of this, as it were, cacophany is the rule itself. So, when a judicially-developed, legal rule is enunciated, it is as if a person who has looked at the score of a symphony hums his impression of what it should sound like. In other words, it is an approximation. There is no correct level of generality of a legal rule of this kind; they are all approximations based on the decided cases, and can be added to or subtracted from by subsequent decisions. The more cases are decided, the clearer the impression may become and the more accurate the approximation. The rule is the outcome of shearing away the immaterial facts, generalizing from what is left so as to create representative rule-elements and reading off the result.

II

This method of reading the facts and decisions of different cases together as if each case were one line in an orchestral score, the totality of which is the underlying rule which is only capable of being approximately enunciated, just as the performed symphony can never without reservation be said to be exactly what the composer intended, is based on the renowned French anthropologist, Claude Levi-Strauss', theory of how to understand myths. Levi-Strauss himself states that the myths of a culture to be understood rather than recounted have to be taken not singly but as an aggregate and read as an orchestral score. In his essay, The Structural Study of Myth,[20] he gives such a rendering of the Greek Oedipus myths, constructing the sort of table which was compiled above for the cases on the rule in Rylands v. Fletcher. Indeed, Professor Edmund Leach's restatement of Levi-Strauss' view seems redolent with echoes of sentiments vented by legal theorists discussing the ratio decidendi of a case.

"The problem, as Levi-Strauss sees it, is roughly this. If we consider any corpus of mythological tales at their face value we get the impression of an enormous variety of trivial incident, associated with a great deal of repetition, and a great deal of harping on very elementary themes ... Levi-Strauss postulates that behind the manifest sense of these stories there must be another non-sense, a message wrapped up in code. In other words he assumes with Freud that a myth is a kind of collective dream and that it should be capable of interpretation so as to reveal its hidden meaning."[21]

Myth, to Levi-Strauss, therefore, partakes of the nature it has for theologians, such as the German, Schneiwind: "the expression of unobservable realities in terms of observable phenomena",[22] and when the observable phenomena are rightly construed, the unobservable reality can be approximately discovered.

Levi-Strauss also stresses the communicative nature of myth. Leach has again expressed his view admirably.

"Myth is not just fairy-tale, it contains a message. Admittedly it is not very clear who is sending the message, but it is clear who is receiving it. The novices of the society who hear the myths for the first time are being indoctrinated by the bearers of tradition - a tradition, which in theory at any rate, has been handed down from long dead ancestors. Let us then think of the Ancestors (A) as 'senders' and the present generation (B) as 'receivers'.

"Now let us imagine the situation of an individual A who is trying to get a message to a friend B who is almost out of earshot and let us suppose that communication is further hampered by various kinds of interference - noise from wind, passing cars and so on. What will A do? If he is sensible he will not be satisfied with shouting his message just once, he will shout it several times, and give a different wording to the message each time, supplementing his words with visual signals. At the receiving end B may very likely get the meaning of each of the individual messages slightly wrong, but when he puts them together the redundancies and the mutual consistencies and inconsistencies will make it quite clear what is 'really' being said.

"Suppose for example that the intended message consists of 8 elements, and that each time that A shouts across to B different parts of the message get obliterated by interference from other noises then the total pattern of what B receives will consist of a series of 'chords' as in an orchestra score thus:

1	2		4			7	8
	2	3	4		6		8
1			4	5		7	8
1	2			5		7	
		3	4	5	6		8

Levi-Strauss' postulate is that a corpus of mythology constitutes an "orchestra score" of this sort. The collectivity of the senior members of the society, through its religious institutions, is unconsciously transmitting to the junior members a basic message which is manifest in the "score" as a whole rather than in any particular myth."[23]

Clearly, therefore, an important message is being transmitted via the myth, just as the judicial decisions also carry an important message. There, the judges in their judgements communicate with the parties and also, perhaps more importantly, with subsequent judges and generations. Thus, the corpus of cases like the aggregate of myths does not merely repeat the same thing, but rather states in collectivity what is not expressly stated by any one case independently.[24]

There is, thus, a structural unity to the judicial decisions and the myths, and a unity also in the method to be used to understand and interpret them. Both judicial decisions and myths carry messages to their hearers or readers. Indeed, the line separating myth from law is far from distinct, as the words of the Iglulik Eskimo, Orulo, in response to questions about the laws of his people, quoted by Hoebel, demonstrate:

"Too much thought only leads to trouble ... We Eskimos do not concern ourselves with solving all riddles. We repeat the old stories in the way they were told to us and with the words we ourselves remember ... You always want these supernatural things to make sense, but we do not bother about that. We are content not to understand."[25]

Levi-Strauss also solved another problem concerning myths with his theory. That problem was what to do when more than one version of a myth was extant. Students of myths had searched for the _true_ version or the _earliest_ version. Levi-Strauss defined the myth "as consisting of all its versions".[26] He wrote:

"If a myth is made up of all its variants, structural analysis should take all of them into account .... We shall then have several two-dimensional charts, each dealing with a variant, to be organised in a three-dimensional order .... so that three different readings become possible: left to right, top to bottom, front to back (or vice versa). All of these charts cannot be expected to be identical; but experience shows that any difference to be observed may be correlated with other differences, so that a logical treatment of the whole will allow simplifications, the final outcome being the structural law of the myth."[27]

The problem of the different versions of myths has its counterpart in jurisprudence in the difficulty of finding the _ratio decidendi_ of a case where there is more than one judge. The same method, slightly adapted, can render service here. If there are five separate versions of the judgement, as there often is in the House of Lords, to find the _ratio_ one has merely to create a table out of the five speeches as was done earlier for the separate cases under the rule in _Rylands_ v. _Fletcher_. The _ratio_ will again be the approximate rendering of what the speeches taken together and read like an orchestral score say. When such a case is a part of a series of cases, then it will be necessary to construct the three-dimensional model of Levi-Strauss with the different judgements forming the depth element in the picture. Thus, the structural unity between judge-made law and myth is extensive and serviceable.

III

This structural unity can be found in other contexts. It will be remembered that Levi-Strauss' theory of myth was said to have affinities with Sigmund Freud's theory of dreams.[28] Freud was not by any means the first person to attempt the task of discovering the meaning of the phantasies that haunt our sleeping hours. However, he was the first to recognize an important aspect of the problem. He recognized that the dream itself, as experienced by the dreamer, was only one level of the experience, and to get at the meaning it was necessary to move from this level to another. This realization was largely absent from earlier attempts at explanation. He wrote:

"Every attempt that has hitherto been made to solve the problem of dreams has dealt directly with their manifest content as it is presented in our memory. All such attempts have endeavoured to arrive at an interpretation of dreams from their manifest content or (if no interpretation was attempted) to form a judgement as to their nature on the basis of that same manifest content. We are alone in taking something else into account. We have introduced a new class of physical material between the manifest content of dreams and the conclusions of our enquiry: namely, their latent content, or (as we say) the 'dream-thoughts', arrived at by means of our procedure. It is from these dream-thoughts and not from a dream's manifest content that we disentangle its meaning. We are thus presented with a new task which had no previous existence: the task, that is, of investigating the relations between the manifest content of dreams and the latent dream-thoughts, and of tracing out the processes by which the latter have been changed into the former.

"The dream-thoughts and the dream-content are presented to us like two versions of the same subject-matter in two different languages. Or, more properly, the dream-content seems like a transcript of the dream-thoughts into another mode of expression, whose characters and syntactic laws it is our business to discover by comparing the original and the translation."[29]

The similarity between this task and that of discovering the ratio decidendi of a case should be immediately apparent. Just as one must move from the facts and the decision to the legal rule for which they are authority, so one must move from the manifest content of the dream to the latent dream-thoughts. The meaning of the dream, like the ratio of the case, is hidden from view. The process of moving from the manifest to the latent content of a dream was called by Freud the dream-work and he divided this process into four stages. The four stages are condensation, displacement, representation and secondary revision. Freud had some doubts as to whether secondary revision was really a part of the dream-work. Each of these stages will now be considered in turn.

Condensation is that part of the process whereby a number of dream-thoughts are condensed or compressed into the content of the dream so that the manifest dream has a smaller content than the latent one. This clearly has its counterpart in the problem of the ratio decidendi. As has been shown, the rule actually enunciated was obtained from the facts of the case, but not all the facts were present in the constructed rule. Also, when a body of decisions had developed, the rule was not stated as being where a mill-owner or burial board or St. John's Ambulance Brigade build a reservoir, plant a yew tree or erect a flagpole, but rather all of these things were compressed into the words, "where a person brings or collects or keeps upon his premises". Thus, the rule contains a condensation of the facts of each case for which it is authority and it is possible to work back to the facts from the rule. A lawyer questioned about the rule would, therefore, react rather like the dreamer about the dream; he would recall the facts and link them to the rule elements just as the dreamer would attempt to link the dream-thoughts to the content. The difference is, of course, that the facts at the time of the decision are the manifest part while the rule is latent, whereas later the facts seem subsidiary to and less important than the rule. The process is thus working in both forward and reverse. One first needs to find the rule; then, when more cases are decided, one has to decide whether the formulation of the rule is accurate and this requires recourse to the facts read according to the orchestral-score method.[30]

The rule, therefore, is a condensation of the facts of each case for which it stands authority, and this is similar to the first stage of the dream-work.[31] The unnecessary facts for the decision are removed. The second element in the dream-work, displacement, also has its counterpart in the finding of a legal rule. Freud used the term, displacement, to signify two features in the dream-work,[32] namely that the dream-content has a different centre from the dream-thoughts, and that elements in the dream-content have to be substituted for elements in the dream-thoughts. This bears a similarity to the fact that the legal rule exists on a different level to the case or cases from which it emerges and that the relevant facts of a case have to be translated into rule-elements, so that it could be said that each rule-element is substituted for a material fact at a higher level of generality.

Freud's third stage of dream-work, representation, involves the transposition of a dream-thought into an image which can be incorporated into the dream-content. Inasmuch as abstract dream-thoughts have to be given some form of symbolic representation in the dream-content, this part of the process would clearly not be expected to have any correspondence with a part of the process of finding a legal rule. However, a similarity may exist, for a rule-element must represent the material fact for which it does duty. The quantity of water, the yew tree, the flag-pole are, thus represented by the phrase "something likely to do mischief if it escapes". This may be seen by some as more akin to displacement than representation, but some sort of representation certainly is present. Perhaps the matter can best be summed up by saying that the displacement is the move from the facts to the rule-elements, but the rule-elements once one has them represent the facts. Two things are involved, therefore, namely the need to move to a higher level of generality, and the need when one arrives there to construct rule-elements which correspond to the material facts; the former is akin to displacement, the latter to representation.

Freud's final stage was secondary revision,[33] which involves the ordering, revising and sometimes even the supplementing of dreams so that they form an acceptable and intelligible whole. This process is similar to what occurs quite frequently in judgements, for judges tend to formulate and reformulate a rule to ensure that it is satisfactory, and quite often supplement it by posing hypothetical situations to see whether it works satisfactorily in them.

A brief example of dream-work producing a dream from dream-thoughts is that of Bismarck's dream, discussed at length by Freud in The Interpretation of Dreams.[34] In short, at a time when his country was facing grave difficulties and the burden of finding a solution lay heavily upon him, Bismarck dreamt that he was riding along a narrow Alpine path with a precipice on one side and steep rocks on the other. The path grew narrower so that his horse refused to proceed and, owing to the narrowness of the path, it was impossible to turn around or dismount. In this portion of the dream, the first three features of dream-work can clearly be seen in action. All the problems facing Bismarck have been condensed to one difficult situation on which they are now centred and which does duty for all of them, that is, displacement has occurred. Also, the problems are represented by the difficult situation. It must be emphasized that this is but a very brief and perhaps crude illustration of dream-work in action, but it is sufficient to bring out the similarities between dream-interpretation and finding the ratio decidendi of a case. The complete dream and its analysis can be read in The Interpretation of Dreams.[35]

Thus, dream interpretation to Freud was a matter of translating the manifest dream-content into the latent dream-thoughts and ordering what was found there. This notion of a latent entity being translated into a manifest one is present in other aspects of his work also, for example his work on jokes, slips of the tongue, forgetfulness and hysteria.[36] The American psychiatrist, Thomas S. Szasz, has adverted to the structure of hysteria. Agreeing with Fairburn that hysterical conversion has as an essential and distinctive feature the substitution of a bodily state for a personal problem, Szasz wrote: "the distinctive feature of hysteria is the substitution of a 'bodily state' for communications by means of ordinary language concerning personal problems. As a result of this transformation both the content and the form of the discourse change. The content changes from personal problems to bodily problems, while the form changes from verbal (linguistic) language to bodily (gestural) language.

"Accordingly, hysterical conversion is best regarded as a process of translation."[37] Szasz thus considers hysteria to be communication by protolanguage.[38] Freud, too, thought of a dream as an abnormal form of communication in which the sleeper's unconscious communicated with his conscious mind in a manner which did not disturb sleep.[39] This communicatory role provides yet another similarity with myths and legal rules.

A further feature in Freud's theory of dreams with an obvious and useful parallel in the theory of the nature of legal rules as presented here concerns the phenomenon of a plurality of dreams. In the development of a legal rule, as has been shown, many cases normally contribute towards the end result. Each case then helps to limit the extent of the generality of the legal rule. Similarly, Levi-Strauss saw the plurality of myths as being a manifestation of the fact that there were repeated attempts to communicate the message. Freud expressed the same view with regard to dreaming:

"Quite often an immediately succeeding dream allows us to confirm and carry further the interpretation we have tentatively adopted for its predecessor. A whole series of dreams, continuing over a period of weeks or months, is often based upon common ground and must accordingly be interpreted in connection with one another."[40]

"When several dreams occur during the same night, they often have the same meaning and indicate that an attempt is being made to deal more and more efficiently with a stimulus of increasing insistence."[41]

Thus, the several dreams could be arranged in the tabular form used earlier for judicial decisions and myths and then read collectively like an orchestral score so as to find their meaning, the equivalent in the dream-table to the rule in the case-table. The more dreams there are available, the better the interpretation is likely to be, just as the more cases there are available, the more exact the enunciation of the legal rule. The similarity is, therefore, striking. Finding the *ratio* from the facts is a process very like finding the meaning of a dream from its content, although the process is seemingly reversed. Whereas the facts are condensed to find the *ratio*, it is the latent content which is condensed to produce the dream. Whereas with dreams one labours to find what has been condensed, with legal rules one strives to discover the result of the condensation. An important difference between the two is that in judicial decisions attempts are made to formulate the rule whereas in dreams the meaning is rarely revealed.[42] However, it must be remembered that such formulations by judges are merely attempts to enunciate the rule and that the rule itself is not made manifest by such utterances but remains, as it were, in the score of decisions. The same is true of dreams. The interpretation of a dream, or even of a series of dreams, is an attempt to get at the latent content from the dream-content. As Freud took occasion to point out, it is never possible to be sure that a dream has been completely interpreted. The same is, of course, true of legal rules. Reading across the table of judicial decisions like an orchestral score, one attempts to formulate the rule for which the cases are authority, but one can never be sure that one's formulation is exact; one is never certain that a novel case may not add to or subtract from one's attempt at enunciation. Thus, it can be seen that a legal rule resembles a dream in that it has, in Freud's words, "a structure with a meaning."[43]

IV

However, the similarly between legal rules and dreams is not confined to this structural unity. There is also a similarity of function, and it has been recognized by leaders in various fields of behavioural study - for example, by Freud in psychoanalysis, by Saussure in linguistics and by Durkheim in sociology - that the function of events in the general social framework is of considerable significance.[44] Dreams according to Freud have a double function. Their first function is to promote the wish to sleep. In this they are in conformity with the ego, or are ego syntonic, the ego directing that sleep should be uninterrupted and the dreams getting rid of the stimuli which would interfere with sleep. In other words, if these stimuli were not translated into dreams, they would awaken the sleeper. The second function of dreams according to Freud[45] is to allow repressed instinctual impulses to be satisfied while sleeping in the form of a hallucinated fulfilment of a wish. Thus, not only is sleep unbroken but the instinctual impulse which threatened to break it is obliquely satisfied by being translated to a different level. Such an explanation of the function of dreams is very similar to Jung's description of the purpose of the symbolic process in all its manifestations. Of the symbolic process, Jung wrote: "Its beginning is almost invariably characterized by one's getting stuck in a blind alley or in some impossible situation; and its goal is, broadly speaking, illumination or higher consciousness, by means of which the initial situation is overcome on a higher level. As regards the time factor, the process may be compressed into a single dream or into a short moment of experience, or it may extend over months and years, depending on the nature of the initial situation, the person involved in the process, and the goal to be reached."[46]

In relation to dreams, Jung's initial situation in which one gets stuck is that one wishes to sleep but also needs to release the repressed impulse, and the two things are not conformable. However, sleep is undisturbed by the dream which overcomes the initial situation at the higher level. However, the judicial process can be characterized so as to fit Jung's description also, although, in this case, the process is not completed in a short moment of experience but is extended over a longer period. There, the initial situation is one of dispute, but not an individual's internal dispute between sleep and impulses, but a dispute between individuals which if not solved could disrupt the peace of the social group in which these individuals live. Thus, if one individual floods the mines of another with his reservoir, the two will be in dispute as to who should foot the bill for the damage caused, as was the case in *Rylands* v. *Fletcher*. If there is no regulated means of settling such a dispute, the mine-owner may well resort to self-help and the order of the community may well be broken. If the parties are left to their own devices, the dispute will be settled, in all probability according to their relative strengths, physical or economic, but settled none the less. If order is merely enforced, the dispute may remain unsettled and the quality of the aggrieved party's membership of that community may deteriorate.[47] The initial situation in which the community has got stuck is therefore the need to maintain order and yet not leave the dispute unsolved. The judicial process, of setting up a court to which the disputants may resort and deciding the issue there, preserves order and settles the dispute, but it does the latter by translating the dispute into litigation, where the disputants are represented by counsel and the court orders compensation to be made. Compensation is often said to restore the parties to the positions they would have occupied if the injury had not occurred, but clearly this is nonsense. The payment of damages to the plaintiff in Rylands v. Fletcher did not restore his mine to its unflooded condition. However, the damages restore the parties to their respective positions symbolically; they too operate on the higher level. After the judicial decision is reached, the parties go away satisfied, for they share in the symbolism that the damages are restorative. Thus, the order of the group is maintained and the dispute settled, but settled symbolically. The analogy with dreams should be obvious.

The fact that the function of law in a community is to settle such disputes has been adverted to by several eminent writers on law and politics. Some such expressions are based on theoretical considerations,[48] but others have emerged from close study of the workings of many legal systems both primitive and sophisticated, ancient and modern. Thus, Diamond in The Evolution of Law and Order states that: "to secure ... a settlement is the whole aim and purpose of such governmental authority as exists."[49] The emphasis here on dispute settlement is clearly correct, but the duality of the function - to settle disputes and maintain order - and the symbolic nature of the settlement are both missed. Professor Alan Watson's conclusion that: "The point of a legal process is the resolution of a dispute, actual or occasionally potential, by means of a decision"[50] is far nearer the mark and it attributes some significance at least to the means employed, and Watson also emphasizes the need to maintain order.[51]

However, whether a decision is actually needed is not entirely clear. Hoebel has described how, among the Eskimos, song duels are used to settle disputes, the disputants coming together and chastizing each other with songs.

"The song duels are juridical instruments insofar as they do serve to settle disputes and restore normal relations between estranged members of the community. One of the contestants receives a "judgement" in his favour. There is, however, no attempt to mete justice according to rights and privileges defined by substantive law. It is sufficient that the litigants (contestants) feel relieved - the complaint laid to rest - a psychological satisfaction attained and balance restored. This is justice sufficient unto the needs of Eskimo society as the Eskimos conceive it."[52] The "judgement' is the winning of the contest either on the merits of the songs or by silencing one's opponent. It is only a "judgement" in that it ends the dispute and can hardly be called a decision.[53] That an end to the dispute is the greatest need in primitive societies together with the maintenance of order, and not the working out of any abstract notion of justice, is noted by Hoebel also in relation to the Ifugao tribe of Northern Luzon[54] and the Kiowa Indians,[55] and the same appears to have been true of the early stages of legal development in Europe.[56] The extent to which the legal process in its early stage is primarily concerned with dispute settlement has been noted by writers treating of such different systems as Roman Law[57] and the customary legal systems of African tribes.[58] Most communities seem to encourage a form of dispute settlement which preserves order but solves the dispute on a higher level. An exception was the customary laws of China which discouraged litigation, preferring to let disputants settle problems peaceably between themselves.[59] Clearly, the Chinese saw judicial settlements as being in themselves harmful, and this is not so amazing as it may at first appear if one remembers that Jung's description of the symbolic process will not only fit dreams but also hysterical conversion, which is still generally regarded today as abnormal and unhealthy. Hoebel has summed up the judicial process very well by saying that law "works to clean up all the little social messes"[60] and noted that as judicial decisions give rise to legal rules, law is usually initially shaped "in the arena of action".[61]

By far the best examples of the double function of the judicial process as being primarily the settlement of disputes and preservation of order can be found in the writings of Sir Henry Maine. In Early Law and Custom, Maine noted how the author of the Hindu law-book called Narada centred his attention on the judicial process, and classified his subject-matter accordingly.

"The principle and meaning of this ancient classification strike me as obvious. The compiler of Narada or his original makes the assumption that men do quarrel, and he sets forth the mode in which their quarrels may be adjudicated upon and settled without bloodshed or violence. The dominant notion present to his mind is not a Law, or a Right, or a Sanction, or the distinction between Positive and Natural Law, or between Persons and Things, but a Court of Justice. The great fact is that there now exists an alternative to private reprisals, a mode of stanching personal or hereditary blood-feuds other than slaughter or plunder. Hence in front of everything he places the description of a Court, of its mechanism, of its procedure, of its tests of alleged facts. Having thus begun with an account of the great institution which settles quarrels, he is led to distribute law according to the subject-matter of quarrels, according to the relations between human beings which do, as a fact, give rise to civil disputes. Thus Debt, Partnership, the Marital Relation, Inheritance, and Donation are considered as matters about which men at a certain point of civilisation do, as a fact, have differences, and the various rights and liabilities (as we should call them) to which they give rise, are set forth simply as guides towards determining the judgment which a Court of Justice should give when called upon to adjudicate on quarrels."[62]

Maine noted the same features in the early Irish, Breton, Roman and Frankish codes.[63]

Maine's great example, however, came with his description of the _legis actio_ procedure of Roman Law. There, the importance of dispute settlement is clear. It demonstrates also the amount of symbolism in the judicial settlement of disputes.

"The subject of litigation is supposed to be in Court. If it is movable, it is actually there. If it be immovable, a fragment or sample of it is brought in its place; land, for instance, is represented by a clod, a house by a single brick. In the example selected by Gaius, the suit is for a slave. The proceeding begins by the plaintiff's advancing with a rod, which, as Gaius expressly tells, symbolised a spear. He lays hold of the slave and asserts a right to him with the words, "_Hunc ego hominem ex Jure Quiritium meum esse dico secundum suam causam sicut dixi_"; and then saying, "_Ecce tibi Vindictam imposui_," he touches him with the spear. The defendant goes through the same series of acts and gestures. On this the Praetor intervenes, and bids the litigants relax their hold, "_mittite ambo hominem_." They obey, and the plaintiff demands from the defendant the reason of his interference, "_Postulo anne dicas qua ex causa vindicaveris_," a question which is replied to by a fresh assertion of right, "_Jus peregi sicut vindictam imposui_." On this, the first claimant offers to stake a sum of money, called a Sacramentum, on the justice of his own case, "_Quando tu injuria provocasti, D aeris Sacramento te provoco_," and the defendant, in the phrase, "_Similiter ego te_," accepts the wager. The subsequent proceedings were no longer of a formal kind, but it is to be observed that the Praetor took security for the Sacramentum, which always went into the coffers of the State.

"Such was the necessary preface of every ancient Roman suit. It is impossible, I think, to refuse assent to the suggestion of those who see in it a dramatisation of the origin of Justice. Two armed men are wrangling about some disputed property. The Praetor, _vir pietate gravis_, happens to be going by and interposes to stop the contest. The disputants state their case to him, and agree that he shall arbitrate between them, it being arranged that the loser besides resigning the subject of the quarrel, shall pay a sum of money to the umpire as remuneration for his trouble and loss of time. This interpretation would be less plausible than it is, were it not that, by a surprising coincidence, the ceremony described by Gaius as the imperative course of proceeding in a Legis Actio is substantially the same with one of the two subjects which the God, Hephaestus is described by Homer as moulding into the First Compartment of the Shield of Achilles. In the Homeric trial-scene the dispute, as if expressly intended to bring out the characteristics of primitive society, is not about property, but about the composition for a homicide. One person asserts that he has paid it, the other that he has never received it. The point of detail, however, which stamps the picture as the counterpart of the archaic Roman practice is the reward designed for the judges. Two talents of gold lie in the middle, to be given to him who shall explain the grounds of the decision most to the satisfaction of the audience. The magnitude of this sum as compared with the trifling amount of the Sacramentum seems to me indicative of the difference between fluctuating usage and usage consolidated into law. The scene introduced by the poet as a striking and characteristic, but still only occasional, feature of city life in the heroic age has stiffened, at the opening of the history of civil process, into regular, ordinary formalities of a lawsuit."[64]

This double function of law is clearly to "institutionalise dispute situations" and disputes are institutionalised in a symbolic process. The latent violence which would have disrupted the order of the community has been sublimated in the process and rechannelled to preserve order.[65] Only the Chinese appear to have considered such rechannelling as itself unhealthy for the community and a thing to be discouraged.

This double function of the symbolic process of solving disputes is present in all its manifestations, whether in primitive or sophisticated societies, just as it is true of all dreams, whether those of infants or of adults. Freud noted that infantile dreams were generally straightforward wish-fulfilments.[66] Freud quotes a dream of his son in which the boy's disappointment at not climbing a mountain and seeing a little hut he had heard much discussed was compensated by his dreaming he had done so. Clearly, the dream performed the double function of maintaining his sleep and satisfying his impulse but did not involve displacement or representation. Adults, on the other hand separate the content of their dreams so that the meaning is kept latent and has to be sought. So also with primitive and sophisticated legal systems. Primitive systems seek only to solve disputes and do not regard the settlement as enunciating or exemplifying any general principles. More sophisticated systems, however, not only settle dispute situations but do so by enunciating general rules or in a manner taken to contain a general rule, the rule being the settlement at a higher level. This step into legal adulthood can be seen occurring in England in the twelfth and thirteenth centuries, when royal writs, which were needed to commence actions in the King's courts, were no longer only granted to meet the needs of the instant case (*brevia magistralia*), but sometimes assumed a stereotyped form into which many causes could be fitted (*brevia formata*).[67]

This last comparison makes particularly clear an issue raised by the whole of the preceding discussion about the function of dreams, that is, that there is a clear parallel between human and social development. Freud himself was more than aware of the existence of this similarity,[68] and indeed devoted an important essay to it.[69] Dreams, symptoms and the peaceful settlement of disputes all mark an important step in the imposition of rule in their respective spheres of development.[70]

V

The discussion so far has treated of two problems

concerning the nature of legal rules. Firstly, it has dealt with the problem of how to find the legal rule from the case or the series of cases from which it derives its authority. In answering this question it was found that Levi-Strauss' theory of myth presented very powerful analogies. Secondly, the discussion has considered how the legal rule comes to be enunciated in the form in which it is enunciated. In this task it was found that Freud's theory of dreams provided an useful analogy. One further question, however, remains, and that is how is it that, when a court is faced with a novel fact situation, it knows under which rule to subsume those facts in order to find its way to the correct decision. For example, when Crowhurst v. Amersham Burial Board came before the courts, or Shiffman v. Order of St. John, the factual situations contained in those cases led to their being classified as cases under the rule in Rylands v. Fletcher. Such classification was of considerable importance in English law prior to the abolition of the forms of action in the nineteenth century, for only if the correct form of action were used could a remedy be given. Thus, the question arises of how do the courts and the parties know under which heading, as it were, to place a novel dispute situation. This is another question where the answer seems obvious until an attempt is made to give it; another situation in which efficient practice clearly precedes the theory of it.

Looking at the several cases, a lawyer would instantly recognize that they were cases under the rule in Rylands v. Fletcher, just as first-year law students have little difficulty in recognizing which areas of the law the facts of a problem require discussed. However, looked at without the aid of legal training, it is not immediately apparent in what way it is possible to say that building a reservoir and flooding a mine is similar to planting a yew-tree and killing a horse, or in what way either or both of these is like erecting a flag-pole and injuring a passer-by.

The problem of how to account for the similarity between situations clearly distinguishable for their dissimilarities is not confined to the activities of the law courts and their personnel. Gilbert Ryle raised the same issue in relation to pretending, as he called it.[71] A forged signature is clearly not the same sort of thing as the signature of which it is a copy, and yet it is similar; a man pretending to be a bear or a corpse is not really like a bear or a corpse, and yet, if his pretence is a success, he will have brought the similarity of his act to bears or corpses to our minds. Likewise, when Tarquinius Superbus struck the heads off the taller poppies in his garden with his stick, that was not the same thing as executing the chief citizens of Gabii, yet his son, Sextus, saw the similarity and knew what to do.[72] This last instance makes particularly obvious something true of all the other examples; in each the similarity is communicated, so that once again a form of communication is under discussion.

To answer this question, it is again proposed to make use of a theory, or possibly more than one, from a separate but related discipline, on this occasion the study of language. In his work, _Tractatus Logico-Philosophicus_, Ludwig Wittgenstein produced a theory of representation which will prove serviceable to our needs here. Wittgenstein later abandoned the position he had taken in the _Tractatus_ but that does not prevent its being used profitably here. Indeed, Wittgenstein's later position, as presented in the _Blue and Brown Books_ and the _Philosophical Investigations_ can also be of use in this discussion, and may not be entirely unreconcilable with his _Tractatus_ position, at least so far as this argument is concerned.

Wittgenstein's theory of representation was developed to show how propositions represented reality. He developed a pictorial theory of such representation, and, clearly, the fact that a two-dimensional picture can instantly be recognised as depicting people, places or events is an example of the problem in hand. To Wittgenstein, "A picture is a model of reality."[73] However, this merely states the problem, which is how is it that the picture is taken to be a model of reality and that the similarity overcomes the obvious dissimilarities. In the _Tractatus_, Wittgenstein explained this by postulating that "There must be something identical in a picture and what it depicts, to enable the one to be a picture of the other at all."[74] The picture to Wittgenstein was related to whatever it depicted and thus stood in a special relationship to that thing. That relationship he called the pictorial relationship. It was for such a relationship to exist that it was necessary for there to be "something identical" in both picture and what it depicted; the two must have the same form, he thought, and this form he called pictorial form. It was this common pictorial form which made them similar. Clearly the greater the similarity between them, the closer the pictorial relationship and the more pictorial form they had in common. The greater the dissimilarity, the less pictorial form they had in common, until they would cease to be similar at all, in other words the pictorial relationship would be at an end. The minimum pictorial form required to set up a pictorial relationship was called by Wittgenstein the logical form. This, then, is the pictorial theory of representation presented by Wittgenstein in the _Tractatus_.

This model works well in accounting for the similarity between cases which leads courts to classify them as being under the same rule or requiring the same form of action. Thus, although _Rylands_ v. _Fletcher_ concerned the escape of water from a reservoir into a mine and _Shiffman_ v. _The Order of St. John_ a flag-pole falling upon a pedestrian, both are alike in that they concern one person harming another by bringing something dangerous onto his land for his own use and allowing it to escape. Similarly, _Crowhurst_ v. _Amersham Burial Board_ shares this similarity although it concerned a yew-tree and a horse. The cases, therefore, although different, have a common form and each represents the same basic situation although in different factual circumstances. They can, therefore, be said to stand in a pictorial relationship to one another and to have a common pictorial form. When a new case arises, it is the presence of the pictorial form which allows the parties and the court to recognize the pictorial relationship which it has with the other instances and state that it is a case under the rule in _Rylands_ v. _Fletcher_, just as when a new painting of the Crucifixion is unveiled it is recognized as a depiction of that event because of its pictorial form and the resemblance it bears to other paintings of the event, no-one living having seen the event itself. The rule in _Rylands_ v. _Fletcher_ must also, of course, have the same pictorial form as the cases under it, otherwise it would not be related to them. However, the rule itself is something more than just another entity with the same pictorial form. It is an attempt to describe the pictorial form of the cases, which they cannot, as factual circumstances, express themselves; they can only display it.[75] The rule, however, wishes to express exactly what will admit a new set of facts to the classification or group of cases and thus seeks to state the minimum pictorial form which a case must have. In other words, the rule attempts to state the logical form of the group. It attempts to do so and is, therefore, an approximation. As has been said, additions and subtractions have to be made to modify the rule as old formulations are found unsatisfactory when newer versions of the pictorial form throw more light on the nature of that form. The more exact the rule becomes the closer it gets to the logical form of the cases from which it derives its authority.

Wittgenstein, as has been said, later abandoned this search for the essence of language and propositions, and spoke of the 'family resemblances' among the entities he studied.[76] The concept of family resemblance can also be used to describe the similarity between the cases under the same rule, and the rule as an attempt to express that resemblance, a departure of which the later Wittgenstein would not have approved. However, A.J.P. Kenny has made a very interesting suggestion concering the family likeness concept. He writes:

"the concept of family likeness leaves room for the notion of convergence on, and divergence from, a paradigm ... I believe that the paradigm on which the notion of proposition converges ... is the proposition conceived according to the logical parts of the picture theory."[77]

Whether one follows the _Tractatus_ or the _Philosophical Investigations_ or makes use of Kenny's hypothesis, it is nevertheless the case that Wittgenstein's theory of language analogically explains a great deal about how cases come to be subsumed under certain headings by the courts. The new case is recognized as displaying the same pictorial form as, or as having a family resemblance to, earlier cases, and is thus admitted to the group.

Wittgenstein also believed that "Language disguises thought".[78] His position in the _Tractatus_ was that the form of a factual proposition would only be apparent when analysed and broken down into elementary propositions. Only when these ultimate components were reached, which would be many in number, could the meaning of the factual proposition they lay behind be properly explained.[79] In other words, the factual proposition disguises its structure of elementary propositions, and has to be decoted for its meaning to emerge. There is an obvious similarity here with Freud on dreams, where the manifest dream-content has to be decoded to discover the meaning of the dream in the latent dream-thoughts. Also, there is a similarity with Levi-Strauss on myth and, of course, with the idea advanced here that decided cases can be decoded to find legal rules. Such similarities should not be surprising. It is clear, for example, that Freud believed that his theory of dreams would have far wider implications. He himself stated that "The interpretation of dreams is the royal road to a knowledge of the unconscious activities of the mind",[80] and held that every result similar to a dream achieved during the daytime, among which myths and legal decisions can be counted, was due to the same mental forces.[81] Thus, those who have thought of judicial decisions as being intuitive or hunches were not far off the mark. What was needed to fill out their theories was an explanation of how such hunches occurred, a theory of the efficient practice already in existence.

C.G. Jung attributed intuition and hunches to the unconscious workings of the mind. He wrote: "Intuition is an unconscious process in that its result is an irruption into consciousness of an unconscious content, a sudden idea or "hunch". It resembles a process of perception, but unlike the conscious activity of the senses and introspection the perception is unconscious. That is why we speak of intuition as an "instictive" act of comprehension."[82] Trained lawyers and judges are often said to reach the correct decision to a problem or case as if by instinct; the proposition is not so far-fetched as at first sight it may appear. Legal reasoning, like dreaming or speaking a language, involves an efficient, unconscious practice, and all such processes are linked in having a common structure or pattern, and to a large extent common functions as well. Nor is it surprising that they should have a common structure as they are all phantasy systems - some shared or social, others, like dreaming, not - and as such are all products of the human brain so that it is not surprising that there are features common to all.[83]

The fact that these processes have common structures had led some thinkers to believe that each individual inherits these methods, that they are innate in each human being. According to Jung, for example, although ideas were not inherited, thought patterns were.[84] Thus, the method of constructing dreams, myths and phantasies was present in the human brain at birth, although no actual dreams, myths or phantasies were so present. The same idea could be extended to the technique of enunciating legal rules and the technique of making meaningful linguistic utterances. Indeed, in the field of linguistics Professor Noam Chomsky has made this analogous claim, stating that, whereas no-one is born knowing a language, the techniques of how to acquire a language and use it meaningfully are present in the human brain at birth.[85]

Whether such structures are innate or not is not of the first importance to the theory here advanced. What is important is that dreams, myths, languages and legal rules are all related to one another in that they are all phantasy systems, and that, to discover the nature of legal rules, it is to these related areas that one should turn for guidance. The fact that they are related becomes clear from the fact that the table constructed to discover how to find a legal rule from the cases in which it is displayed will serve equally well to understand the message of a body of myths, the meaning of several dreams, or to find the pictorial or even logical form of pictorially related entities. Law belongs to the family of phantasy systems to which it bears this family resemblance;[86] the amount of space devoted here to examining these other systems has been with the object of displaying that resemblance. Legal reasoning is a process akin to dreaming, myth-interpretation and speaking a language, and can only be fully understood according to the terms of the phantasy systems to which it is related.

VI

The legal rule chosen to illustrate the theme of this chapter was the rule in _Rylands_ v. _Fletcher_, which was developed in the courts and enunciated by the judges during the course of settling disputes. It is thus a common law rule. The discussion proceeded from such a rule in order that there should be no doubt that the theory of law which will emerge from this work is applicable to the common law as it has developed and not just to law as produced by legislatures. Some dissatisfaction has been expressed with previous theories of law on the ground that they do not really fit the common law centred as they are upon enacted or statute law.[87] However, it might be said that the present discussion, although nominally beginning with a common law rule, is not really doing so, because the rule in _Rylands_ v. _Fletcher_ is not really a representative common law rule. Two reasons might be given for making this criticism. To begin with, the rule was enunciated in the very first case in which it was applied,[88] and did not change its form substantially afterwards. Secondly, and largely because it had been so enunciated, the rule was treated in the subsequent cases in which it was applied as though it were a statutory enactment. However, despite these possible objections, the rule serves its purpose well in this context. Indeed, any rule of common law would do the same, for all that is needed is the data of decided cases with which to build up the table from which the legal rule can be read off as though one were reading an orchestral score. Provided it is remembered that if the judges enunciate a rule that does not alter the fact that the enunciated rule is still no more than an approximation, no harm will be done and the rule in _Rylands_ v. _Fletcher_ will do service. Where no rule is enunciated by the court, the exercise is obviously purer but perhaps less suited to acting as an example with which to introduce the topic currently being discussed.

This explanation of the nature of a legal rule fits, as has earlier been said, even the very early development of the common law when it was based around the royal writs. Thus, the early writs, or _brevia magistralia_, could be tabulated so as to be able to read off from them a generalization of the situations in which such a remedy would be given, and such a generalization was to be later embodied in the _brevia formata_, which were designed to fit more than one cause of action and the structure of which could not be altered. At a later date, the decided cases rather than the writs would be read off to discover the legal rules on which the decisions were based. An excellent, modern example of an unenunciated rule which can be read off from a three-dimensional chart would be the rule which has been developed in the nineteen-seventies making occupiers of premises liable for injuries to trespassers in certain circumstances. This rule began its career in the House of Lords in _Herrington_ v. _British Railways Board_,[89] has never been authoritatively enunciated, but has been discussed and applied in several, subsequent cases. Another modern context in which the model could be useful would be in decoding the rule concerning negligent misstatements which originated in _Hedley Byrne_ v. _Heller_.[90]

The criticism of legal theories which stated that they do not fit the common law also drew attention to the customary basis of the common law.[91] The current theory of the nature of legal rules will also serve to discover rules of customary law. There, instead of placing decided cases in the table, one would place examples of rule-governed activity concerning a certain issue and then, once again, read off the customary rule from the resultant orchestral score. In other words, the current theory meets the objection of that criticism.

However, although it meets the objection of that criticism and serves as a satisfying model for explaining the nature of both customary law and common law rules, it is not limited to explaining the rules of such systems. It will work equally well with rules produced in other ways. Thus, rules of enacted law, of which statutes are an example, can be accommodated in the model. Such rules, of course, are not shaped "in the arena of action", but are enunciated by the legislature, not to solve one dispute, but rather with a view to solving many. Obviously, in enunciating such rules, the legislature will usually have past disputes and their content in mind, but future needs and hypothetical dispute-situations and their supposed content will also serve to shape the finished product. These rules then are shaped less in the arena of action and more in that of abstract thought, but the process by which they are shaped is nevertheless the same as that described for rules generally, with its great similarity to the formation of dreams. Such rules, in addition, have still to be applied in solving disputes and when this stage is reached, everything which has been said about the importance of pictorial form or family resemblance in subsuming cases under the rules will still apply. Indeed, once a body of cases has been subsumed under one of these rules, it will quite often be seen that the interpretation of the rule by the courts will have been influenced by the decisions made under it. In other words, the rule of enacted law, although the most important line in the score, will nevertheless only be one line in it when the rule comes to be read off from that score, and the harmony provided by the cases is by no means insignificant. The situation is not that far distant from where, in a strict system of _stare decisis_, a highly respected common law judge has enunciated a rule in deciding a case, as occurred in _Rylands_ v. _Fletcher_, and that enunciated rule becomes the theme which subsequent decisions follow. That even legal rules got from statutes should be only a part, albeit the dominant part, in the score should not be too surprising, for even these rules are only approximations of what is needed to solve actual disputes. Likewise, the enacted rules of civil law jurisdictions, the rules to be found in the various codes, are enunciated by one or more persons and emerge according to the same pattern and have the same structure as their statutory and common law counterparts, and their application is also governed by the same need to subsume concrete cases according to whether they resemble the rule or not. Even where, as in ancient Rome, the opinions of those learned in the law are given the force of law, the rules they adumbrate will be enunciated and applied according to the same pattern.

Thus, across the board, legal rules are enunciated to solve disputes and maintain social order, but are only approximations to the actual dispute solutions which are needed. As products of the human brain, both in their enunciation and application, they betray their provenance, and are similar in structure as well as function to other phantasy systems, displaying like them the unconscious workings of the mind.

****

1. (1866) L.R. 1 Ex. 265.
2. Vide, H. Kelsen, General Theory of Law and State, p. 135.
3. Vide, Ross v. Fedden (1872) 26 L.T. 966, at 968.
4. Maine, AL, 37-8.
5. Vide, infra, on enunciation.
6. ILS, p. xvi.
7. Lord Diplock has suggested that legal reasoning combines both induction and deduction; vide, Home Office v. Dorset Yacht Co. [1970] A.C. 1004. This view runs into both sets of difficulties.
8. A.L. Goodhart, "Determining the Ratio Decidendi of a Case", (1930) 40 Yale Law Journal, 161.
9. J. Stone, "The Ratio of the Ratio Decidendi", (1959) 22 MLR 597; A.W.B. Simpson, "The Ratio Decidendi of a Case", (1959) 22 MLR 453.
10. [1932] A.C. 562.
11. J. Stone, op.cit., 603.

12. G. Ryle, _op.cit_., 31.
13. _Ibid_., 57.
14. [1936] 1 All E.R. 557.
15. (1878) 4 Ex.D. 5.
16. [1894] 2 Q.B. 281.
17. (1890) 24 Q.B.D. 656.
18. [1947] A.C. 156.
19. Vide, _Rylands_ v. _Fletcher_ (1868) L.R. 3 H.L. 330.
20. Levi-Strauss, _SSM_, 212-3.
21. Leach, _LS_, 57.
22. _Ibid_., 54, citing. J. Schniewind, "A reply to Bultman" in H.W. Bartsch (Ed.). _Kerygma and Myth_, (London, 1953).
23. Leach, _LS_, 59-60; cf. G. Ryle, _op.cit_., 10.
24. Leach, _LS_, 70-1.
25. Hoebel, 69.
26. Levi-Strauss, _SSM_, 216-7.
27. _Ibid_., 217.
28. Leach, _LS_, 57.
29. _PFL_ IV, 381; cf. II, 38.
30. Cf. E. Leach, _Culture and Communication_, 40.
31. This is similar to Goodhart's reduction of facts to material facts; vide, _supra_, n. 8.
32. Vide, Wollheim, _Freud_, 70.
33. _Ibid_., 72.
34. _PFL_ IV, 498 ff.
35. It must be emphasized that this is but a very brief and perhaps crude illustration of dream-work in action, but it is sufficient to bring out the similarities between dream-interpretation and finding the _ratio decidendi_ of a case.
36. Vide, S. Freud, _The Psychopathology of Everyday Life_, _PFL_ V.
37. Szasz, _op.cit_., 102.
38. _Ibid_., 118-20.
39. _PFL_ II, 38.
40. _PFL_ IV, 671.
41. _PFL_ I, 212.
42. _PFL_ IV, 650.
43. _PFL_ IV, 671.
44. J. Culler, _Saussure_, 7-8.
45. _PFL_ II, 48.
46. Jung, _CW_ 9(1): 38-9.
47. Traditional Chinese jurisprudence took a different view, vide, _infra_.
48. Lucas, _PP_, 31-3; H. Kelsen, _General Theory of Law and State_, 273; _Oxford Essays_ (2), 10 (A.M. Honoré), 279 (J. Raz); _LMS_, 91-2 (J.R. Lucas).
49. _ELO_, 113.
50. A. Watson, _The Nature of Law_, 8.

51. *Ibid*., 13-5.
52. Hoebel, 98-9.
53. *Ibid*., 98.
54. *Ibid*., 114-5.
55. *Ibid*., 172.
56. *CLH* VI, 69.
57. *ILS*, 2-3 (J.A.C. Thomas).
58. *Ibid*., 145-6; 150. (A.N. Allott).
59. *Ibid*., 123. (H. McAleavy).
60. Hoebel, 279-80.
61. *Ibid*., 332.
62. Maine, *ELC*, 381-2.
63. *Ibid*., 382.
64. Maine, *AL*, 396-8; vide F.M. Pollock's Note 5 (*AL*, 417) and A. Watson, *The Nature of Law*, 22.
65. Cf. R. Wollheim, *Freud*, chapter 2; and vide, *CLH* VI, 5.
66. *PFL* IV, 206.
67. Vide, E. de Haas and G.D.G. Hall, *Early Registers of Writs* (Selden Society, vol. 87), (London, 1970).
68. *PFL* IV, 699.
69. "Civilization and its Discontents", Freud *CW*, XXI 64, especially pp. 97 and 140.
70. R. Wollheim, *Freud*, 106.
71. G. Ryle, *op.cit*., 245-6.
72. K. Olivecrona, *op.cit*., 29-30.
73. *TLP* 2.12.
74. *Ibid*., 2.161.
75. *Ibid*., 2.172.
76. *BBB*, 20; *PI*, 1.67.
77. Kenny, 223-4.
78. *TLP*, 4.002; cf. *PI*, II 224.
79. D. Pears, *Wittgenstein*, 58-9.
80. *PFL* IV, 769.
81. *PFL* IV, 774.
82. Jung, *CW*, 8: 132.
83. Vide, E. Leach, *Culture and Communication*, 26.
84. Jung, *CW*, 7: 138.
85. Vide, J. Lyons, *Chomsky*, 66-82.
86. Cf. J. Culler, *Saussure*, 55.
87. *Oxford Essays (2)*, 77 (A.W.B. Simpson).
88. Ignoring the views of Blackburn J. on this issue.
89. [1972] A.C. 877.
90. [1964] A.C. 465.
91. *Oxford Essays* (2), 94. (A.W.B. Simpson).

CHAPTER TWO

THE NATURE OF LEGAL VALIDITY

I

Legal rules are meant to settle disputes and preserve order. They do this by outlining a principle for solving a dispute at a different level from that at which the dispute manifests itself and at which, if allowed to take its course, it would disrupt the order of society. By rechannelling the disruptive forces prevalent in the dispute situation and resolving them at the higher level, order is preserved and the dispute solved. The rules which perform this function emerge in different ways. At the lowest level, they can emerge through customary practice and not really be enunciated at all. Thus, if a particular procedure is seen to work the double oracle of resolving a dispute and maintaining the order of the community, it may be adopted by other disputing parties at a later date. In such circumstances, there is no apparent rule in existence as far as the members of the community in question are concerned, and they merely apply the solution to similar situations without referring to a generalized concept. Such a concept could, however, be enunciated if one or more members of the group possessed the necessary sophistication to do so, and an external observer might well generalize from the wilderness of single instances which confronted him.

Where such generalization has taken place, then one is clearly confronted with the phenomenon of a legal rule. It is still, however, no more than a generalization of what to do to solve the dispute without disturbing the good order of the community. As a generalization, it is open to inaccuracy and must be taken as an approximate guideline of how disputes are solved without ruining order, an approximation the accuracy of which will vary according to the ability of the enunciator or enunciators to generalize from the single instances. The enunciation may be the work of the people who live in the community, or it may be the work of external observers. It may, if it is an internal enunciation, be by common argument, agreement or realization, or, as with judicial decisions, such as the rule in Rylands v. Fletcher, or statutes, it may be the work of specialist enunciators. Such specialist enunciation may emanate from those whose task it is to solve disputes, as with enunciation in the course of resolving disputes judicially, or it may take the form of enunciating rules to meet dispute situations which have arisen or are likely to arise. The latter form of specialist enunciation is the sort which produces statute law, codes and constitutions. Thus, legal rules can emerge into the social limelight in different ways. However, although anyone might theoretically give vent to a dispute-solving, order-preserving principle, not every such principle enunciated constitutes a legal rule. To be a legal rule, it is necessary that the rule should be accepted or ratified by the community in question as such, and the question, therefore, must be asked as to why certain enunciations are treated as law, that is, are valid, efficacious or binding.

Once again, the same problem can be found in different contexts. Thus, one might inquire as to why it is that the rules of association football are treated by players of the game as binding upon them, or the rules of chess, or cricket. Sports and games clearly offer a fairly direct analogy with law as they are alike in being rule-governed activities. A less obvious analogy, however, is that of language. When an English-speaker utilizes the word dog in the presence of another English-speaker, the latter will interpret this to mean the four-legged, domesticated animal that barks. Thus, when an English-speaker says dog, he expects his listener to interpret this to mean 'dog', and if the listener speaks or understands English, he will interpret the sound dog as meaning 'dog'. However, the question remains as to why this success, not only with individual words but with whole sentences and conversations, is continually achieved. The problem of why rules are binding is very much akin to the problems of how words, written as well as spoken, have meaning.

One thing is quite clear and that is that the mere fact of external conformity to rules is not enough to explain their validity. Professor H.L.A. Hart has made this point very effectively by stating that the externally-observable feature of conformity to a pattern of behaviour is not enough to state that a rule exists; there must also be an internal aspect to the behaviour, the people who conform to the externally-observable pattern must do so out of a sense of obligation. This sense of obligation Hart has called the internal aspect of rules. Thus, the fact that people go to the pictures regularly on Saturday evenings does not mean that there is a rule to that effect because, although they may do so out of habit, they do not do so out of a sense of obligation. On the other hand, the fact that men regularly bare their heads on entering a church is the manifestation of a rule because there is an internal aspect to this externally-observable pattern of behaviour, a concomitant sense of obligation, that one is obligated to remove one's hat on entering a Christian place of worship. Likewise, it is not merely a matter of habit that players of association football, other than the goalkeeper, do not handle the ball during play, or that players of chess regularly move the piece called the bishop diagonally; in both cases, the players feel that they ought to conform to this pattern of behaviour and this internal sense of obligation makes this pattern of behaviour a rule of the game in question. When actually entering the church, playing the game or speaking the language, the rule may be observed automatically, but the internal aspect may still be inferred from the fact that if stopped and asked why the pattern was being conformed to, the answer would contain a reference to the necessary sense of obligation.[1]

The question, however, remains as to why this sense of obligation should exist. One thing, however, is by now clear and that is that the sense of obligation which transforms a habit of behaviour into a rule of behaviour exists in the minds of the participants only, and does not exist in the way that mountains, streams and grandfather clocks exist. Once again, the validity of rules and the meanings of words must be recognized for what they are if questions concerning them are to receive satisfactory answers. The validity of rules and the meaning of words are phantasies, but not the phantasies of one mind but the phantasies of whole communities or social or linguistic groups. They are shared or social phantasies which form an externally-observable system. R.D.

Laing has called this phenomenon of collective ratification of phantasy by the term collusion,[2] thus signifying both that it is shared and that it is a game in which two or more participate. Thus, footballers collude in believing that it is wrong to handle the ball during play unless one is a goalkeeper; chess-players collude in believing that the bishop should be moved diagonally, and English-speakers collude in believing that the sound _dog_ means 'dog', the four-legged, domestic animal which barks. Ludwig Wittgenstein expressed this idea of collusion in the _Tractatus_ when he wrote that: "If everything behaves as if a sign had meaning, then it does have meaning."[3] This statement could be adapted to apply to laws or the rules of games. The adaptation would run: "If everyone behaves as though the rule were valid, then it is valid." One objection will, however, be taken and that is that the universal 'everything' is too extreme; 'a sufficient number' would, it is submitted, be more accurate for reasons which will emerge in due course.

The question, however, still remains as to why people should collude, as to why they should behave as though words were meaningful and rules binding. Again, the answer given to this question will be true with adaptation of all the social phantasy systems. However, legal rules will be taken as the starting point. Legal rules are enunciated to provide pointers as to how to solve disputes without destroying the good order of the social group. It is clear, therefore, from the start that it is important to members of the group that order be preserved and disputes solved in order to do this. The existence of disputes is a threat to order, and that trouble is taken to preserve order means that order is taken to be a premium of social life. That this is so is clear from what has been said by courts of law in situations where the validity of legal rules has been in question. After the Unilateral Declaration of Independence by Rhodesia in 1965, the effective government of Rhodesia passed emergency legislation allowing for, amongst other things, detention orders to be made. The validity of these detention orders was challenged in the High Court. In September 1966, the High Court held that the orders must be upheld "on the basis of necessity and in order to avoid chaos."[4] The need for order is apparent from this decision. The reason for this need, it is submitted, is not far to seek. Human beings, the ultimate product of evolution, take part in the struggle to survive which is common to all creatures. Along with other creatures, they have learnt that the chances of survival are greater if they band together to form groups than if they attempt to exist singly. Their social groups, therefore, whether families, extended families, tribes or nation-states are formed with the object of increasing the chances of survival, and clearly, therefore, the preservation of the group becomes in itself an important goal. If the individual is to survive, the social group to which he belongs must also survive; it must be made to cohere. Equally clearly, therefore, anything which threatens the cohesion of the community must be removed, and disputes which clearly threaten that cohesion, must therefore be settled.[5] When ways of settling disputes and preserving social cohesion are found, therefore, these ways will be followed, and when the way of doing so is described in a rule for doing so, then clearly it is in the interest of the community and of each individual that the rule be obeyed. Such rules, therefore, will be accepted as binding upon the members of the community and will be ratified by them.

It is for much the same reasons that the rules of games and clubs are treated as valid by the players and members respectively. If the enjoyment to be obtained from playing a game is to be obtained, then the rules of the game must be followed. If they are not followed then the game will deteriorate and the enjoyment will be lost. Thus, for their enjoyment to survive, the players must conform to the rules, and, as they are playing for this enjoyment, they accordingly feel that they must obey the rules in question. On a more serious level, the members of a club or professional body may have banded together to protect or promote their interests. The rules of the club or body will be expressions of what members must do if those interests are to be aided. Thus, to break the rules will lead to a decreased chance of those interests being helped by the club's existence, and accordingly, the members feel obligated to observe the rules in order to protect or promote their interests.

On an even higher level comes the ratification of the meanings of sounds which make up a language. Here, the stake is far more like that which underlies the validity of legal rules. Human beings communicate with one another in the language of their social group, so that clearly the need to communicate is a social need, and the level of sophistication that languages have reached reflects the importance with which communication with the members of one's group is regarded. To live together in a community requires a degree of communication, and so the need for a means of communication is a part of the need to form groups which cohere, which, as has been said, is a manifestation of the need to survive. Thus, the need to communicate is related to the urge to survive. For this reason, to refuse to give meaning to the sounds which make up a group's language would lead to a breakdown in the communication and, thus, in the cohesion of the group and accordingly present a threat to survival. Responsibility, therefore, dictates that the meanings given to certain sounds should be ratified in the interests of survival, and the individual members of social groups accordingly ratify the meanings given by the community to those sounds. A failure to ratify will be treated as abnormal, and a deliberate and regular failure may be treated as insanity.[6] Much the same is true of other patterns regarded as essential, such as the basic postulates of logic and mathematics, and the difficulties which confronted Wittgenstein in attempting to investigate the bases of these disciplines are very instructive.[7]

If there is no ratification, then, clearly, the rules are not regarded as being so important and are not valid, or the means of communication not so important as to be treated as a language. Wittgenstein himself noted that if a different set of arbitrary symbols were substituted for the words of a sentence with the intention of carrying the same meaning, it was difficult to ratify the meaning of these new symbols immediately.

"I say the sentence: "The weather is fine"; but the words are after all arbitrary signs - so let's put "a b c d" in their place. But now when I read this, I can't connect it straight away with the above sense. - I am not used, I might say, to saying "a" instead of "the", "b" instead of "weather", etc. But I don't mean by that that I am not used to making an immediate association between the word "the" and "a", but that I am not used to using "a" <u>in the place of</u> "the" - and therefore in the sense of "the". (I have not mastered this language.)

"(I am not used to measuring temperatures on the Fahrenheit scale. Hence such a measure '<u>says</u>' nothing to me.)"[8]

Only if it were of some importance would such alternative systems be mastered. Thus it is that persons who have to live in a foreign country develop abilities in the linguistic, monetary and other systems of that country more readily than do casual tourists.

In the legal sphere, one of the most vexing, theoretical questions concerns the standing of International Law, the body of rules which purports to govern the dealings of sovereign states with one another. A great deal of energy has been spent in arguing as to whether International Law is really law at all or merely a form of inter-state morality. From the viewpoint of the present theory, this question can only be answered according to the attitude of states to the rules of International Law. If states regard those rules as binding, that is, if they have the necessary internal aspect which ratifies them as binding, as necessary for cohesion and therefore for survival, then it is submitted that they are laws in the proper sense of that term. However, if, on the other hand, they are not so ratified and are not treated as being necessary for survival, then they do not constitute laws according to the theory here presented. Clearly, the theory does not answer the question; it merely provides the test according to which the question can be answered empirically. It is submitted that, at the time of writing, the answer to the empirical question of whether International Law is law at all is in the negative, for it is not generally regarded as being necessary for survival. This circumstance may, of course, change. It is also a fact that it may come to be regarded as binding by some nations sooner than by others according to the present theory, but this, as will be shown, is true of all legal systems. The same test, subject to the same conditions, could equally be applied to ascertain whether the laws of the European Economic Community are properly so regarded. The same sort of procedure could also give guidance as to whether Esperanto was a language in the full sense of the term. All of these questions relate to social phantasy systems, which exist only in the minds of the colluding participants in the phantasies. Statements about such phenomena are not, however, meaningless, but are on the contrary very meaningful, as they deal with, as things stand, essential features of human life in society. The matter has been well summed up by the analytical psychologist, C.G. Jung. He wrote that, "Psychological truths are not metaphysical insights; they are habitual modes of thinking, feeling and behaving which experience has proved appropriate and useful."[9] Provided that it is borne in mind that their appropriateness and usefulness have led to experience demanding that these modes should be followed not merely out of habit but as a rule, this statement can be taken to express an important truth about social phantasy systems generally, and law in particular.

Legal rules, therefore, are approximations, usually enunciated, of principles which aid social cohesion and survival in situations of dispute which if unresolved would threaten both, and are treated as binding by those persons who belong to those groups whose cohesion is guarded by the existence of the rules, because their survival is regarded as being dependant upon such cohesion and thus upon the existence of the rules in question. The theory as it stands, however, although it explains why legal rules are binding, does not explain why they are binding in the particular form in which they exist. In other words, whereas any member of the community, if asked, would probably be able to enunciate what he thought to be the correct principles to follow to promote cohesion and resolve disputes, all such enunciations are not treated as binding law. Rather such treatment is reserved for enunciations by particular persons or according to particular methods or procedures. Any explanation of why legal rules are binding must take into account that only some enunciations are treated as having binding force so as to qualify as legal rules. Thus, whereas a Royal Commission may make proposals or a national newspaper advocate a certain policy, only if their principles are adopted in statutory form will they be treated as legally binding. The question, in other words, now is why are some enunciations treated as binding, that is, as legal rules. It is submitted that this fact is yet another manifestation of what experience has taught the individuals who form a social group to be appropriate, useful and good for survival. At some stage, probably when the group was faced with a serious threat to its existence, such as external attack, internal revolt or disease, it became clear that certain people or certain methods produced more reliable enunciations of the course which promoted cohesion and survival than those produced by other people or procedures. These people or procedures henceforth became regarded as those best-suited to enunciate the survival principles, and their enunciations were subsequently treated as of considerable authority. The extent of this authority will come in for discussion at a slightly later stage.[10]

One issue, however, calls for comment at the present stage and that is that according to the present theory, the best-suited persons or procedures enunciate the survival principles which will be followed. Clearly, therefore, the correct principles for social cohesion and survival are regarded as being capable of discovery, and are discovered rather than invented by their enunciators. Theories such as this have been extant for centuries. Thus, the common law was often stated to reside in the bosom of the common law judges; the German historical school of jurisprudence spoke of a *Volksgeist* which produced the laws of the group; French writers such as Duguit thought laws were created by the *solidarité sociale*, which was only declared by statutes and other juristic acts. All these theories are, to some extent, Natural Law theories which see law as being sought and found, rather than made, by human agency. The present theory probably belongs to this family because it sees law as a manifestation of human nature, but differs from them in that it seeks to explain the particular phenomenon of human behaviour called law in the light of what has been discovered about similar phenomena in disciplines such as psychology, anthropology and linguistics.

II

Legal rules are ratified and obeyed by members of the communities to which they relate because they are accepted as being the principles which will further the cohesion of the social group in question, and the social cohesion is in turn desired and preserved as being in itself a cardinal necessity for the survival of the individuals who form the group. If men were to live without the protection of such groups, they would be in competition with one another and stand less chance of surviving. If, however, they were in competition, they would naturally regard each other as competitors and aggression between individuals to obtain food, shelter and mates would be the shape of life for such individuals. Living together, however, in a community, such competitive aggression must give way to co-operation, and the competitive element made subservient to a certain extent to the co-operative element of life. However, when a member of the group is injured in some way, either in body or goods, by another member, clearly his survival chances are hampered despite his membership and there is obviously a temptation to resort to aggression to restore the balance. It is at such moments, moments of dispute, that the rules of the community meant to restore order and solve the dispute come into play so that the community as a whole is not injured by the disputing parties. The rule seeks to overcome the aggression and rechannel the instinctive urge so as to utilize it in preserving rather than destroying the cohesion of the group. Thus, the pressure to conform is great, for the consequences of failing to conform are severe. This position has been described by Professor Hart: "The rules supported by the serious pressure are thought important because they are believed to be necessary to the maintenance of social life or some highly prized feature of it. Characteristically, rules so obviously essential as those which restrict the free use of violence are thought of in terms of obligation. So too rules which require honesty or truth or require the keeping of promises, or specify what is to be done by one who performs a distinctive role or function in the social group are thought of in terms of either 'obligation' or perhaps more often 'duty'. Secondly, it is generally recognized that the conduct required by these rules may, while benefiting others, conflict with what the person who owes the duty may wish to do. Hence obligations and duties are thought of as characteristically involving sacrifice or renunciation, and the standing possibility of conflict between obligation or duty and interest is, in all societies, among the truisms of both the lawyer and the moralist".[11]

This conflict between what the individual wants and what the community expects has a parallel in the psychological make-up of each individual according to Freud's theory of the psyche. In its maturest form, Freud's theory of man's mental apparatus viewed the mind as having a three-fold structure, and Freud termed these three parts the ego, the superego and the id respectively. The id corresponded to what Freud had called in earlier versions of his theory the Unconscious and contained those elements and energies which were repressed and not allowed access to the conscious mind of the individual. One can conclude that the instincts which were so repressed were those adjudged disadvantageous to survival. These instincts, however, often attempt to find access to the conscious mind and their force has to be rechannelled in some way. Dreams and hysterical conversion illustrate ways in which such forces find egress without admitting their associated instinctual impulses into the conscious mind of the individual concerned. The individual's conscious mind, or the greater part of it, Freud later termed the ego. The ego, amongst other things, has the task of keeping the instincts of the id at bay. It also contains those elements of the mental reservoir which are not repressed. The superego, however, was the last of the triad which Freud discovered, and it consists of the agency which judges and criticizes the individual and his actions. Freud believed that the superego exists in every individual's make up, and is that part of the mind which the individual sometimes feels is giving a critical commentary on his activities - "Now he's crossing the room", "Now he's sitting down", and so on. This superego, according to Freud, sets the standard by which the individual judges his activities, in particular the operation of his ego, and it is also the agency which criticizes the ego's achievement. The ego, therefore, in striving to do its work, for example, in keeping the instincts of the id at bay, is constantly trying to live up to the standard set for it by the superego, or, as Freud earlier termed it, the ego-ideal. Nor is Freud silent on the subject of the genesis of this critical agency. The superego, according to Freud, is an internalization or introjection of the earliest influences which an individual has upon his character, namely the individual's image of his parents, particularly his father. The young child's need to be like his father expresses itself in identification with, and introjection of, the father's character which becomes the child's superego. Later influences, such as teachers, admired friends and other heroes of the environment, also play a part in shaping the critical agency of the superego. The energy which fuels the superego, according to Freud, is internalized aggression; the aggression which fuels the instincts repressed in the id finds an outlet in the superego where it is applied in demanding that the ego keep the aggressive instincts of the id at bay. "The superego confronts the rest of the ego, and imposes demands upon it of a normative kind".[12]

Looked at from the point of view of survival, the workings described make perfect sense. The individual is subjected to various instinctual impulses, some of which promote, and some of which hamper, survival. He must clearly, therefore, repress those which hamper and develop those which promote this goal. In deciding which are which, clearly resort will be made to those who have, as it were, done well in the survival game. Equally clearly, the father figure is just such a person having secured a mate and produced offspring, which is, in the long term, that on which the survival of the species depends. Thus, the standards of the successful parent are adopted as those which the individual must himself attain and are taken to be the standards against which self-criticism will be carried out. The examples of other successful persons are later used to modify this parental basis, although the model remains, by and large, parental in nature. The individual thus carries on his part in the survival game according to the standards he has accepted from the previous generation. Obviously, there is stress present in such a mental structure, the stress caused by repressing certain instincts. However, on Freud's model, the energies bottled up in the id are released through the superego to aid the process of repression, rather than to undermine as would be the case if they had entered the ego directly and had not been rechannelled.

This same model can clearly be drawn up to suit a community of individuals as well as, if not better than, it can be for one of its members. Freud himself was fully aware of this.[13] Having stated, very like Professor Hart, that the urge towards personal happiness in an individual often stood in hostile opposition to the urge towards union with others, Freud continued:

"The analogy between the process of civilization and the path of individual development may be extended in an important respect. It can be asserted that the community, too, evolves a super-ego under whose influence cultural development proceeds ... The super-ego of an epoch of civilization has an origin similar to that of an individual. It is based on the impression left behind by the personalities of great leaders - men of overwhelming force of mind or men in whom one of the human impulsions has found its strongest and purest, and therefore often its most one-sided expression.... Here, indeed, we come accross the remarkable circumstance that the mental processes concerned are actually more familiar to us and more accessible to consciousness as they are seen in the group than they can be in the individual man. In him, when tension arises, it is only the aggressiveness of the super-ego which, in the form of reproaches, makes itself noisily heard; its actual demands often remain unconscious in the background. If we bring them to conscious knowledge, we find that they coincide with the precepts of the prevailing cultural super-ego. At this point the two processes, that of the cultural development of the group and that of the cultural development of the individual, are, as it were, always interlocked. For that reason some of the manifestations and properties of the super-ego can be more easily detected in its behaviour in the cultural community than in the separate individual."[14] Freud reckoned that the cultural super-ego had developed its ideals and set up its demands, and that among its demands were those concerning the relations of human beings with one another comprised under the heading of ethics. Freud is clearly using the term, ethics, in a sense wide enough to include laws within its ambit. He thought that ethics was a therapeutic attempt to deal with "the sorest spot in every civilization"[15] namely, the problem of how to get rid of the greatest hindrance to civilization, the constitutional inclination of human beings to be aggressive towards one another.

In dealing with this problem and others related to it, which is, of course, basically the dispute situation which has already been postulated, the cultural community sets up as its super-ego, the ideals and standards of those who have survived and can be taken as showing how the trick is done. These are, according to the theory here presented, those taken as being best-suited to enunciate the principles for cohesion and survival. Those who are best-suited to do this form, in Freudian terminology, the super-ego of the community or social group in question. Before such persons or procedures emerged, the community would grope in the dark to solve each problem on a hit and miss basis. Once, however, a best-suited person, group of persons or procedure is discovered, it takes over the function of providing a model with which the problems can be solved and cohesion and survival guarded. Clearly, the best-suited principle has to be discovered; it cannot be enunciated because, before it emerges, no one is best-suited to enunciate it. Nor, once they are in existence, can the best-suited persons or procedure enunciate the best-suited principle, for if they did, their enunciation would itself be dependent on the best-suited principle, that is itself. It can of course be described, but it must be remembered that such descriptions, like the enunciations, are only approximations. The best-suited principle is displayed rather than enunciated in the workings of the legal system.

While the best-suited persons or procedures succeed in enunciating principles which aid cohesion and survival, the enunciations made will be ratified as binding laws by the members of the social group. That they are so obeyed displays the fact that they are regarded as the best-suited to enunciate. Once the best-suited principle is in operation, laws can originate in two ways: firstly, they can emerge as previously from well-established practices of the community which are settled as aiding cohesion and survival, and, secondly, by enunciation by the best-suited persons or procedures. The best-suited principle itself emerges according to the former method. Rules which emerge according to the former method do not rely on enunciation for their validity; they are accepted as valid.[16] Thus, if a rule which has emerged by the former method is subsequently enunciated, its basis of validity is not altered and remains the first method. If a principle is enunciated according to the best-suited method which is against what is accepted as being necessary for cohesion and survival according to the primary method, the enunciated principle will not necessarily be ratified as binding. This does not automatically invalidate the authority of the best-suited persons or procedures, but clearly they are weakened by such an occurrence. If they regularly enunciate unacceptable principles, then this may lead to a partial or even complete withdrawal of the belief that they are the best-suited persons or procedures, and a change in the best-suited principle may take place. The best-suited persons or procedures can, of course, produce prescriptions for disaster and yet have their judgements ratified; such a community is clearly unlikely to cohere and survive for long. This in outline is the best-suited principle. This outline must now be considerably developed.

III

According to what has been stated above, legal rules can now be divided into two categories - those which are accepted by the community as aiding survival as a result of practice and those which are accepted because they have been enunciated according to the best-suited principle. The best-suited principle, that certain persons or procedures are able to enunciate best the survival principles needed by the community, is itself accepted, as has been said, as a result of practical experience. Both methods of acceptance lead to valid or efficacious legal rules emerging because the rules which emerge according to either method have the necessary internal aspect and are, therefore, binding. The first kind have the necessary internal aspect because they are accepted as being necessary for cohesion and survival; the second have this aspect because they have been enunciated according to the principle accepted as producing the best guidelines for these purposes. Some theorists distinguish the concepts of legal validity and efficacy fairly strictly while allowing for a connection between the two. Kelsen, for instance, regards validity and efficacy as two entirely different concepts, but having an important interrelationship. To him, a norm is considered to be valid only on the condition that it belongs to a system of norms which is, on the whole, efficacious.[17] He regards efficacy as a condition, not the reason, of validity. According to Kelsen, a norm is not valid because it is efficacious, but rather if the order to which it belongs is, on the whole, efficacious. The system, according to Kelsen, is efficacious if there is a presupposition that the laws of the system should be obeyed. The presupposition, Kelsen terms the basic norm or grundnorm of the system. Thus, behind the rules accepted from experience, there is the notion that they ought to be followed, that is, according to Kelsen, a basic norm which validates them. Similarly, rules enunciated according to the best-suited principle are obeyed because it is believed rules so enunciated should be obeyed, because, in other words, of the basic norm. From this, all the rules of the system derive their validity.

Kelsen, however, as the title of his theory - the Pure Theory of Law - suggests, does not ask why the basic norm is followed. According to the present theory, the reason why legal rules are followed, the factor which accounts for the internal aspect, is that they are accepted as being the correct principles for social cohesion and survival. It is the lack of this reason for following rules or norms, basic or otherwise, which it is submitted led Kelsen to make the unnecessary distinction between validity and efficacy. According to Kelsen, there is no inconsistency in saying that a valid norm is nevertheless inefficacious.

For example, although the rules enunciated by the best-suited principle are generally followed, that is, the system is, on the whole, efficacious, it may occur that one particular enunciation will not meet with acceptance from the community, that is, will not be efficacious. This situation, it can be argued, occurred in England and Wales in relation to the Industrial Relations Act, 1971. The enunciation, even though made in accordance with the best-suited principle, may not be accepted as a good guideline for cohesion and survival. If this occurs, it is submitted that there is nothing to be gained from calling such a rule valid though inefficacious. It is more realistic to incorporate within the basic norm the limitation which allows for such an occurrence. This, the best-suited principle does, for it recognizes that the rules enunciated according to the best-suited method will be accepted as valid provided they can be accepted as good for cohesion and survival. Clearly, the fact that they are so enunciated will be very persuasive that this is the case, particularly if the best-suited method is well-established. However, where a rule, even though enunciated according to this method, is not so accepted, it is not a valid rule of law for the social group concerned.

Professor Hart, in his theory of law, regards law as a system of rules. Hart's rules are of two kinds, primary and secondary. Primary rules are the rules of conduct which the members of a community observe. Secondary rules are rules concerning the proper enunciation, change and application of such primary rules and are of three kinds, namely, rules of recognition, rules of change and rules of adjudication. Secondary rules are rules for the officials of a legal system instructing them as to how to discover, alter or make determinations with the primary rules. Hart himself states that these rules need only be observed by the officials so interested. One argument for separating validity from efficacy would be to say that even though a particular enunciation was not accepted as efficacious by the members of the community, nevertheless the officials who apply the law would recognize it as valid according to the rule of recognition, and would try to apply it, and in doing so they would not be acting illegally. This argument, however, exposes a weakness in Hart's theory. By stating that secondary rules are meta-rules for officials, Hart makes it clear that such rules are not laws. These rules belong to a different game, connected to, but distinct from, the game of legal validity. The secondary rules are approximate enunciations of what officials should do in administering the law, and, if these rules are followed, such officials will be regarded as having acted properly, their conduct is unimpeachable. However, the best-suited principle, unlike the rule of recognition, is not a standard for officials to use in their meta-game activity, but a standard according to which the acceptability of enunciations made according to the best-suited method is adjudged by the members of the community generally, the standard by which it is determined whether an enunciated rule is to be accorded the internal aspect which makes it binding. This is a feature missing from Hart's theory, but one which is essential to a complete theory of law. Again, it is probably missing because Hart, although recognizing the goals of social existence, does not incorporate them sufficiently into his theory of law. While the secondary rules which officials follow are meta-rules connected with the legal system, the officials being the personnel of the best-suited method in its operation, they are not laws themselves, but are rules of a higher activity or meta-game. The best-suited principle on the other hand is the standard by which the activities of the officials in enunciating rules and determining disputes are criticized and deemed worthy of acceptance. Validity in the narrow sense refers to the officials' meta-game. When dealing with the level of laws on the other hand, there is no merit in stating that a rule though validly enunciated for the officials is not acceptable according to the need for cohesion and survival. Only those rules which are acceptable need to be regarded as binding, efficacious and valid. Likewise, even though a rule is not properly enunciated according to the meta-rules of officials, it is nevertheless likely that it will be accepted as binding by the members of the community if it aids their goals. The distinction might be rendered as being between technical and actual validity. For present purposes, valid is used synonymously with binding and efficacious; the narrower sense, where needed, will be rendered by the phrase technically valid.

An important feature of the best-suited principle is that it accepts the content of a rule as being significant in determining its validity. This feature can be illustrated by making use of an example taken from Kelsen. A child is told that he ought to go to school. If he asks why he ought to go to school, he is told that he ought to go to school because his father wishes it, and he ought to obey his father. The norm which gives the child a reason for obeying the first norm is, therefore, a norm of a higher order. If the child asks why he ought to obey his father, he may be told that he ought because God so commands. Again, recourse is had to a higher order norm to find a reason for obeying a lower order norm. Finally, it may be presupposed that God ought to be obeyed - the highest order norm of all, the basic norm of the system, which provides the ultimate reason for obeying all the norms in the system. However, the father instead of instructing the child to go to school may have forbidden him to say his prayers. This may put the child in a quandary because, on the one hand, he ought to obey his father, while on the other hand he may recognize that God commands him to say his prayers. According to Kelsen, the father's command not to pray is valid within the system but may prove inefficacious. According to the present theory, it may be technically valid, but is not really valid because it will not be ratified by the child. This is because, again according to the present theory, the situation would be presented differently. The child would obey the father as the father is the best-suited person to enunciate principles for the child's welfare. If, however, the child is aware that a particular principle does not promote his welfare, that principle will not be obeyed. In other words, the best-suited principle must be ratified on each occasion that it is exercised, and the content of rules enunciated according to the principle is the factor which determines whether the rule is accepted or not. If it is, then the best-suited principle is ratified and becomes stronger; if not, then it is somewhat weakened. The degree to which it is weakened by non-ratification depends upon its strength prior to non-ratification. Its prior strength will also influence the willingness of the members of the community to ratify a suspect enunciation. In short, no rule will be accepted unless it is regarded as aiding cohesion and survival, and the method according to which a rule is enunciated is never sufficient to guarantee its acceptance. Without such acceptance, the rule will lack the necessary internal aspect to make it a binding law, so that even if the members of the community are forced to comply by powerful officials, they will be obeying the officials to, survive and not the rule itself.[18]

In this last example, the officials who enforce the rules will have the requisite, critical, reflective attitude towards the notion that they ought to enforce the rules, and the other members of the community will have the critical, reflective attitude towards the notion that the officials must be obeyed if they, the other members, are to survive. However, although they are coerced into conforming to the rules in question, the other members of the community will not have the critical, reflective attitude towards those rules which is needed to make them laws. Indeed, the notion that the officials must be obeyed will be accepted from practical experience not enunciation, and, for these other members, a new best-suited principle will have to develop, a sort of _imperium in imperio_, before this notion can itself be enunciated. This sort of society, where the mass obeys officials out of fear and only the officials enjoy the internal aspect of the rules, has been dubbed a mameluke society.[19] Unfortunately, those theories of law which equate legal validity with technical validity are rooted historically in the notion that laws are commands backed by threats, that is, that the mameluke model is the basic model for legal systems. The most cogent expression of this view of law was that of John Austin who saw laws as the commands of an habitually obeyed sovereign to his subjects, which commands, were backed up by the threat of a sanction.[20] Professor Hart has criticized this theory and shown that in failing to account for the internal aspect of legal rules, it fails to distinguish between the concepts of being obliged and being obligated. Where an order is obeyed out of fear, as in the mameluke society, the members of the community are obliged to follow the rules; where, however, they obey out of the internal, critical, reflective attitude, they feel obligated to obey. What Hart, however, fails to take account of is why they should feel obligated. The answer is that they accept the standards of conduct involved as being guidelines for survival. If they do not so accept, they must either be obliged to follow the standards, or the standards will be rejected. The best-suited principle takes account of this necessary feature. It also shows that where persons are obliged to obey, there, too, they act from the survival motive, but the rule which is followed is not that being enforced, but that they must obey the commands of the officials to survive.

The command and obedience theory of law continues to haunt theories where validity is something for officials rather than all members of the group, and clearly it takes no account of the content of the commands. The fact that the sovereign so commands is in itself treated as sufficient to attract obedience. There is an obvious similarity here to the best-suited principle, but the similarity stops at the point where content becomes a relevant feature of the latter. One of the offshoots of the command theory is the search for the sovereign in any community, the law-creating agency which is habitually obeyed by its subjects yet renders habitual obedience to none. In English legal theory, the classic exposition of the doctrine of sovereignty is that of Albert Venn Dicey. According to Dicey, Parliament was sovereign in England. He expressed his views in both positive and negative terms: positively, any Act of Parliament, or any part of an Act of Parliament, which makes a new law, or repeals or modifies an existing law, will be obeyed by the courts; negatively, there is no person or body of persons who can, under the English constitution, make rules which override or derogate from an Act of Parliament, or which will be enforced by the courts in derogation of an Act of Parliament.[21]

Dicey, however, believed that, despite the wide statement of the doctrine, certain limitations had to be recognized. These limitations were of two kinds: there were internal limits - the sovereign could not act out of character - and external limits, and it is these latter which are of interest here. Dicey wrote that: "The external limit to the real power of a sovereign consists in the possibility or certainty that his subjects, or a large number of them, will disobey or resist his laws". Thus, Parliament would not enact that all blue-eyed babies should be killed as it would not be obeyed. Dicey is here clearly anticipating the content-test which is an essential feature of ratification under the best-suited principle. Unless the rule enunciated can be taken as aiding cohesion and survival, it will not be accepted as valid. The function of ratifying resides with the members of the community generally and not with officials. It is acceptance by these members which gives the enunciations of best-suited persons or procedures the force of law. Dicey was groping towards this sort of conclusion when he quoted Hume's words that government is founded on opinion only,[22] but was hampered from reaching the conclusion because the concept of which he was treating, sovereignty, was itself rooted in the inadequacies of the command theory. Just how close Dicey got can be seen from his comments when treating of constitutional conventions,[23] where he postulates that although legal sovereignty rests with Parliament and it is the elected not the electors who are obeyed, political sovereignty resides with the electors.[24] In other words, although technical validity can be given to laws by Parliament, actual validity requires that the laws be accepted by the people. This view is clearly a harbinger of the best-suited principle which is here set forth, and which accepts that the content of a rule is very relevant to the question of whether it is a valid, binding, efficacious law.[25]

Rules of law, then, emerge in two ways. Either they are accepted as a result of practical experience or they are enunciated according to the best-suited principle of the community. The best-suited principle itself is accepted on the basis of practical experience. If a rule has been enunciated by the best-suited method, this is a reason for accepting it as a valid, but not in itself a sufficient reason. If the content of the rule is deemed not to aid survival, then it will not be accepted as a rule of law by the community despite its being enunciated by the best-suited method.

Whether a community has a best-suited method of enunciation, and, if it has, just what exactly that method is, are both empirical questions. In particular, any answer given to the latter question must be realized for what it is, an approximate description of what a particular community regards as the best-suited method of enunciation at a particular moment of time, and as such the answer may be incomplete and indeed, in time, the method itself can undergo important changes. Examples of best-suited methods include what the leader or leaders of the community enunciate, the leaders being the strongest or the eldest men or whatever. On the other hand, faith may be placed in a popular assembly or religious institution. The persons who actually settle disputes may be trusted as enunciators, for they actually encounter the situations which present dangers to cohesion. Alternatively, principles laid down by the founders of the community may be regarded as unalterable, and are sometimes regarded as having divine origins. Thus, constitutions, codes, statutes and judge-made rules are all examples of laws laid down according to a best-suited method. The best-suited principle exists then in all legal systems which have gone beyond the stage of being purely customary in nature.[26] It takes over the role accorded to sovereignty, rules of recognition and grundnorms in other theories. Certain questions which have posed difficulties in relation to these rival key concepts must now be asked of the new concept to see if it can provide better answers. It will be seen that the best-suited principle provides a better theoretical structure, within which answers to these questions can be given, than do its earlier counterparts.

IV

In certain countries, particularly in those where the people feel that under an earlier method of enunciation they were subject to oppression, those principles regarded as the most fundamental and important to cohesion and survival will be enunciated in the form of a written constitution or Bill of Rights. These principles will be enunciated by best-suited persons or procedures, and, in earlier times, such enunciations were often ascribed to a deity. The Ten Commandments belong to this sort of enunciation as do the legal tenets of the Qur'an. However, the fact that the fundamental survival principles have been enunciated does not end the task of enunciation for all time for disputes will still have to be settled, and in difficult situations more principles and rules of cohesion and survival may have to be formulated. Thus, in the United States of America, for example, despite the existence of a Bill of Rights, courts have to settle disputes, and Congress and state legislatures have to enunciate survival principles from time to time. A problem which arises in such contexts is what is to be done where the current dispute-deciders or enunciators, the courts and the legislature respectively, think that the correct survival principle at the present time is not that contained in the constitution. The problem normally arises in the form of a statute declaring a principle contrary to some fundamental principle enshrined in the constitution. The question faced at such moments is which is the principle which really aids cohesion and survival. It is possible that the question will be answered on its merits each time such a conflict arises, but it is more usual in this sort of conflict between statute and fundamental right for the question to be determined according to the best-suited principle of the community. Thus, if the drafters of the constitution are still regarded as having enunciated the best principles for survival, the statute will be abrogated; but if the current legislators, with their contemporary knowledge of facts and events, are now regarded as best-suited, their enunciations will be accepted despite the constitution. The latter view is taken, for example, by the Swiss; in the United States, the former opinion is held.

An interesting feature of the United States solution is that the issue is decided by the courts. It was the Supreme Court in _Marbury_ v. _Madison_[27] which held that it could review legislation to see if it offended against the constitution, and it is that court which continues to carry out that function. It must have been open for the people to accept or not to accept that ruling of the Court with regard to review, and they clearly accepted the Court's decision on the merits, and thus also accepted that the Supreme Court is best-suited to enunciate what is the better survival principle between competing alternatives, and who are the best-suited to enunciate such principles. Nevertheless, it is the members of the community, the people of the United States, who accept and thereby ratify these rulings of the Supreme Court, that is, they ratify it as best-suited to make these enunciations. Thus, the question "Is this law in America?" is answered by the Supreme Court, and their rules of recognition for determining between different enunciations are part of a metagame structure.

That such a function is entrusted to the courts should not provoke surprise, for it is the courts which traditionally enunciate principles for dispute-settlement and thus for cohesion and survival. The difference here is that the dispute is actually between competing principles. Nevertheless, the courts are given the task of shaping the law "in the arena of action". The qualities which the judges of the Supreme Court need to be best-suited, and the consequences for the community should mistakes be made, were aptly described by Tocqueville in _Democracy in America_, and the relevant passage has been quoted by Sir Kenneth Wheare in his book, _Modern Constitutions_.

"'The Federal judges must not only be good

citizens, and men possessed of that information and integrity which are indispensable to magistrates, but they must be statesmen - politicians, not unread in the signs of the times, not afraid to brave the obstacles which can be subdued, nor slow to turn aside such encroaching elements as may threaten the supremacy of the Union and the obedience which is due to the laws.' And he added, 'if the Supreme Court is even composed of imprudent men or bad citizens, the Union may be plunged into anarchy or civil war'. What he said of the Supreme Court of the United States, applies with almost equal force to other countries where judicial review of the Constitution prevails."[28]

Very much the same sort of problem has been discussed in relation to the doctrine of sovereignty and is termed the problem of continuing sovereignty. Basically, that problem amounts to this: if the best-suited persons enunciate a principle for survival which contradicts an earlier principle enunciated by the same method, one principle has to be treated as the correct principle and the other has to be rejected. The problem of which to accept as valid is similar to that where a constitutional provision is at odds with a statute, except for the fact that here the same best-suited mechanism produced both of the principles involved. Again, each case could be taken on its merits, or it could be held that the earlier principle was the correct one, or it could be held that it was the later. If the earlier were preferred, then clearly the persons who enunciated that principle are regarded as better-suited than those who enunciated the later; and if the later is preferred, then clearly the current best-suited persons are always to be trusted. It is this latter solution that is generally accepted as being correct. The issue is settled in favour of the current best-suited persons and a guide to dealing with such disputes is given in the form of the principle, <u>lex posterior derogat priori</u>. The role of such principles will be examined later. This solution used to be expressed by saying that there was a principle of continuing sovereignty. It is better expressed under the new theory by saying that the best-suited principle states that those who are currently best-suited to enunciate are best-suited to enunciate not only as against their contemporaries, but also as against their predecessors within that role. The question must, however, be answered empirically for each society at any given moment of time.[29] In England and Wales, it is currently answered by the courts according to the maxim mentioned above, so that clearly once again the courts are trusted as best-suited to enunciate what is law in this jurisdiction, and their enunciations are accepted and ratified.

Another related problem concerns the phenomenon of legislative entrenchment. If a survival principle which is enunciated by the best-suited mechanism is regarded as of fundamental importance, such as the provisions of a Bill of Rights, then the best-suited persons at the time of this enunciation may wish to guard against its repeal at the hands of their successors in that role, whom they accordingly do not really regard as being necessarily equal to them in skill at enunciation. One of the techniques used to prevent such a subsequent repeal is to state at the same time as enunciating the principle that it can only be repealed by a special procedure, such as for example requiring a majority of three-quarters of the legislature being in favour of repeal, or requiring both Houses of a bicameral legislature to sit together to effect such a plan. If such a course is adopted, the question arises as to whether their successors in the role must follow the special procedure to repeal the principle or whether they can repeal the principle and the special provision by following the general procedure, that is, by a bare majority or while sitting separately. This question, too, really turns on asking who are the best-suited to enunciate on this point. If the answer is the former, then the special procedure will have to be followed; if the latter, then the principle and the procedural provision can be abrogated by an enactment in the ordinary manner. On that issue, if the former view is taken, the best-suited principle will have undergone a change.[30]

The same problem can be examined at a far more general level. It is possible that the best-suited persons would attempt to change the community's best-suited principle itself. Thus, they might state that in future only enactments carried by a three-quarters majority were to be binding, or, in the classic example, they, in the United Kingdom Parliament, might enunciate that in future their powers be exercised by the Greater London Council. Such an unlikely event, however, would still fall to be treated empirically under the present theory. Thus, if the community ratified this particular enunciation, a point of some doubt, it would in future accept the enunciations of the Greater London Council in the place of those of Parliament. However, it might be obeying the G.L.C. because of the Parliamentary enunciation, in which case it would clearly still regard Parliament as best-suited, or it might now regard the G.L.C. itself as best-suited and, therefore, worthy of obedience. It is likely that at first the former would be true, but that as the enunciations of the G.L.C. were regularly ratified, then confidence in that body would grow so that in time it would be obeyed in its own right as best-suited to enunciate. Parliament would then have difficulty in taking back its own powers. Such changes in the best-suited principle may have occurred within this jurisdiction this century by virtue of the Parliament Acts.[31]

The so-called problem of autochthony is nothing more than a special instance of this situation between states. The problem arises when a colonial power grants independence to one of its colonies. The imperial Parliament will pass a statute granting independence to the colony and the statute will probably contain the new, independent state's first constitution. The difficulty is that it may appear as though the new state's constitution and all the laws that it generates are based ultimately upon the statute of the imperial Parliament, and that that enactment is the source of the validity of all the new state's laws. Such new states frequently wish to sever all connections with their colonial past; they wish their laws and legal system to be autochthonous. The best-suited principle provides the answer to their question by treating the question of what is the basis of the validity of the laws of the new state as an empirical one. If the reason that the community regards the decisions of the courts and the enunciations of the legislature of the new state as valid is that they are carried out in accordance with the provisions laid down by the imperial Parliament, then clearly the body regarded as being best-suited to enunciate the community's survival principles is still the imperial Parliament. However, if the constitution is itself now treated as being the enunciation of the fundamental survival principles, and the legislature and the courts as being best-suited to make further enunciations, then as far as the members of the new state community are concerned there has been a change in the best-suited principle of the community. Once that change has occurred, and as in the previous example it may take time to occur, the time involved in acquiring confidence in the new legislature while reliance upon and veneration of the old weakens, the community will be autochthonous, entirely independent of the mother Parliament. It may even be the case that the new state community already accepted the suitability of local enunciations before the technical hand-over, in which event complete autochthony is very much the case from the outset. The problem of what is the position of the mother Parliament, if it wishes to repeal the statute granting independence, raises an issue which will be dealt with below.

Having looked at problems which arise when an older enunciation is in conflict with a more recent one, it is only fitting to look at the question of how long an enunciation remains binding once ratified by the community. This problem is not difficult. The answer to it applies not only to rules which are accepted because they have been enunciated according to the best-suited principle, but also to rules accepted as a result of practical experience, of which the best-suited principle is one. All rules are valid while they continue to be accepted and ratified by the community. Regardless of their provenance or importance, once they are adjudged to be a hindrance to cohesion and survival rather than an aid, they will no longer be accepted and are thus no longer valid. Questions concerning the continuing technical validity of enunciated rules and whether such rules can be abrogated by desuetude or negative custom are generated by the residues of the command theory of law. The problem of desuetude is no problem once the validity of a law is treated as an empirical question to be answered according to the test of whether it is accepted by the community either as the result of practical experience or as a consequence of the best-suited principle. If a dispute about the validity of such a rule arises, it is again the courts who are likely to adjudicate on the issue. They may act on the principle that enunciations remain valid until formal repeal. If so, then enunciations based on this principle have to be ratified and accepted. Indeed, the best-suited principle itself is an example of a survival principle which has changed with time and the old forms of which have been abrogated through desuetude.

Disputes as to whether an old or recent enunciation is the law, or as to whether an old enunciation is still binding, tend to end up for decision in the courts. The courts, in other words, are accepted as having the last official word on what is the law, and it is their enunciation of what is law which is accepted and ratified or rejected by the community. Clearly, therefore, the courts, shaping the law as they do in the arena of dispute situations, have a strong claim when resorted to over such matters to be _the_ best-suited institutions to enunciate the survival principles of that community. Other persons or bodies enunciate - the founding fathers, Parliaments, and so on - but the courts are left to make the final determination. What they say, therefore, about whether the constitution is sounder than legislation, whether recent legislation is better than more dated, and about other like matters, is merely enunciated to lay down guidelines to help them get at the enunciation of the survival principle for the community. Such guidelines - whether single principles like the _lex posterior_ maxim or whole rules of recognition - are instructions to enable them to get at the enunciation and guidelines therefore for the courts and not the community, although they may also be utilized by non-best-suited persons in discussions and speculations about the law. Such guidelines are part of the metagame of finding the survival principle and not part of the legal regulation of the community. They are not rules of law but metarules; they refer to a related but distinct activity. They exist, however, in order to keep the courts on the right track, as it were, when enunciating. They are meant to ensure that the principles which the courts enunciate will be accepted and ratified by the community, and contribute also, indirectly, to preserving and increasing the strength of the community's best-suited principle.

As well as developing guidelines to help solve disputes between competing survival principles and the like, guidelines like the _lex posterior_ maxim or a rule of recognition, the courts also develop guidelines to help them in solving other kinds of disputes with which they are faced. All such guidelines are enunciations of lessons they have learnt from practical experience. Such enunciations are intended to help them survive as the best-suited institution to enunciate for their community.[32] One of the difficulties which can be overcome by deriving guidelines from practical experience is how best to apply a rule enunciated elsewhere to a particular dispute situation. Sometimes this difficulty will be whether the rule should be interpreted so as to apply or not to apply to a given set of circumstances. Canons of statutory interpretation are evolved to meet such difficulties and are examples of metarules which the courts follow in solving disputes and enunciating the dispute-solving principles. Rules of this sort decide whether words are to be given their natural or a technical meaning, whether the mischief which Parliament was trying to solve should be borne in mind when looking for the meaning of the rule, and whether preliminary reports, what the French call travaux préparatoires, are to be consulted in performing the task. On a wider ambit, the whole doctrine of precedent can be viewed as the principle the courts follow in deciding whether to treat their own previous decisions as such guidelines, and the rule of recognition as how best to decide between different forms of enunciation - earlier decisions, statutes, the constitution, juristic opinion, and so on. Individual principles may also be used as guidelines of how to solve particular types of case. Thus, the principle that "Equality is equity" is a guideline as to how to settle disputes over fractions of ownership, and nemo dat quod non habet a principle as to what to do if property is sold by a person who has no title to it. Such principles are not laws of the community. It is not the case generally that "Equality is equity" or that nemo dat quod non habet; exceptions to such principles exist, and the finished rules of law, the enunciated survival principles, incorporate such exceptions. The principles are only guidelines for the manufacture of rules of law. The rules themselves are the finished product according to which the process of manufacture is judged. Often such rules have to take account of conflicting principles.[33] It is according to the quality of the rules that the best-suited institution is judged, although the fact that it follows acceptable manufacturing processes will probably sway the members of the community into accepting and ratifying its normative products. Thus, where a dispute-settlement may be unpalatable, the fact that it is a principled decision may be the sweet which succeeds in getting the child to take the medicine.[34]

On occasion, a dispute may arise for which there is no established principle of settlement. In such an event, the courts nevertheless are faced with the task of solving the dispute, and have to enunciate a new survival principle. Clearly, in shaping this new rule of law, they will use their metarules of enunciation to find the best solution. Such cases, to which no predetermined answer exists, have been termed hard cases. In solving these, the courts enunciate new rules of law, and it is in such situations that the courts find themselves most at the mercy of the need for acceptance and ratification from the community members at large. The courts, always in the front-line of the best-suited principle, are here at their most exposed. If the rules they enunciate under these circumstances are accepted, their position as the best-suited to enunciate is strengthened; if they are not, their position is accordingly weakened.

A question which exercises legal theorists is whether or not there is a right answer to such hard cases. Under the present theory, the right answer would be that which aids cohesion and survival, and the task of the courts is presented as being to find the principle which does that. If the courts come up with the principle which is regarded as doing that, then it will be accepted as the right answer. Also under the present theory, the metarules of interpratation and so on are presented as methods of discovering the right answer to the problem. They are a sort of technology for finding the correct survivial principles.[35] Whether the principle enunciated actually aids survival is a distinct question from whether the people believe it will. In accepting and ratifying or rejecting, the people may be mistaken, so that wrong principles may be ratified while the right may be rejected.

The type of hard cases which has just been considered is one to which no enunciated rule already applies. Originally, all disputes which came up for settlement would be hard cases of this sort. Only as a result of the practical experience of solving such hard cases, were the courts able to formulate metarules of dispute-settlement and rule-enunciation. Sometimes, however, a different sort of hard case may arise as a result of such metarules having been formulated. Such cases arise where the courts recognize that an established rule which according to their metarules ought to be applied to a dispute situation does not solve the dispute in the best manner to guarantee social cohesion and survival. This situation involves, as it were, a crisis of confidence in the metarules. If the metarules are regarded as the best available for good enunciation, they are likely to be followed; but if they are not so well established, they may be altered or disregarded. Thus, in such a situation the courts may ignore the metarules and reach what they think is the best survival principle as it appears to them at the moment. Alternatively, they may strive to stay within the metarules by finding some feature in the instant situation which distinguishes it from the earlier cases in which the unsatisfactory rule has been applied. If this feature is not really present and is continually resorted to, it may form one of the fictions around which a substantial part of the common law has developed. The last solution, of course, is for the courts to stick resolutely by the metarules and apply the unsatisfactory rule, possibly with the rider that the legislature ought to abrogate it as soon as possible. This last solution with the rider may well lead to the current metarules being adversely criticized as they are being condemned as techniques for enunciating the best rules by the very persons who use them. If the last solution is adopted without the rider, and is found to be unsatisfactory by the people, particularly if the phenomenon is of frequent occurrence, the best-suited principle of the community may be in for a change. Thus it was, for example, that the rigidity of the mediaeval common law led to the development of the Court of Chancery - in effect a change in the best-suited principle of the mediaeval English community. It is perhaps salutary to remember that all these rules, whether the survival principles or the metarules used to discover and formulate them, are only approximate enunciations of what is required to achieve the respective goals, and to treat them as anything more may endanger survival, either that of the institution or that of the community.

Each time a survival principle is enunciated according to the best-suited method, it must be accepted and ratified by the community. This is particularly crucial where the principle emerges from either of the two sorts of hard cases which have been described. If the principle is rejected, then clearly the best-suited method has on that occasion not worked and the community's best-suited principle is accordingly weakened. To what extent it has been weakened depends upon how injurious to social cohesion and survival the enunciated principle was regarded as being. A suspicion that a strong best-suited method has failed may not lead to rejection; constant suspicions over a weak method may destroy it altogether. Most, established best-suited methods are probably strong enough to overcome occasional rejections. Thus, the best-suited method of England and Wales adapted to the rejection of the Industrial Relations Act. However, a really serious aberration might destroy even a very strong method. Thus, if Parliament were to enact, as in Dicey's example, that all blue-eyed babies should be killed at birth, it is more than likely that it would totally destroy its position as best-suited to enunciate for the community, and whether the courts would accept such an enunciation according to their metarules would also probably seal their fate. Where, after a gradual process of weakening or after a sudden manifestation of unfitness, the best-suited method is not gradually altered but itself flatly rejected and replaced by another best-suited method, the problem known as that of revolutionary legality arises.

V

When a best-suited method or person is rejected, it is normally replaced by another. Sometimes it will be found that the person or persons who replace the deposed best-suited persons will already have been recognized, at least by some members of the community, as making better formulations of the correct principles, than the best-suited persons, and, thus, their enunciations will be accepted and ratified by this section of the community immediately. This section will form the nexus of those who accept and ratify, and, therefore, feel obligated to follow the enunciations. Around this core of faithful supporters, the authority of the new best-suited method will grow, extending to the other members of the community. Until it extends in this way, the new principle exists in a sort of mameluke society. Eventually, the new best-suited principle may become that of the whole community. Of course, while some feel obliged rather than obligated to obey, there will always be an *imperium in imperio*, and this may never be wholly eradicated. This section of the community may still adhere to the old best-suited principle. An example of such a group are the so-called White Russians who still feel bound by the tenets of the Tsarist regime and do not accept the validity of the new, Soviet republic.

A problem closely related to that of the authority of a new regime which has replaced the old by *coup d'état* or revolution is why in such circumstances some laws, perhaps the vast majority, passed by the old regime continue to be treated as valid. In point of fact, the theory here put forward is not really presented with this problem. According to the new theory, each and every enunciation of the best-suited institution has to be accepted and ratified to be valid. The validity of an enunciation, or of any rule, depends upon its acceptance and ratification. Thus, enunciations of the old best-suited institution which have been accepted and ratified as being good for cohesion and survival are valid and continue to be so once accepted, despite the fact that the institution has ceased to be accepted as the best-suited to enunciate and has been replaced by another. The problem of revolutionary legality arises from theories that treat legal validity as being due to the provenance of a rule. By squarely stating that validity is due to acceptance and ratification of a rule by the members of the community, the new theory avoids this pitfall and its problems altogether. The rules are accepted and ratified by the people in the same way as are the meanings of words in their language and the rules of logic and mathematics. They are accepted as correct and are, therefore, valid, being ratified on each occasion that resort is had to them and they are used.

One problem which has not been discussed so far, however, is the fact that not all the members of a community may ratify a particular principle. Indeed, not all may accept and ratify the best-suited principle of the community. Those who do not accept the best-suited principle may be obliged to follow the rules but will not feel obligated to do so. From their point of view, they obey the officials not the rules, and the society is a mameluke society where almost everyone is a mameluke except them. Such a problem can be particularly acute in a society with discrete minority groups who do not accept the best-suited principle. Some communities with such minorities forming a part of them attempt to overcome the problem by ensuring that the personnel of the best-suited institutions are representative of these groups. Thus, for example, a Canadian cabinet must contain both English-speaking and French-speaking Canadians.[36] However, such discrete minorities may come to develop their own best-suited institution to counsel them as to what to do if they wish their group to survive. This best-suited institution may counsel that they obey the rules of the larger community, completely or in part, so as to avoid persecution and to protect their chances of survival. However, if the group is regarded as being strong enough to survive attempts at persecution, the best-suited institution may counsel the group to break away from the larger community.

If this occurs, then a conflict will develop if the larger group believes that it must retain control over the smaller if its cohesion and survival are to remain unthreatened. It is a conflict of this sort which has faced the United Kingdom over the Unilateral Declaration of Independence by Rhodesia, and it is also a problem of this sort which is contemplated as supervening when it is asked what would occur if an imperial Parliament attempted to repeal a statute which granted independence to one of its colonies. The question turns on what is regarded as necessary for cohesion and survival, as do all such questions. If in the smaller state the new best-suited principle is accepted and ratified, whether given by bilateral grant or taken unilaterally, then their system is to them legal as necessary for their survival, and the attitude of the larger community will be interpreted as aggression which threatens their survival. If the larger group, however, accepts and ratifies the principle that it still has or has again taken the right to enunciate over the smaller group and believes such to be necessary for its survival, then the smaller group will appear to it as a robber band whose existence as a disobedient unit threatens the cohesion and survival of the community. The new theory allows such situations to be described in this fashion from the outside, as it allows that legality depends upon acceptance and ratification. Such a conflict cannot be resolved according to rules unless rules have been accepted and ratified as guidelines for solving such disputes. International Law promises such a system, but, as yet, it is submitted that the validity of such rules is not regarded as necessary for cohesion and survival so that they are not accepted and ratified as valid. Conflicts, such as those postulated, cannot be solved by a recognized process of dispute-settlement. However, patterns of settling such disputes may eventually emerge and be accepted as proper guidelines. Institutions may even emerge which will be accepted as being best-suited to enunciate such guidelines. Until that time, however, such issues pose a threat to cohesion and survival rather as would internal disputes within a community if it had no survival principles with which to solve such disputes while maintaining order. The international community is currently attempting to find its survival principles and dispute-settlement procedures.

VI

Legal rules, therefore, are approximate enunciations of the principles which it is believed the members of the community must follow if the community is to cohere and the members are to survive. These rules are accepted and ratified by use, either as being the result of practical experience or because they have been enunciated by the persons or procedures which the community accepts as being best-suited so to enunciate its survival principles. The best-suited institution in turn will develop metarules to aid it in its task of enunciation. This model of how laws are enunciated and accepted provides the criteria by means of which problems concerning legal validity and legality can be reduced to series of empirical questions.

****

1. Vide, generally K. Olivecrona, _Law as Fact_, 216; A. Ross, _On Law and Justice_, 13-8.
2. R.D. Laing, _Self and Others_, 108.
3. _TLP_, 3.328.
4. Judgement GD/CIV/23/66, quoted in G. Marshall, _Constitutional Theory_, 65.
5. Lucas, _PP_, 10-11.
6. There is social pressure to collude; vide, R.D. Laing, _op.cit_., 142-3.
7. Vide, D. Pears, _Wittgenstein_, 135-41.
8. _PI_, 508.
9. Jung, CW, 9(2): 27.
10. An instance of such authority being attained is the Bretwalda of Anglo-Saxon England, vide, C. Brook, _The Saxon and Norman Kings_ (London, 1978), 81-82, 91-3, 101 and F.M. Stenton, _Anglo-Saxon England_ (3rd Ed., Oxford, 1971), 33-7.
11. Hart, _CL_, 85.
12. R. Wollheim, _Freud_, 196.
13. Freud, _CW_, XXI 141-4.
14. _Ibid_., 141-2.
15. _Ibid_., 142.
16. Thus, Kelsen believes that the validity of the basic norm, or grundnorm, is always postulated, never derived; vide, H. Kelsen _General Theory of Law and State_, 110-1 and H. Kelsen _Pure Theory of Law_, 200-1.

17. H. Kelsen, _General Theory of Law and State_, 41-2.
18. This is what J.R. Lucas has called a "mameluke society"; vide, _infra_, n.19.
19. Lucas, _PP_, 75 ff.
20. Kelsen also requires a sanction in his theory.
21. A.V. Dicey, _An Introduction to the Study of the Law of the Constitution_, 40.
22. _Ibid_., 77.
23. _Ibid_., 59.
24. _Ibid_., 430.
25. The modern view of sovereignty, which defines the concept "from within its own four corners, as it were" is, it is submitted, merely a description of a current best-suited principle. The modern view is classicly stated in R.F.V. Heuston, _Essays in Constitutional Law_ (2nd Ed, London 1964), chapter 1.
26. Vide, _infra_, chapter 4.
27. 1 Cranch 137 (1803).
28. K.C. Wheare _Modern Constitutions_, 119.
29. Where it is not wished to admit that a clash can or has occurred, the conflicting view may be subjected to harmonization. The outstanding example of this is the way in which the Glossators explained away the discrepancies in the _Corpus Juris Civilis_, culminating in the _Glossa Ordinaria_ of Accursius in the thirteenth century.
30. An example of such a question arising is _Harris v. Minister of the Interior_ (1952), (2) S.A. 429 (A.D.).
31. 1911 and 1949, modifying the role of the House of Lords.
32. Among such materials, it is submitted, are to be found the canons of statutory interpretation, legal maxims and principles and Hart's secondary rules.
33. Vide, Ronald M. Dworkin, "Is law a system of rules?" in Robert S. Summers (ed.) _Essays in Legal Philosophy_, and J.M. Eekelaar, "Principles of Revolutionary Legality" in _Oxford Essays (2)_.
34. Legislatures also have guidelines in enuncaiting. Such guidelines are termed policies and some scholars have argued that one of these policies, namely economic efficiency, is paramount; vide, e.g. R. Posner, _Economic Analysis of Law_ (Boston, 1972). It is submitted, however, that such policies are only followed if they are believed to aid cohesion and survival, and that these latter are the basic goals.

35. Vide, d'Entrèves, _NL_, 147-51.
36. K.C. Wheare, _op.cit._, 131-3.

CHAPTER THREE

THE NATURE OF LEGAL CONCEPTS

I

Attention has until now been focussed squarely on the macrocosm of the legal system and its workings. The questions which have been examined are how it is that legal rules are discovered and enunciated, and, then how it is that they come to be regarded as binding upon the community. These questions related to the processes by which the legal system of a community operates and are obviously, therefore, questions of considerable importance. Having discussed these questions, the next step would appear to be to describe just how it is that a legal system comes into being and develops. However, before doing this, it is proposed to make a brief discursion and to focus attention away from the macrocosm of the legal system onto the microcosm of the individuals who are affected by the operations of the system. To the individuals who are the members of a particular social group, it is not the processes by which rules are discovered, enunciated and deemed to be valid which most directly affect them. Rather they are most directly affected by how those rules which have been discovered, enunciated and deemed to be valid regulate their lives and, in particular, their relations with other individuals. It is this microcosm which will now be examined.

The terminology in which this microcosm of legal relations within the community is normally described is that of the so-called, fundamental legal concepts, that is, of rights, duties, powers, and so on. Before commencing an analysis of what these concepts amount to under the new theory, it is perhaps instructive to consider briefly the controversy which has surrounded their nature according to earlier thought on the subject. Thus, to Natural Law thinkers, the natural rights of individuals were granted to them by God or by nature, and were transformed into legal rights by discovery and recognition at the hands of legal systems. This view, it will be seen, is not that far removed from the stance which will be taken on this subject by the new theory. For the Natural lawyers, these rights were entities which certainly existed.

The existence of rights has not however, met with general acceptance, and this is a matter of note for the present discussion. The English philosopher, Jeremy Bentham, was the first to deny the existence of legal rights and duties. Rights and duties were according to Bentham, fictitious entities, because they could not be empirically ascertained.[1] Remarkably similar views to Bentham's were to be adumbrated a century later in Germany by such theorists as Julius Binder, who thought rights mere representations of the mind without any objective reality. The attitude taken by such thinkers is clearly that rights do not exist other than in the imagination. According to the theory here advanced, they are phantasies. However, this comes as no surprise under the new theory as law itself has already been described by it as a social phantasy system. Thus, if rights and duties are phantasies that does not remove them from the ambit of meaningful discussion. Rather it helps to indicate the terms in which that discussion must take place. One of the thinkers who came close to actually using the word "phantasies" was Petrazycki, who denied that rights were real and thought of them as psychological phenomena which exist only in the mind. He called them "phantasmata", and likened them to aesthetic judgements about "attractiveness" or "ugliness".[2] In this, he came close to establishing the realm of discourse to which "Phantasmata" or phantasies belong.

It is the same failure to follow up the judgement that the legal concepts in question are phantasies with a reasoned discussion of what follows from this if anything like a full understanding of these concepts is to be achieved, which mars the work of the Realists, both American and Scandinavian. Cohen's judgement that such concepts were supernatural is typical of the American school as is his conclusion that such words were bankrupt because they could not pay up in the currency of fact.[3] Cohen clearly had a narrow interpretation of the word, "fact". The Scandinavian Realists also doubted the existence of rights and duties. To Axel Hägerström, the founding father of the school, they were a species of meta-physical concepts, against which genus he virtually pursued a vendetta.[4] Hägerström did not, however, undervalue such metaphysical ideas as psychological facts.[5] Lundstedt followed in Hägerström's footsteps and called rights, "chimeras", imaginary somethings to be resisted at all costs.[6] The Danish jurist, Alf Ross, has followed up this line of thought, but has maintained that, despite their lack of semantic reference, the words can be interpreted so as to have a realistic content.[7]

What was said about Bentham, Binder and Petrazycki, pertains also to the Realists with perhaps some partial exemption for Ross. Their failure lies in not having used their conclusions about rights so as to construct a meaningful theory of them. The theory here advanced accepts that rights, duties, powers, and all the fundamental legal concepts are phantasies, but does not for that reason dismiss them as meaningless chimeras. These phantasies reflect the influence of law upon relationships within a community. Just as the community as a whole observes the phantasy of the existence of legal rules and of their validity, so do the members of the community think of their relationships one with another according to those laws in terms of further phantasies of rights, duties, and the like. Again, these concepts are no less real for being phantasies; they belong to a different order of reality from tangible objects and that is all.

The most widely-acclaimed discussion and classification of these legal concepts is without doubt that of W.W. Hohfeld.[8] Hohfeld stressed that these concepts could not be considered in isolation. Although complete acceptance of this is not possible here, nevertheless it is accepted as being a significant recognition of the fact that law is a social phenomenon, a phenomenon which cannot exist outside of a community with a common goal. Hohfeld identified eight, fundamental legal concepts, namely, right, no-right, privilege, duty, power, liability, immunity and disability. He ranged these concepts into four pairs and stressed that they had always to be thought of in pairs. To begin with, there were four pairs of jural opposites, in the sense of contradictories. These were right/no-right; privilege/duty; power/disability; and immunity/liability.[9] The first of these - right/no-right - illustrates the relationship between the members of each pair. Either an individual has a right to something or no-right; there is no other alternative. This is clearly a logical relation -

either _p_ or _not-p_, nothing else is logically possible. Thus, either a person has a right to £500 from X or he has no-right to it. Either he has a power to rescind a contract with X or he has not, that is he is under a disability. Either he is immune from having his position changed by X or he is not, that is he is under a liability. Either he has a privilege to walk down the street or not as he chooses, or he has not and is, therefore, under a duty to do so or not to do so. This last example brings out a possible inadequacy in Hohfeld's discussion, for Hohfeld's theory never clearly expressed the fact that a duty was the contradictory of a privilege either if it obligated an individual to do or not to do an act.[10] Thus, if a man is told that he is free to eat chocolate or not as he chooses, this could be contradicted by telling him either that he ought to eat chocolate or its contrary, that he ought not to eat chocolate. This never emerges clearly from Hohfeld's discussion. A further criticism of Hohfeld's concept of privilege will be made later.

As well as ranging the eight concepts into four pairs of opposites, Hohfeld also arranges them into four pairs of jural correlatives, namely right/duty; privilege/no-right; power/liability; and immunity/disability. According to this classification, where-ever one person has one of these concepts, another must have the correlative. Thus, if A has a power to rescind a contract, there must be a person X who is under a liability to have his contract rescinded. If A has no such power to rescind, then he is under a disability, so that there must be a person X who is immune from having his contract rescinded. Thus, the pairs, as can be seen, have their opposites too.[11]

With the other two pairs, however, a problem arises. It is a problem of terminology. If A has a privilege that he can walk down the street, then X has no-right that A should or should not walk down the street. This illustrates the correlation of privilege/no-right.[12] However, this could be properly expressed by saying that A has a right to walk down the street and is, indeed, frequently so expressed. Hohfeld, however, uses right in a different sense, for if one says that A has a right to walk down the street, this means, in Hohfeldian terms, a privilege and postulates a correlative no-right not a correlative duty. The right which Hohfeld correlates with duty, he terms a claim-right. Thus, if A has a right to £500 from X, X is under a duty to render A £500. It is in this sense that Hohfeld uses the word, 'right'. In common parlance, however, even in common legal parlance, the word, 'right' does service both in Hohfeld's sense as the correlative of a duty, and in the sense of Hohfeld's privilege. Clearly, Hohfeld had to distinguish the concepts in some way. It is, however, submitted that his method of distinction was unfortunate in its consequences, and therefore a different nomenclature will be used here. The word, 'right', simpliciter. will be used here to indicate what Hohfeld termed privilege. For Hohfeld's use of right, claim-right will be used, and accordingly its opposite will be designated no-claim rather than no-right. The other concepts - duty, power, immunity, liability and disability - will be used according to their respective meanings in the Hohfeld analysis. The purpose of making these alterations will become apparent as the discussion proceeds.

The concepts are normally, for convenience, arranged into two rectangles, with the jural contradictories set diagonally opposite one another, and the jural correlatives vertically above and beneath one another. This pattern is followed in figure 2.

Figure 2

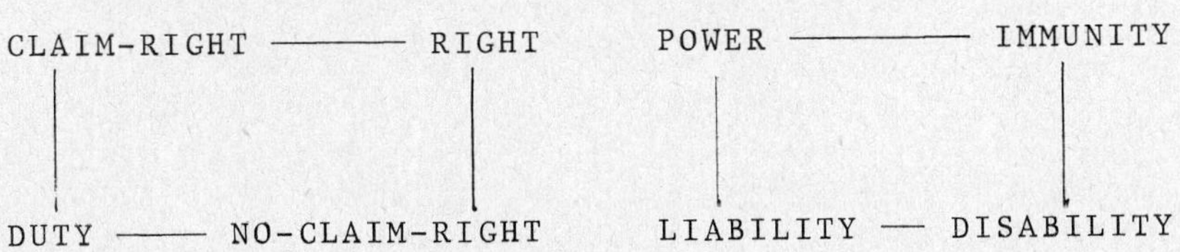

The only other objection which will be taken to the Hohfeld analysis is the need for a duty always to have a correlative claim-right. This will be discussed later. It is now proposed to examine each of the fundamental legal concepts in turn, to see how they relate to the social phantasy of law as viewed by the new theory here advanced. It is proposed to begin with the concept of a right, that is, Hohfeld's privilege, although the term, 'right', will not here be restricted to its fundamental sense.

II

It has already been postulated in considering the nature of legal rules and their validity that social groups are formed in order to promote the survival of their members. Once such groups are formed, it is clear that, if the purpose of survival is to be achieved, these groups must cohere. The goal of the community can therefore be described as to promote social cohesion and, thus, survival. Legal rules, and other social phantasies, are meant to advance these twin purposes by preventing disputes which endanger these goals from arising, and by providing a form for resolving those disputes which actually do arise and threaten to disrupt the community. It can also be taken as the norm that the individuals who make up the groups also wish to survive, and accordingly expect that the social group of which they are members will protect their survival interests. Certain activities will be marked as being necessary for survival so that individuals must be free to pursue such activities. Thus, individuals will regard it as necessary for survival that they should be allowed to eat, breathe, have some form of shelter in which to live and sleep, and so on. Similarly, in certain communities, a premium may be placed upon individuals being allowed to express their views without restriction, to come together for this purpose, to move about the community territory freely, and to worship the divine being. Where individuals believe that the freedom to indulge in these activities is necessary if they are to survive, then this view will probably be expressed in the form that individuals have a right to free speech, freedom of assembly, freedom of movement and freedom of worship. In other words, in this sense, a right is something which an individual has in relation to an activity if he regards that activity as being essential to his survival or well-being.[13]

Of course, as far as the community is concerned, what exactly these things are, which are necessary for survival, is something which has to be ascertained. Each individual cannot follow his own ideas if there is to be a community in any real sense. Thus, what rights must be protected if cohesion and survival are to be achieved must be discovered by means either of practical experience or else by enunciation by the best-suited persons or procedures. Once these rights have been discovered, then clearly the community will allow its members these rights in the interests of cohesion and survival. Each individual will probably have some idea of what he needs in the way of things he must be allowed to have or to do if he is to survive, but it is the decision of the community through practical experience or enunciation according to the best-suited method that will determine what are to be the needs which the community regards as being so essential. What the community so regards are the individual's legal rights. If the individual agrees with the judgement of the community, then clearly he is in tune with the rest of the community and is one of the people who will accept and ratify this enunciation of individuals' rights. If he does not agree, he may nevertheless accept and ratify the enunciation in the belief that the best-suited method is better-suited than he to make such determinations. This is also a form of agreement. On the other hand, his disagreement may be so fundamental that he does not accept and ratify the enunciation, because he feels it does not promote survival. In such circumstances, he will either obey the rule grudgingly, feeling obliged rather than obligated to do so, or he will reject it, and perhaps the best-suited method, altogether. While individuals are members of such communities, however, their legal rights are so determined by the community. Whether the enunciations actually do aid cohesion and survival is a question of fact in each case. Some may believe that there are definite principles which aid survival and which are discoverable. Such principles, in this field, could be termed natural rights. What an individual must actually be allowed if he is to survive may then be termed his natural rights. What, however, the community to which he belongs determines he must be allowed if he is to survive are his legal rights. The two may or may not coincide.

If a community has actually enunciated these rights according to its best-suited method, then they will be treated as fundamental rights[14] which must on no account be violated. Often, they will be incorporated in the constitution or in a bill of rights. Thus, in the United States, freedom of speech is a protected, fundamental right, having been so enunciated in the Bill of Rights. In the United Kingdom, on the other hand, freedom of speech is regarded as being something which must be allowed each individual even though it has never been enunciated as such. Rather, the lesson has been learnt from practical experience. This does not make it any less a fundamental right.

It is perfectly possible, of course, for freedom of speech not to be accounted necessary for survival at all. This attitude may be apparent in some countries currently.

At this point, it is necessary to indicate a weakness in the Hohfeld analysis. Hohfeld regards these rights as privileges to do or not to do. Thus, an individual in a society which regards free speech as necessary for survival will be free, have a privilege, to speak or not to speak as he chooses. Hohfeld sees such rights as privileges coupled with immunities, so that as well as there being an absence of duty to speak or not to speak on the individual's part, there is also a disability on the community's part to impose either kind of duty. In viewing the situation in this fashion, a view made unavoidable by his wishing to examine the fundamental legal concepts, Hohfeld overlooks an important point, namely that even where a community has no bill of rights, so that no immunities and their correlative disabilities are present in law, nevertheless there may be, probably are, fundamental rights in existence which cannot be altered by the group. Thus, until a few years ago, motorists in Cardiff were free to drive their vehicles westwards along Queen Street towards the castle, that is, they had a Hohfeldian privilege to do so. Late in 1975, however, that portion of Queen Street between the Park Hotel and the castle was closed to traffic and designated a pedestrian precinct. The privilege was thus withdrawn, and motorists now had a duty not to drive in that part of Queen Street. This change could occur because the right to drive in the area in question was not a fundamental right. The right to speak, on the other hand, is regarded as fundamental by some groups. If an attempt were made to take away the right to free speech, therefore, it might not be so successful. It might come unstuck because the courts would hold that it was unconstitutional, so that it went against the clear instructions of the best-suited persons or procedures as to what was best for cohesion and survival. In such circumstances, the Hohfeldian description of privilege cum immunity would be apt, but only if the paramount position of the constitution had previously been established. If the persons or procedures which the courts had previously regarded as best-suited, according to their metarules for discovering the best enunciations, were to make the attempt then the courts might be forced to alter their metarules in order that their own enunciations might be accepted and ratified. Again, the privilege *cum* immunity view could be taken to fit, but here the fit is less comfortable. The fit is least comfortable of all, however, in the situation where the courts accept the attempt, enunciate that free speech has gone, and either have that enunciation rejected by the community or have the community reject them as best-suited enunciators. There, although the privilege *cum* immunity view can be argued, it is submitted that it is weak. It is better to recognize that some rights are fundamental even if not recognized by the community as being the subject of immunity from change, their fundamental nature being realized from practical experience only when they are challenged,[15] while others are not; Professor Ronald Dworkin calls rights of these sorts rights in the strong sense and rights in the weak sense respectively. Here, it is proposed to speak of the former as fundamental rights and the latter as privileges, thus to some extent returning to Hohfeld. Privileges are, then, rights which can be interfered with or negated without, in the opinion of the community, any risk to cohesion and survival. Fundamental rights, however, are not regarded as being susceptible to such tampering. Of course, what were once fundamental rights may dwindle into privileges and what were once privileges strengthen into fundamental rights. In wartime, for example, freedom of speech is often restricted in a manner which would not be tolerated in peacetime. Fundamental rights and privileges are subdivisions of what were initially called rights, and were so represented in figure 2.[16] They have this in common, that individuals are free to do or not to do those things to which they have rights, but if the rights are only privileges, then interference by the community with the right will not be regarded as dangerous to cohesion and survival. The distribution of fundamental rights and privileges amongst the members of the community will be effected according to what the community believes to be the distribution which will best aid cohesion and survival. This distribution may be equal or far from equal, and may vary from time to time according to the prevailing opinion of what is best for cohesion and survival. One of the contexts in which what an individual must be allowed if the community is to cohere and survive, that is, his legal rights, are enunciated is in so-called hard cases. There, legal rights like rules are discovered and shaped in the arena of action.

III

If a right is defined as what subsists in the situation where the law allows a person either to indulge or not to indulge himself in a particular activity, then a right is contradicted if the law demands either that a person do or that he not do that thing. Thus, a person does not have a right to drive along Queen Street if he is told by the law that he must not do so, and a person does not have a right, as the word is used here, to give X £50 if he is told by the law that he must do so. In both cases, either where a person must or where he must not do something, he is said to be under an obligation or duty. Just as it was seen that a person was given legal rights to those things which he must be allowed if cohesion and survival were to be promoted, or in the weaker sense of privilege if it was not regarded necessary for cohesion or survival to command or forbid a particular activity, so a person is placed under a duty if the community considers that it is necessary in the interest of cohesion and survival that something be done or not done.[17] Thus, because killing disrupts the community and threatens cohesion and survival, members are under a duty not to kill other members. Similarly, if a right to personal posessions and property is regarded as necessary for survival, the unauthorised taking of such property will be vetoed - members will be under a duty not to steal. Individuals are placed under duties to do or not to do certain things in order to prevent disputes, and thus to promote cohesion and survival. The concept of a duty, therefore, which is the contradictory of the concept of a right as here used, is clearly a concept which only makes sense given a community setting, or at least a relationship with another person or other persons. The concept of right might be used in a vacuum, although this is unlikely. However, a duty is more of a community concept than a right.

Just as in the case of right, an individual may or may not agree with his social group that a certain activity is obligatory. Thus, he may accept the community's judgement that a certain course of conduct is a duty because he himself believes it is so, or he may accept and ratify the enunciation because he regards the method of enunciation as being better suited to indicate the correct course for cohesion and survival than he himself is. Again, however, he may think the enunciation incorrect but obey it out of fear of the consequences of disobedience to himself, that is through feeling obliged to obey rather than obligated, or he may be so certain of the correctness of his own view as to disobey the enunciation or even to reject the method of enunciation altogether. Only a very strong best-suited principle will withstand repeated and widespread disagreement with its enunciations.

According to the present theory, both rights and duties are, of course, phantasies, but social phantasies in that their content is shared by more than one person. Indeed, these phantasies are shared by a whole community. If a person needs something to survive, he is regarded as having a right to it. If he must or must not do something to promote cohesion and survival, he is regarded as having a duty to do or not to do that thing. In both cases, the relation between the individuals and the activities exists only in the minds of the members of the community. The Hohfeld analysis, and other theories of rights and duties, do not however look behind this veil of phantasy to see why such phantasies are called into existence. For this reason, they are subject to weaknesses. Hohfeld insisted that a duty could not exist without its correlative of claim-right. Thus one could not be under a duty to pay X £50 unless X or someone had a right to claim that £50. For a duty to exist, someone had to have a corresponding claim-right which enabled the duty to be enforced. This is also sometimes put in the form that before a duty can exist, there must be a sanction for non-performance which the person with the claim-right can call upon the authorities to put into effect. Thus, if the £50 is not paid, X will go to court and the court will order that the £50 be paid. If it is still not paid, the debtor may have his goods seized or be imprisoned until he does so. Thus, the duty is enforceable. Without a sanction, some theorists hold, there can be no duty.[18]

The idea that a duty cannot exist without its correlative claim-right, and the connected idea that a duty can only be said to exist if a sanction is attached to the opposite behaviour, or delict, are both based upon study of Western systems of jurisprudence.[19] The ideas cannot gain support from oriental legal systems. Thus, in Jewish law, acts are classified as being either obligatory, meritorious, allowed, forbidden or invalid.[20] Whereas four of these classifications can be fitted into the scheme of the Hohfeld analysis,[21] one, that of meritorious acts, clearly cannot. There is in such a system clearly not only a duty of obligation but also a duty of aspiration.[22] Western theorists might well argue that such duties of aspiration are part of the realm of morality rather than that of law, but this is to fly in the face of how the members of the community governed by the system in question treat the concept. The same is true of other oriental systems. Thus, in Islamic law, there are certain duties which have no corresponding claim-rights and to which no sanctions are attached. An example is the duty placed upon the husband of one wife not to take any more wives unless able to make proper provision for their maintenance and support.[23] Hindu law is also composed of a mixture of duties, some of obligation and some of aspiration.[24] The Islamic and Hindu instances can, of course, be interpreted as cases where the sanction belongs to the next world or existence rather than this, and the claim-right is thus in divine hands. However, the Jewish classification of meritorious acts does not allow even this. All that can be said here is that by attaining the highest standard of conduct, divine favour for the community is promoted so that its survival is better assured, but this does not allow in either a claim-right or a sanction either in this world or the next. If one accepts that legal duties of aspiration can thus exist, and that they aid cohesion and survival and can lead to rewards for the aspirant in the here and now, then the concept of a duty can be classified in two ways.[25] First, there is a duty in the sense used by Hohfeld, the duty which has a corresponding claim-right. The second sense, however, is that of duty where there is no such claim-right. This second sense can be subdivided itself into those duties which are obligatory despite the lack of a claim-right, like the Mohammedan's obligation to his wives, and those duties of aspiration which when fulfilled constitute the Jews' meritorious acts. Again, therefore, although the Hohfeld analysis provides a good starting point for examining the concept of duty, its fundamental approach makes it too narrow to give an entirely satisfactory account of the concept under the new theory. Under the new theory, a duty can be defined as something which a member of a social group is either obligated to perform or should aspire to perform in order to ensure or to promote respectively the cohesion of his community and the community's goal of survival.

IV

As has been stated, according to Hohfeld every duty had to have its corresponding claim-right. Although the present theory denies this, it accepts that some duties do have corresponding claim-rights. Thus, in England and Wales, where a husband is under a duty to maintain his wife, the wife has a corresponding claim-right to be maintained by her husband. Where X owes A a debt of £50, X is under a duty to pay the sum and A has a claim-right to it. Where D injures P in an accident through negligence, D is under a duty to compensate P and P has a claim-right to be compensated. From the point of the individual who has the claim-right, which is the level on which these concepts operate, a claim-right is his relation to what the community states that others must render him in order to ensure or promote cohesion and survival, and which the community is prepared to see that those others do render him by supplying the means by which the claim-right can be enforced. The person with the claim-right therefore, is the one who can call the sanction into play when a duty has been broken; he is the person who can enforce the duty through the courts. It can, thus, be seen where the sanction theories of duty have their origins.

It is submitted that the best way to understand how the concept of claim-right arises is to concentrate on the function of the group in avoiding disputes and seeing that disputes which cannot be avoided are settled without disrupting the peace and order of the community. The person whom the community invests with a claim-right is the person whom the community fears will cause a dispute if in a given situation he is not rendered what is necessary for cohesion and survival. In other words, if others will not play the cohesion and survival game with him and grant him what he needs, he will not play it with them and preserve order. Thus, when such a person is not granted his requirement, that is, of course, what the community states he requires, rather than allow him to settle the issue for himself at the cost of disrupting the peace of the community and thus endangering its cohesion and, therefore, survival, the community gives him a right to claim that the community should help him to enforce the duty it has imposed for his benefit. Clearly, the claim-right is similar to a right _simpliciter_ in that the holder is allowed to enforce the duty or not at his discretion.[26] The community will, if he chooses to enforce his claim-right, attempt to solve the dispute without disrupting the order of the group. Thus, if X owes A £50 and doesn't pay, rather than let A resort to self-help and risk a disruption, A is given a claim-right to enforce X's duty to pay him the sum in the courts of the community. Where the community considers that a person is not likely to cause a disruption if he is disappointed, then it will not give him a claim-right. Thus, in England and Wales, where X contracts with Y to pay A £50 and X fails to pay A the sum, Y is given a claim-right to enforce the contract against X but A is not. Under the present theory, the reason for this is that English law does not regard A's disappointment as being likely to disrupt the community, whilst Y's, as a party to the contract, is so regarded. Some other legal systems take a more cautious view and give A a claim-right. More generally, in Equity, a person who has not given consideration will not be aided with equitable remedies. The maxim is, "Equity will not assist a volunteer". Again, under the present theory, this can be rationalized by saying that a person who has not parted with something of value is not likely to be able to disrupt the order of the community if disappointed in his expectations.

Even though a particular individual may not be able to cause a disruption himself, the community may recognize that others may do so on his behalf. Thus, the claim-rights of children are allowed to be enforced by their next-friends because it is recognized that such individuals might cause disruption on the children's behalf if the children were not rendered their due. The fact that the law does not regard such intervention as likely on behalf of animals or persons long dead probably explains why trusts of imperfect obligation have come to be frowned upon, and why such obligations remain imperfect. Indeed, this approach would allow a rationalization of the whole issue of _locus standi_.

According to Hohfeld, the contradictory of a claim-right was merely no-right, or in the current terminology, no-claim-right. The concept merely fills a slot demanded by logic, marking as it does the correlative of a right in the current sense of being free to do or not to do a particular thing. Thus, whenever a person is not considered likely to be able to disrupt order because he has not been rendered something, as regards that person Hohfeld would say he has no-right, that is, no-claim-right, and that the person, from whom he might expect whatever it is, has a privilege to render or withhold as he chooses. Thus, a person may have a right to do as he chooses as against one, but under a duty in relation to the same conduct as regards another. In the example given above of X contracting with Y to pay A £50, X would have a duty to pay the sum as against Y but have a right to pay or not to pay as against A. This may, at first blush, seem a misleading way of looking at the situation, but by so treating it, Hohfeld brings out a great truth according to the present theory. That truth is that disputes arise between individuals and that whereas a dispute between X and Y is adjudged likely so that, to ensure cohesion and survival, X is placed under a duty as regards Y, a dispute between X and A is not deemed likely so that no duty is placed upon X as regards A, so that X has a right to pay or not to pay as against A. Whether this is really what is necessary to avoid disputes is a question of fact in each society. All that is said here is that this is how one society, rightly or wrongly, views this situation. The fact that A has no-claim-right is then a judgement by the community that he is unlikely to cause a dispute if his requirements in this situation are not met.

An interesting example of a no-claim-right situation is the situation surrounding an expired debt, where the expiry is due to limitation or laches. Although X may have owed £50 and Y had a claim-right to enforce the debt, if Y waits too long, the debt will be said to have expired, either because the limitation period for bringing actions of debt has run, or because, under the equitable doctrine of laches, which does not involve a fixed period, it is considered that the debt has become stale through Y's delay. In both cases, therefore, Y loses his claim-right so that he has no-claim-right and X is no longer under an enforceable duty to pay. In such instances, and perhaps it is particularly clear with the second, the new theory would explain this by saying that if Y has waited so long he is unlikely to be able to cause a disruption if he now claims the sum, so that the community is not threatened and therefore need not entertain his claim.[27]

The first four of Hohfeld's eight, fundamental legal concepts have now been examined, namely right, duty, privilege and no-right. Although the Hohfeld analysis will accommodate the legal concepts presented here, it was decided to take the concepts in a non-fundamental sense so as to preserve the meanings which they have in normal usage. Thus, right has been used here in the sense of Hohfeld's privilege, and has been allowed an ambit wide enough to incorporate Hohfeld's privilege cum immunity under the name of fundamental right, reserving the meaning of privilege for non-fundamental rights. Fundamental rights, or rights in the strong sense, are those things which a community must allow an individual to do or not to do at his choice if there is to be cohesion and survival.[28] Privileges, or rights in the weak sense, are those things which the community currently allows individuals to do or not to do because they present no dangers to cohesion and survival, although freedom in relation to these activities is not regarded as essential to attaining those goals. Likewise, Hohfeld's concept of duty is not quite so broad as that presented here. To Hohfeld, a duty had to have its correlative claim-right. Under the present theory, a duty is something which an individual must do if cohesion and survival are to be guaranteed or something which he ought to do if cohesion and survival are to be furthered. Some duties will, thus, have correlative claim-rights, such as the duty in England and Wales to maintain one's wife; others, like the Muslim duty of impartiality between wives, will not have such correlative claim-rights but will nevertheless be regarded as duties by the community. The Hohfeld analysis would classify such duties as privileges, but this, it is submitted hides the realities of the situation behind the intact classification. Hohfeld's analysis cannot accommodate the Jewish concept of a meritorious act. This also would have to be classified as a privilege, but, again, in reality is probably seen as an aspiration, a form of duty rather than a freedom to do or not to do.

An objection may also be taken to the notion of a claim-right under the Hohfeld analysis. This, as has been seen, is the correlative of a Hohfeldian duty, and allows the holder to call for that duty to be enforced. The analysis, however, cannot properly accommodate the question as to whether such claim-rights ought to be enforced by their holders. In traditional Chinese law, individuals are discouraged from litigating, the community preferring to see disputes settled peaceably out of court between the parties if at all possible. Thus, although the individuals concerned have claim-rights, there is a duty -

which has no correlative claim-right and which Hohfeld would accordingly classify misleadingly as a privilege - to settle out of court.[29] This relationship between claim-right and duty-not-to-exercise-it-unnecessarily cannot be expressed properly under the Hohfeld analysis. It is submitted that all these factors are masked because Hohfeld deals with the surface phenomena of his legal concepts only, without looking at the social foundations for their existence. Once these foundations are examined, the hidden distinctions are revealed. This is not to deny the undoubted usefulness and appropriateness of the Hohfeld analysis at its chosen level of operation.

V

Hohfeld's second group of concepts, which consists of the concepts of power, liability, immunity and disability, causes less problems as it does not mask any distinctions which are important under the new theory. A power, according to Hohfeld, is what an individual has if it is within his volitional control to change a given legal relation. Thus, an individual may have a power to enter into a contractual obligation, to make a gift of a part or all of his property, or, if he is a trustee, to pay capital sums to the beneficiaries so that they become absolutely entitled to them. In all these instances, one person's expression of his wishes alters one or more legal relations, and powers are said to have been exercised. In such cases, the community to which the individual belongs clearly considers that it is in the interests of cohesion and survival that the individual should have the ability to do this. A power, then, is the recognition that an individual should be able to alter certain legal relations in the interests of cohesion and survival. Thus, it may be adjudged that in the interests of cohesion and survival individuals should be able to acquire and dispose of property, and, thus, they are given powers to do so.

One example of such a power to alter legal relations is the ability of the best-suited persons or procedures to change the survival principles of the community. This power is accorded to them by the community in the belief that the enunciations made will aid cohesion and survival, and, while the enunciations are deemed to do this, the existence of the power will be accepted and ratified. That the community accepts that over a smaller area of legal relations, a particular individual should, in the interests of cohesion and survival, be allowed to alter those legal relations is an acceptance that, over that area, the individual in question is really best-suited to determine exactly what is best to promote those social goals, or at least that to allow him such powers is the best way of furthering the community's social goals. Clearly, therefore, one would expect that powers would only be given to individuals who, generally speaking, were likely to use those powers in a manner which would avoid disputes and promote cohesion and survival, and that powers would be withheld from individuals whose manner of exercise might create disputes and hinder those objectives being realized. Indeed, this appears to be the case, for powers to enter into contractual relations and to make wills and so on are withheld from infants and mental patients, because, according to the new theory, their exercise of such powers would probably cause rather than avoid disputes. A second expectation would be that, just as the enunciations of the best-suited persons or procedures, which are exercises of their powers, will not be followed if not accepted as being good for survival, so if an individual exercises a power in a manner likely to cause dispute and disruption, his exercise of the power will not be accepted by the community as valid through the judgement of its courts, those best-suited to determine whether the exercise furthered the social goals or not. Again, this is the case, as even where an individual is regarded as suitable to be given powers, he will not be allowed to exercise them against the community's interests. Thus, if a power to enter into a contract is used so as to set up an illegal contract or one which is immoral or against public policy, the exercise will not be accepted and ratified as valid. As with the best-suited principle, one faulty exercise does not necessarily lead to a repudiation of the power in question, at least not unless it is a major aberration - which may lead to the individual being judged delinquent or insane. Continual aberrations may lead to loss of the power; thus, trustees are sometimes removed for unfitness, agents have their authority revoked, and so on.

Even where it is regarded that in the interests of the community a person should be given such powers, there may still be disputes over the exercise of such powers. Such disputes are particularly likely in relation to matters or things which are vital to the community, its cohesion and survival. Thus, the land of the community may well be so important that disputes about it are highly likely, and the same may be true of beasts of burden in an agricultural community, boats in a fishing community, and so on. To prevent disputes from arising in relation to these things while preserving the beneficent powers of individuals to alter legal relations pertaining to them, formalities may be demanded to clarify that an alteration in the legal relations concerning such basic property has taken place. Thus, land in mediaeval England had to be transferred with livery of seisin which involved a ceremony on the land, and _res mancipi_ in Roman Law also had to be transferred by means of a ceremony, namely _mancipatio_. The circumstances of the exercise of a power may also make it likely that disputes will arise. This is the case with transfer at the time of death, where the power-holder will not be available to clarify his wishes if a dispute should arise. Such exercises may have to be carried out according to formalities also. In most modern societies, the required formality is that the transaction should be executed in, or evidenced by, writing.

VI

The other three concepts in this group can be dealt with fairly quickly. The jural correlative of a power, according to Hohfeld, is a liability. In the terms of the new theory, a person has a liability if, in the judgement of the community, it is best for cohesion and survival if his legal relations can be altered by the enunciations of another. The community, of course, will not accept a liability in relation to the improper exercise of powers. The individual who has the liability may not consent to the community's view that he should be liable. In such circumstances, he may accept the liability grudgingly rather than willingly, and may not accept it at all. Where a power/liability relation exists with regard to a legal relation, the situation is given to change and the relation can be described as dynamic.

On the other hand, it is possible that the community may deem it best for cohesion and survival that an individual's legal relations should not be prone to alteration according to the decisions of another. In such a situation, the individual will have an immunity and the other persons will have a disability in that they are unable to alter the legal relations in question. Again, individuals may disagree with the community's judgement on the merits of disabilities, so that they may be accepted willingly, deferentially, grudgingly or not at all. Where a legal relation is not given to change, it may be described as static, and individuals will stand in an immunity/disability relationship with regard to it.

The last four concepts - power, liability, immunity and disability - have been defined according to the terms of the new theory without any need to subject them to the sort of criticism which the first quartet attracted. One thing, however, must be stressed and that is that, clearly, the existence of an element from the second set does not preclude the existence of an element from the first. Hohfeld himself accepted this. Thus, for example, an individual and the community may consider that persons should have a right in the strong sense to have a power with regard to a particular legal relation, or that a person should have a right in the strong sense to an immunity with regard to a particular relation. With regard to a person's power to acquire and transfer property, for example, the community may feel that each individual has a right in the strong sense to such a power and also that the individuals should have an immunity as against other individuals in relation to having that power taken from them. The different concepts, however, operate, as Hohfeld insisted, between different persons and, therefore, at different levels.

VIII

The concepts which have so far been examined have all been taken from, or at least based on, Hohfeld's fundamental legal concepts. Hohfeld thought of his concepts as being the smallest, indivisible particles of the legal world. The criticisms which have been levelled at Hohfeld's concepts do not question Hohfeld's belief that his concepts were fundamental. Nor is it denied that some of the concepts used here, such as fundamental right, can be described according to the Hohfeld theory as combinations of more than one of his concepts. The point made here is that such concepts are not generally thought or spoken of as being combinations, and it is artificial to treat them as being so considered.[30] The concept of a right as used here, therefore, is not necessarily fundamental in Hohfeld's sense, but it is nevertheless a concept used by individuals in relating to the social phantasy system of law in their community. These individuals no more think of such rights as being composed of privileges with immunities than they think of the chairs and tables which they use as combinations of atoms. To insist that when an individual speaks of a chair, he is speaking of the particles which compose it, or that when he speaks of the number four, he has in mind $2 + 2$ or 2^2 or $3 + 1$ or $1 + 1 + 1 + 1$ or $\sqrt{16}$ would clearly be artificial. So, also, it must be allowed that certain legal concepts, which may be divisible into more fundamental concepts, can be spoken of meaningfully in their own right. Thus, among the phantasy concepts which make up a legal system, one will find the concepts of contract, delict, crime, property, ownership, and so on. Each of these concepts can be used in its own right, so that when an individual wishes to impart that the community regards a certain agreement as being binding in that to treat it otherwise might give rise to disruption, he refers to that agreement as a contract; similarly, he refers to acts likely to cause disputes or disruptions as delicts or crimes, and so on.

The examples given in the introduction of this book were all concerned with phantasies of this kind. Thus, the idea that the slave was the property of or was owned by a particular master was a phantasy, as was the fact that this property could be and was transferred to another. The same was true with the apple in the modern example. These phantasies of ownership could be broken down into fundamental concepts, for example that the owner had a claim-right to expect others to treat the property as his, and that the others had correlative duties to do so, and that the owner had a power to transfer, and so on. However, the legal concept of ownership can be described quite properly at its own level of abstraction as the shared phantasy that the title, use and enjoyment of one person in a particular thing must be recognized if the community is to cohere and survive, or some such description. Thus, all legal concepts derive their validity from their part in the social phantasy system of law, and it is not necessary to reduce them to basic jural relations in order to understand their existence, validity and meaning, although a complete understanding may require such a reduction. To say that a person has come of age or is married or single is as meaningful to a member of the community, and perhaps more so, as cataloguing the fundamental legal relations into which such statements can be atomised. If such statements are to be considered a sort of legal shorthand, it is as well to remember that there is no more reason why the symbols of shorthand should be taken as representing ordinarily written words than that the opposite conclusion should be reached. Both obtain their validity as systems of representing sounds from their representative functions and contexts.

Communities construct and ratify other phantasies as well if they consider that their existence will aid the twin goals of cohesion and survival. Thus, corporations are phantasies of this kind, considered necessary for the good of the community, as are other institutions such as clubs and societies. Some are treated as legal persons by the community, another phantasy which has greatly exercised the minds of legal theorists. Indeed, the community itself or, as some are termed, the state, is a phantasy concept of this kind, for it is only in the minds of the individuals who compose the group or who witness the combination that the group has any existence as a distinct entity. The same is true of its connection with a particular territory.

It has been the purpose of this chapter to focus attention on the way in which individuals adapt to social phantasy systems of their own creation by relating themselves to those systems. To do this, yet more phantasies are brought into existence, and these phantasies are the legal concepts used by the individuals who make up the community. Perhaps, in discussing such concepts here, too much time has been allotted to secondary issues concerning them, such as the supposed need to reduce them to fundamental concepts or to criticizing Hohfeld's deservedly admired attempt to do so. It is, however, probably as well that this has been done so that what has been said here concerning legal concepts has clearly been said in full awareness of such issues. The analysis of legal concepts presented here, however, stands independently of such peripheral discussion. The concepts themselves, by helping the members of the group to relate to its phantasies of laws and their validity, help to promote the goals which the rules themselves are designed to further, namely dispute-avoidance and settlement, cohesion and survival. These concepts, therefore, represent the same phenomenon of legality looked at from a different angle, that of the individual adapting to the group, rather than that of the group and its institutions directing individuals. This is the crux of the new theory in relation to legal concepts. Now that this viewpoint has been examined, a return must be made to the perspective of the social group.

****

1. K. Olivecrona, Law as Fact, 168 ff.
2. Ibid., 171.
3. Ibid., 172.
4. Vide, A. Hägerström, Inquiries into the Nature of Law and Morals (Ed. K. Olivecrona, 1953).
5. K. Olivecrona, op.cit., 174.
6. Ibid., 176.
7. Ibid., 178.
8. W.W. Hohfeld, "Some Fundamental Legal Conceptions as applied in Judicial Reasoning", (1913) 23 Yale Law Journal, 16.
9. Sir John Salmond used the word liberty instead of privilege; vide, Salmond on Jurisprudence (12th Ed. by P.J. Fitzgerald) (London, 1966) § 40.
10. Vide, Re Kay's Settlement [1939] Ch. 329 for an example of such a confusion, and (1960) 76 L.Q.R. 100 (Elliott) for a criticism of it.
11. Thus, right/duty is contradicted by no-right/privilege, and power/liability by disability/immunity.
12. This difficulty is present in Salmond's terminology too.
13. This sense, it should be noted, is not fundamental.
14. Again, here, the word right is not being used in Hohfeld's fundamental sense.
15. The privilege cum immunity view is regarded as weak here because the fundamental nature of the right is not recognized until the crunch comes, so that not even the phantasy of an immunity is present. However, once the possibility of its being lost is contemplated, its existing fundamental nature is recognized.
16. Hindu law recognizes this sort of distinction in relation to rules which it classifies as seen and unseen, the unseen being incapable of abrogation; vide, ILS, 92 (J. Duncan M. Derrett).

17. If an act is banned because it is bad for cohesion and survival, this is somewhat different from banning an act as part of an overall policy. This, it is submitted, is the basis of the distinction between mala in se and mala prohibita.
18. Cf. A Giddens, Durkheim, 65.
19. Vide, e.g. H. Kelsen, General Theory of Law and State, 58-61.
20. ILS, 45 (Ze'ev W. Falk).
21. Obligatory and forbidden acts would both be classified as duties by Hohfeld, allowed acts would be accommodated as privileges and invalid acts as those subject to disabilities.
22. Cf. Fuller ML, 5-9.
23. ILS, 75 (N.J. Coulson); R. David and J.E.C. Brierly, Major Legal Systems in the World Today (2nd Ed., London, 1978), 421.
24. ILS, 90 (J.D.M. Derrett); David and Brierly, op.cit., 448-9.
25. Hohfeld would classify them as privileges.
26. Hohfeld realized that his fundamental concepts were not mutually exclusive. Indeed, Hohfeld realized that to be in existence at all, every claim-right or power had to be combined with a privilege to exercise it.
27. Indeed, there would be more danger from X if it did.
28. This entails an immunity from change being coupled with it, and the best-suited persons being under the concomitant disability.
29. Thus, Western systems often contain checks against vexatious litigation.
30. The same artificiality was a hindrance to the acceptability of Ludwig Wittgenstein's Tractatus theory of representation, as he saw all propositions as being composed of numerous elementary propositions. Ultimately, he abandoned the necessity for such reduction in the Philosophical Investigations.

CHAPTER FOUR

THE NATURE OF LEGAL SYSTEMS

I

So far, the concepts which have been examined - legal rules, their validity and legal concepts such as rights and duties - are those which make up the parts which form the whole of a legal system. Having worked out a theory to explain these concepts, the last stage in completing that theory seems naturally to be to construct from it the model of a legal system. To exist even as a phantasy, a legal system must have legal rules, and those rules must be regarded as valid. Likewise, to those individuals who make up the community to which the legal system appertains, it must consist of rights, duties, powers, and so on. In this chapter, it is proposed to construct an account of the development of a legal system. This account will be speculative in that it is based on the conclusions as to the nature of legal rules, validity and concepts which have previously been reached. However, by littering the account with examples taken from the actual development of legal systems, it is hoped to show that the account which follows is not mere speculation, but rather that the account of the development of a legal system which will now be constructed around the new theory of the nature of law is such that the historical evidence concerning the development of actual legal systems can be slotted into the various stages of the account without difficulty. In other words, the theory will be seen to fit the facts. It must be stressed, however, that considerations of space dictate that the historical examples must be selected sparingly; much more evidence could be incorporated to buttress the theory's accuracy. The theory as here constructed can be used to explain the development of any legal system. To describe the evolution of any one system in detail would require more space than can be devoted to this chapter. The theme is therefore one which it is hoped will be developed in relation to individual legal systems in later works.

The starting point for this account of how a legal system develops, which is meant to illustrate at the end the nature of legal systems generally, will be the individual human being, for without such human beings there could not be legal systems. For human beings, like animals, one of the fundamental goals of life, if not the fundamental goal, is to go on living, that is, to survive.[1] From the very first, a human being is dependent upon others to achieve this objective. At the moment of birth, and for a considerable time thereafter, a child is dependent upon its parents for the wherewithal to survive. This very dependence is the root of a great deal that shapes the character of the individual and of the species.

The fact that the child is dependent upon its parents means that to a certain extent if it is to survive, it must play the game of life during its early stages according to their rules. Moreover, in its parents, the child is presented with two human beings who have, as it were, stood the test of time, who have survived to adulthood. The child, therefore, if it wishes to survive in turn, will accept that the parents know what is in its best interests if it wishes to survive. The parents, in other words, are the persons whom the child regards as best-suited to communicate to it the precepts which it must follow if it is to survive. For the sake of example, the position of a male child will be considered and it will be supposed, in our example, that the father exercises the greater influence over him. That the facts can be different is obvious, but the variations can safely be left to the reader to provide. As the child grows up, he will learn a great deal from his parents. He will learn a language, good manners, how to dress, and so on. As he is instructed by his father, he will follow his father's example and instructions in the belief that what his father shows him or tells him is in his best interests if he wishes to be like his father, that is, to grow up to manhood and achieve a family of his own. This need to be like his father will result in his making his father, according to Freud, his ego-ideal. He will model his own personality upon that of his father because that is the best thing to do to survive. In time, the example of other persons whom he regards as good examples of survivors will be incorporated into the ego-ideal so that the parental imago will be mixed with those of other educators and of heroes of the community. The child will assess his own achievements by comparing his performance to the standards of his ego-ideal, and he will criticize his achievements by means of this process. The criticizing agency by which the ego is judged by the standards of the ego-ideal was called by Freud the super-ego. This agency will continue to set the standards and criticize according to them throughout the individual's life.

A factor which must not be left out of the picture, however, not even at this early stage, is that the father himself came into the world as a helpless child and he, too, had to struggle to survive. He, in his turn, needed to model his behaviour on that of his father so that he took his father as his initial ego-ideal. In bringing up his child, in turn, his actions were governed by the activity of his superego, so that the standards he exemplifies to his son and which his son takes as his ego-ideal are the standards of the father's superego. In turn, the father's father brought up the father according to the dictates of his superego, and so on back to the primiaeval slime. The standards which the child incorporates into his personality as being best for survival have, therefore, been communicated over the generations. They are traditional standards for living and survival. Freud recognized that the superego was the vehicle of tradition, and that it could render important assistance in understanding the social behaviour of mankind.[2]

The child will learn from the father both by imitating his example, as with learning a language, and also from instruction and correction. The basic points of this system of learning will perhaps be clarified by an example. Given a small family - father, mother and son - living in a rural setting and supporting itself by means of growing food, cutting timber and the like, a sort of pioneer set up, one can readily imagine the child finding the father chopping down trees one day and subjecting the father to a series of questions. The child might begin with: "What are you doing, Daddy?", to which the father would reply, if he had the patience, that he was chopping wood. The child might continue: "Why are you chopping wood, Daddy?" Father: "To have firewood for the winter". The child might then, as children do, begin an infinite regress of questions: "Why do we need firewood for the winter?" - "To keep warm"; "Why do we need to keep warm?" and so on until ultimately either the father loses patience or the answers reach the stage of: "Unless we keep warm, we perish", so that the question, if it comes, "Why don't we want to perish?" meets with an answer of the "No one wants to perish" variety; in other words, everyone wants to survive. The child now realizes why his father chops wood; wood-chopping is a necessary activity if they are to survive in their environment.

The child, having satisfied his curiosity, may now ask to help his father in the task, clearly a form of emulation. The father agrees and gives the boy a small hatchet. The child wields it about the place dangerously, risking an injury to himself and his father, so that the father is forced to show him how to use the hatchet properly. In other words, the child has to learn that merely cutting wood is not enough; there is a right way and a wrong way of doing it, the method itself being linked with avoiding injury to self and others, and thus to survival. The child now handles the hatchet as he has been shown by his father.

The next day, the father goes for a walk and finds his son chopping merrily away at some saplings. He immediately stops him. The child is surprised as he thinks he is doing what his father does to aid survival and in the way his father has taught him. His father now realizes that the previous day's lesson is still incomplete; the lesson only approximated to what was needed in the way of instruction. He therefore points out to the child that one only cuts as much wood as is needed, and that to cut saplings is foolish for, if they were allowed to grow to maturity, they would provide even more wood, and so on. This enunciation is, therefore, an improvement on what has gone before.

Already, at this very primitive level, there are clear resemblances to what has been said about legal rules and their validity. The father enunciates by word and action to the child what is necessary for survival. The child, by piecing together what the father has told and shown him, assembles the survival precept. The more he is instructed, the closer the precept gets to what is required. The child obeys the father because he recognizes that the father is the best-suited person to enunciate the survival principles, and the father harks back to what he has learnt in teaching his child, a sort of metagame like the courts on earlier decisions, the constitution and so on. What the father gives to the child are survival precepts, but one would stop short of calling them laws. If the child were to disobey, to continue cutting down saplings, one would not term his conduct illegal. One would call it wrong, and, if he did it deliberately, possibly even immoral. Even if his father punished him for disobedience having warned him that he would do so, one would still not call the conduct illegal. For law and a legal system to exist, something extra is clearly required.

The fact that the child may wish to disobey his parent, may wish deep-down inside to fell every sapling in the neighbourhood, raises another important issue. If he wishes to continue in his conduct, he is faced with a choice. The choice lies between obeying hisfather, which he feels he ought to do because his father embodies what is needed in the way of qualities and behaviour to survive, and satisfying his own needs and impulses. He must choose between satisfying his impulses and obeying his ego-ideal. The need to follow his father to survive involves, then, sacrificing a part of himself, his impulses, in order to do so. The benefit of survival and parental love involves the burden of sacrificing certain of one's wants to achieve those goals. Some modern psychologists refer to this denial of self to gratify others, this conforming to what one thinks others want one to be rather than allowing oneself to be what one is, as alienation, and argue that it can lead to psychological disturbance. Freud, himself, recognized that each individual is forced to repress impulses arising in his id if his ego, the repressing agency, is to live up to the standards set by the superego.

The structure according to which one learns by example is common in many walks of life. The concept of apprenticeship is rooted in the notion that standards can be learned from one who has mastered the skill, and many skills and trades are taught by example.[3] Religious creeds also acknowledge the need to emulate paragons of excellence, as is clear in both Christianity and Islam.

Human beings, however, live in larger groups than their families, and usually recognize a need that those larger groups should cohere. Two important theories of social organization accept that the human condition is such that some form of social organization is necessary if human beings are to have any assurance of survival. Thus, Professor H.L.A. Hart has shown how a minimum content of natural law can be postulated from the fact that human beings are vulnerable to injury, are approximately equal and have limited altruism, resources and understanding and strength of will.[4] Similarly, Mr. J.R. Lucas has demonstrated how some form of political organization is required as a result of the fact that humans have some shared interaction and some shared values, but are not infallible in their judgements, have not complete information and are limited in their altruism, so that they need to organize themselves to overcome their imperfections, to live with each other rather than against one another.[5] The new theory also accepts that, in order to survive as individuals, human beings need to form groups which can be maintained as social units meant to aid survival. Hence, the basic need of social rules is to cohere to survive. The child necessarily sticks by its parents because it cannot survive alone; so also individuals must try to forge alliances with others to promote their own survival and that of their kind. Thus, raised in one type of group, the family, an indivdual pools his interest eventually in a larger group, called here the community or social group.

Sir Henry Maine believed that the earliest forms of social groupings were families, and, although no evidence of such groupings has survived, he suggested that the Homeric stories of the Cyclops, who were family groups, point to the belief among the Greeks that societies more primitive than their own were organized on a family basis.[6] Maine also held that the larger social groups or communities were formed out of families by means of extension or amalgamation.[7] Thus, early communities regarded themselves as being composed of individuals with a common ancestor, however unlikely such a notion may sound or may have sounded even to them. The Romans, for example, always responded favourably to the designation, "Quirites", meaning sons of Romulus. Also, Maine pointed to the fact that adoption was an important institution in ancient times, and allowed new members to be taken into families and thus allowed families to be artificially enlarged.[8] Strangers to communities could not become members of the group until they were admitted by initiation, normally being allowed to attend sacrifices to the gods, usually ancestors, and thus being treated as of common descent.

Although Maine's account of the family as the original basis of social groups, with a patriarchal structure, has not met with universal approval,[9] his account fits in well with Freud's concept of what it takes to form a social group. Clearly, if the object is to survive and the precepts for survival emanate, via the superego, from one's ancestors, if two groups of people can share the same precepts or even have the same precepts for survival, it might well be assumed that this implied that somewhere their forefathers must have been related. To modern eyes, it might not appear so for one would probably say that it is not surprising that the same social conditions should produce the same precepts in different groups with the same aim, but all Maine postulated was that the ancients assumed consanguinity not that it actually existed. In the terms of the new theory, the belief was that as the survival precepts came from one's ancestors, then if one had the same set of precepts as another, one must have a common ancestor with that other and be of a common stock. That other was a suitable person, therefore, with whom to make common cause in the aim of survival, and one's family could join with his in pursuing that common goal. The notion of relationship was interpreted by the ancients as a blood relationship, but was, in fact, a related system of adaptation to the human condition, and in particular a related response in the way of precepts for survival. Freud defined this form of group as "a number of individuals who have put one and the same object in the place of their ego ideal and have consequently identified themselves with one another in their ego".[10] The common ancestor is assumed owing to the common ego-ideal, which is manifested in the shared survival precepts. Such shared precepts are necessary obviously if the community is to cohere.[11]

The relationship between family and group, or perhaps more accurately the resemblance between them,[12] manifests itself in another manner here. It was very common for the oldest members of the group, usually the oldest male members, to be venerated by the other members. The term, "elder", as a term of respect remains to this day. These men would be seen as embodying the correct standards of behaviour for cohesion and survival, and were, therefore to be obeyed and emulated. They would form the successors to the parental imagos in the formation of the ego-ideal and the superego. Sir Henry Maine noted this feature of life amid the South Slavonian house communities. He wrote:

"Not only the legal writers, but all travellers in South Slavonian lands, have noticed the extraordinary respect of the South Slavonians for old age. 'Without reverence for old men there is no salvation', is a Servian proverb. 'A father', says another Slavonian maxim, 'is like an earthly god to his son.' A less reverent adage runs, 'The reason why the devil knows so much is that he is so extremely old'."[13]

The Chinese too regard filial piety as the cornerstone of the social structure, and many more examples could be supplied.[14] The words of the ancestors are often the fundamental laws of the community, and the ancestors are often deified.

Much of the role of elders must be left until the role of the best-suited persons in relation to legal systems is discussed. However, it must be stated here that often a very distinguished person may become the ego-ideal of a community, and his example followed by his contemporaries and conveyed to posterity together with his name. Thus, again among the Chinese, the example and teachings of Confucius are traditionally accepted as embodying the genius of the people.[15] How far Mao has now taken over is at the time of writing an open question. Mohammed plays a similar role among followers of Islam, and Jesus Christ among Christians. There are some ego-ideals, of course, that have no memorial, perhaps the vast majority, but their precepts live on in the standards of those who follow their examples. Some ego-ideals are abstractions; thus, in English law, the standard of the reasonable man, the man on the Clapham omnibus, is the yardstick against which so many litigants are measured by the courts.

Another important likeness between the family and the community is that just as a child in the family is faced with the awkward choice of following his impulses or the example set by his father, so in the group, the individual is expected to forgo his own wants and needs if they conflict with what the community requires for cohesion and survival. Social life, like family life, requires sacrifices from the individuals who go to make up the group.[16] Freud has described how the ego has to strike the difficult balance between the demands of the id, the superego and the external world.[17] The individual in society has to strike a similar balance between outside forces, his own wishes and the demands of the group.

Freud also recognized that, without the formation of a group, an individual would be at the mercy of his stronger neighbours. He saw the formation of the group as the victory of the community interest of all surviving together over that of one indivdual surviving at the expense of his neighbours. The power of the community then became 'right' as against the individual's brute force. Freud concluded that: "The replacement of the power of the individual by the power of a community constitutes the decisive step in civilization. The essence of it lies in the fact that the members of the community restrict themselves in their possibilities of satisfaction, whereas the individual knew no such restrictions."[18] Again, therefore, sacrifice is seen as the price of the achievement. The benefit of survival in the community requires the burden of the achievement. The need to sacrifice one's own ends for those of the community is a feature of every legal system, and is particularly prominent among the Hindus.[19] It can, of course, lead to the problem of alienation mentioned earlier, as the individual seeks to do what he feels the group expects of him, and not what he wants to do. An individual in a group is, to a certain extent, torn between what he should do to promote cohesion and what he wishes to do which might destroy it. Thus, the evolution of civilization represented to Freud the struggle between Eros and Death. Eros is the instinct of life, seeking to combine single human individuals into groups, and Death, the instinct of destruction, man's natural aggressive instinct, the hostility of each against all and of all against each. Civilization evolved as this struggle worked itself out in the human species. "This struggle" wrote Freud, "is what all life essentially consists of, and the evolution of civilization may therefore be simply described as the struggle for life of the human species."[20] So far, this discussion has centred on the fact that groups form around shared survival precepts which are transmitted by example and teaching from generation to generation. It must now move on to consider what occurs when a member of such a group offends against such a precept, for here, it is submitted, will be found the beginnings of law and of the group's legal system. Given the forces involved and the sacrifices individuals have to make, that such events occur should not be found surprising.

II

At the outset, it must be realized that not all the precepts for survival are regarded as having equal importance. Some precepts will be capable of being broken without any real risk of dispute. Others will cause disputes only if broken by certain persons, and yet others will be dangerous dispute causers whenever they are transgressed. Thus, for example, to return to the example of the wood-chopping, it is unlikely that if the child were to persist in cutting down saplings on his father's estate that this would lead to a dispute which would threaten the cohesion of the community and the survival of its members. The child's transgression will probably be left to the father to punish if he wishes. The situation might be different if saplings were protected by the community for survival purposes or regarded as sacred to the community's gods, but, in the normal run of things, what has been said will probably hold good. Indeed, where communities are composed of families rather than of individuals according to the group perspective, as is the case with many early forms of social organization, disputes within a family are rarely considered to concern the group, because it is the inter-family bonds which the community wishes to cohere and upon which it pins its survival hopes. Even homicides within a family may not be considered to be a group concern.[21]

However, a slight change in the example will suffice to construct an instance of a dispute-causing breach of precept. If the child, having finished off his father's saplings or having been frightened off them by his father's remonstrations, decides to glut his desires upon the saplings of a neighbouring homestead, the reactions of the neighbour can be readily imagined. The breach of the precept that one should not destroy another person's saplings, a precept which recognizes rights of ownership, duties and so on, is very likely to cause a dispute between the offending and offended parties, which in early, social groupings are the respective families, and not just the individuals, involved. Likewise, if it were a neighbour and not the child that the father found felling trees upon his land, a dispute would be likely to ensue. Now, if a premium is placed upon keeping families united in peaceful co-existence within the community, so that the cohesion of the group may be assured and the survival and welfare of its members furthered, such disputes between families, leading perhaps to frequent breaches of precepts, strife within the group, violence and possibly even killing, is clearly a matter of great concern to the group. It is, therefore, in the interests of the group to see that peace is maintained. However, the survival interests of the offended parties, the interests which their membership of the group was intended to further, have clearly been adversely affected by the offence. Their reaction is, therefore, not unnaturally, to see themselves as having to compete rather than cohere with the offenders to survive, and their aggressive instincts come into play. To their way of thinking, the community has failed to protect their survival interest, so they must fall back on aggression to survive. The community, however, still sees cohesion as the best bet for survival and wishes to prevent the offended parties from ruining that cohesion by giving vent to their disruptive, aggressive impulses. The community, therefore, wishes to prevent disruption but at the same time needs to solve the dispute which has arisen. This is the sort of problem which, as has been shown, requires a dream-like construction in its solution, and the methods adopted to solve the dispute while maintaining peace involve, like dreams, a rechannelling of aggression so as to maintain rather than disrupt the peace, while solving the dispute on a higher level. The solution in the present problem occurs, of course, unlike dreams, on a social rather than an individual level. It is also, as a result of the need to solve disputes while maintaining peace, when the survival precepts of the group have been transgressed, that it is submitted, law emerges for the first time within the social group. Until this sort of situation arises, the community can be said to have rules of conduct, etiquette or even of morality, but not legal rules. The legal rules, which will now emerge, have as their object the preservation of the group. In this, they are like some of the survival principles which have already been discussed. In particular, they derive from those which cannot be broken without actual or threatened social disruption. The object of preserving the group is frequently recognized, even by primitive communities, as the end of law and legal procedure.[22]

The social group, however, is faced with a choice at this point in its development. It must decide whether it is better for survival purposes to force the disputing individuals or families to settle the quarrel amongst themselves or for the group to provide a procedure for settling it for them. In chapter one, it was stated that the procedures for settling disputes not only resembled dreams but also other psychological processes, including hysterical conversion. Although hysterical conversion solves a personal problem at a higher level and thus purchases a sort of peace for the individual concerned, the price is considered high in that hysteria is adjudged abnormal and unhealthy by most people. It could similarly be concluded that legal procedures produce an hysterical and thus unhealthy society and are, therefore, to be avoided if the problem can be solved on a normal, healthy level. Most societies, indeed the vast majority, regard legal procedures as normal and as socially healthy as dreams, but the possibility of their being regarded as socially unhealthy and undesirable, like hysteria, cannot be discounted. The traditional law of China presents the case of a society which opted against free resort to legal procedures and preferred to encourage individuals to reach peaceful settlements according to their own devices. Following Confucius, the traditional law thought it better to induce men to perform their correct social functions spontaneously,[23] and litigation was accordingly discouraged. Thus, civil procedure was totally lacking amongst the Chinese and considerable odium attached to commencing a criminal prosecution. The great, seventeenth-century emperor, K'ang Hsi, desired that "those who have recourse to the tribunals should be treated without any pity, and in such a manner that they shall be disgusted with law, and tremble to appear before a magistrate."[24] Litigants before a magistrate were compelled, accordingly, to kneel, and were harassed with menacing cries and gestures.[25] Likewise, the giving of legal advice was proscribed as an encouragement of litigation,[26] so that traditional China produced no corpus of jurisprudence.

Luckily for lawyers and students of jurisprudence, the vast majority of social groups have not decided with the Chinese against litigation. Most societies have decided to solve disputes for their members, and to rechannel the aggression involved in dispute situations so as to preserve rather than disrupt the cohesion of the community. As has earlier been stated, the preservation of cohesion is the main object, so that clearly this part of the process will be preferred to the other, namely solving the dispute for the parties. Thus, one would expect from this that the earliest procedures would be directed at restoring peace rather than reaching a satisfactory resolution of the dispute from the parties' point of view, for it is the interests of the group and not of the individuals which are primarily being protected. This is borne out by the evidence. Among the Trobriand islanders, for example, native litigations or *yakala* are used to preserve the peace when disputes break out. In them, the two parties meet and, assisted by friends and relatives, hurl insults and recriminations at one another, and this is merely a peaceful alternative to an all out fight with spears and clubs which would clearly harm the cohesion of the group.[27] The *yakala* settles nothing between the parties but preserves the peace. It illustrates remarkably well the idea of shifting the disruption to a higher level, where it doesn't threaten the community, but it does not resolve the dispute. Here, then, the fact that the group's interests are paramount is clearly visible.

One stage up, as it were, from the Trobriand *yakala* come the song contests by which the Eskimo prevent disruption of their social groups and, to a certain extent, solve their disputes. The Eskimo show two stages in institutionalizing disputes. Some eskimos settle homicidal disputes by recourse to regulated combat in the form of wrestling, buffetting and butting. These combats, organized in that they are announced and usually take place before the assembled community on festive occasions, mean that the fight which threatened disruption will take place in a manner which will not affect the cohesion of the community.[28] The facts which caused the dispute are irrelevant to the outcome, for he who wins, wins social esteem.

These duels are elevated to a higher level yet in the song-contest where blows are transformed into words, hurled by the disputants at one another in the face of the community. These song duels call to mind the song-contests described in the pastoral poetry of Greece and Rome, and these, too, probably had some connection with dispute solving. Hoebel has described well the function and achievement of the Eskimo contests.

"The song duels are juridical instruments insofar as they do serve to settle disputes and restore normal relations between estranged members of the community. One of the contestants receives a "judgment" in his favor. There is, however, no attempt to mete justice according to rights and privileges defined by substantive law. It is sufficient that the litigants (contestants) feel relieved - the complaint laid to rest - a psychological satisfaction attained and balance restored. This is justice sufficient unto the needs of Eskimo society as the Eskimos conceive it."[29]

The main object is clearly to preserve order and not to solve the dispute to the satisfaction of the parties. The parties are allowed to work off their aggressions, and that solves the dispute and removes the risk of disrupting the community. Among the primitive, food-gathering tribes of Australia, peace is preserved by 'growling', a procedure which again solves the problem of working off the parties' anger.[30] The mediaeval, European institution of trial by battle was meant to signify a divine judgement as to where right lay. The object, however, is clearly to reach a settlement peacefully rather than to satisfy the conflicting needs of the parties. Sir Henry Maine summed up the position with characteristic lucidity when he wrote that "the most ancient Courts deliberately established by mankind were intended to be what we should call Courts of Arbitration. Their great function was to give hot blood time to cool, to prevent men from redressing their own wrongs, and to take into their own hands and regulate the method of redress."[31]

The first concern, therefore, of emerging legal systems is to preserve the peace of the community, and the main function or at least one of the main functions of the leaders of such communities will be the making of peace between parties to disputes.[32] Indeed, among the Cheyenne Indians of North America, this need for obtaining cohesion after a dispute is illustrated by the fact that the renewed unity of the tribe after a dispute solution has to be symbolized through a ritual, the Renewal of the Medicine Arrows. The ritual had great, emotional force in integrating the tribe after a homicide and made manifest that the social bond had not been broken merely because one precept had been transgressed and a disruption had occurred. The ritual purified the tribe and restored its unity of purpose.[33]

The more sophisticated a social group becomes, the more sophisticated one would expect its dispute-solving procedure to be. This belief is again borne out by the evidence.[34] Thus, one would expect principled decision making to resolve disputes rather than just facilities for letting off steam. However, even when principles for solving disputes emerge, the primary purpose of keeping the peace is still paramount. Among African tribes, therefore, rules will still be departed from if they are unlikely to heal the breach,[35] so that the community interest is still the basis of the procedure even when the stage of finding a satisfactory solution in the parties' eyes has been reached. Indeed, if such a situation cannot be found, recourse may still be had to an institutionalized, violent confrontation. The mediaeval trial by battle thus remained available for settling serious disputes long after higher levels of resolution were reached, although its use became less and less common. In mediaeval Germany, however, the inability to solve serious disputes at a higher level was recognized in the setting up of an institution meant to provide a via media between peaceful settlement in the courts and self-help, in the form of an institutionalized, violent encounter or a permitted feud. These feuds were allowed by statutes called Landfrieden when a judicial determination had been unable to settle satisfactorily a dispute arising from a serious crime.[36]

However, although it has been necessary to show that institutionalized violence remained a method of solving disputes even after the increase in sophistication which brought principled dispute solution, in order to show that the preservation of community cohesion is still the primary object of dispute settling in such communities, it has not yet been explained how the move from procedure designed to give vent to aggression to procedures designed to give a satisfactory solution to the parties occurred. The need for these latter type of procedures was probably the opposite of the need for the landfrieden, namely, that some disputes could never finally be settled by means of song-contests and the like, and that even after such events resort to violence would still occur and disrupt the peace of the group. The group would then need to find a way of bringing such disputes to an end and restore a lasting harmony. Only by satisfying the parties could this be done, unless the community chose to rid itself once and for all of the disputants, a device resorted to on occasions by the Eskimo, and other societies of this equivalent stage of development.[37]

If a solution, satisfactory to the parties, is to be found in dispute situations then the community is doing for them what the society of traditional China encouraged the parties to do for themselves. However, it would clearly be to invite disruption to bring the parties themselves together unless the coming together was institutionalized, but that, of course, would be the song-contest situation. If the parties cannot be brought together, then the alternative is for them to communicate less directly in an attempt to reach a satisfactory solution. Early societies provide evidence that the device of using a go-between to reach a satisfactory solution, while avoiding the risk of an outbreak of violence inherent in bringing the disputants themselves together, was indeed used to solve disputes. Thus, the Ifugao use a go-between to reach a solution in all disputes except homicide cases calling for direct blood-revenge - this latter exception to the rule being a neat analogy to the mediaeval, German _Landfreiden_. The Ifugao call their litigational go-between a _monkalun_. The role of the _monkalun_ has been described by Hoebel.

"The existence of a _monkalun_ represents a first step in the development of juridical institutions. He explicitly expressed the general societal interest in the clearing up of tensions, the punishment of wrongs and the reëstablishment of social equilibrium when the normal balance has been disturbed by an alleged illegitimate act. He is to be recognized as a quasi-public official: the "disinterested" third party who represents the public interest in seeing that justice is done. He is not an outright public official, because his office is not explicit; he is a _monkalun_ only when acting as a _monkalun_, and he is not chosen by the public to serve in that post. He is not a judge; for he makes no judgments. He is not an arbiter; for he hands down no decrees. He is merely a forceful go-between - an admonishing mediator of limited authority but of usually persuasive effectiveness."[38]

The _monkalun_ is, then, the precursor of the establishing of an official to determine disputes to the satisfaction of the parties and for the preservation of the peace of the group. He is not himself recognized as being the best-suited person to settle disputes, but it takes but little imagination to see that a _monkalun_ who did his job well might be employed frequently afterwards and become an established go-between. The situation is very similar to that postulated by Maine in the passage from _Ancient Law_ quoted in the first chapter, where Maine believed that the office of praetor in the Roman world had its beginnings in the settling of disputes by a third party.[39] In Ethiopia, it is a generally recognized duty that a disinterested party who finds himself confronted by a dispute situation as he travels on the road, should accept the office of reconciler if called upon to do so. If he is unsuccessful in providing a satisfactory solution, he should then take the parties and their dispute to a judge for peaceful settlement. Again, therefore the main object is to prevent disruption. In early mediaeval Scandinavia, reconciliation after a crime of violence was also usually effected by means of go-betweens, or the Voldgiftsmaend as they were called.[40]

The effective solution of disputes by means of go-betweens to the satisfaction of the parties and without breaking the peace of the community probably gave rise to two consequences. One has already been noted, that is, that certain people were recognized as successful go-betweens and these probably became the community's first judges. The second probable consequence was to give rise to the idea that a dispute must have a solution if only such could be found. Just as the first consequence gave rise to judges and courts, so the second gave rise to the idea that rules existed to guide the satisfactory determination of disputes, and these rules mark the emergence of law. Again, it has been observed how in primitive societies the two institutions of courts and laws emerge together.[41]

The stages of this emergence must again be detailed for the institutions clearly did not emerge all at once. Just as the solutions found by go-betweens were solutions to the instant disputes and no more, so also the first judgements given by judges in courts were meant to govern no more than the actual dispute in question at that time. The judge pronounced the verdict for that one dispute only and this would not be taken as a rule of precedent for other disputes at first. It was probably thought that judges derived their judgements from divine inspiration; their dispute solutions were given them by the gods. The Greeks used the word _Themistes_ for these isolated judgements, and, as Maine noted, it is the plural form of _Themis_, the name of the divine agent who suggested judicial awards to judges, kings and gods.[42] Maine's speculation holds good for other peoples, and is confirmed by the form of reconciliatory proceedings among the Ashanti tribe of Nigeria. They settle disputes by taking them to a respected elder who represented the revered ancestors of the group. The mediator then pronounced a judgement which was not of his own making but which was the will of the ancestors.

The next step involves the realization that if a solution has solved one dispute satisfactorily, it will solve identical disputes also and probably similar ones as well. There then develops the idea or custom of settling disputes according to well-tried methods which have a proven record of success.[43] The development of the common law provides an interesting illustration of this stage in the growth of the jurisdiction of the royal courts during the thirteenth century. Originally, writs to commence actions for wrongs, or trespasses, in the royal courts were always framed with a particular dispute in mind, but owing to restrictions placed upon the writ-making agency, the Chancery, in 1258, no new writs could be issued. The established writs were still used, however, to decide identical cases to those which had been decided, and by the end of the century the restriction had been lifted to allow changes to be made in the writs so as to accommodate similar situations as well.[44] In all systems, once a body of isolated decisions can be seen to be dealing with a certain topic, those decisions can be read like an orchestral score, the method Levi-Strauss advocated for understanding myths, so as to establish the correct principle for solving such disputes, and the principle enunciated is, of course, a legal rule, for it marks the method for solving the dispute in question at a different, higher level while maintaining the peace of the community. The judges may not themselves enunciate these rules until the system is well-developed, as was the case with the development of the common law. Sir Henry Maine noted how the role of kings in early societies always included the office of judge. This illustrates how the ability to solve disputes is the key element in the recognizing of political power in a community, but this topic must be left until the emergence of the best-suited principle is discussed, a matter closely connected with these developments.

Inasmuch as the disputes which require the solutions are caused by the breaking of survival precepts, it is not a matter for surprise that the isolated judgements and first legal rules bear considerable affinity to those precepts. The survival precepts are what must be obeyed if the community is to cohere and survive, and the legal rules of the community are the solutions to disputes which threaten to thwart those two aims. The emergence of law, therefore, marks the incorporation of the survival principles into legal rules by a process akin to hardening because those precepts which cannot be broken without risking disputes have to be spelt out by the group to its members. Legal rules are, therefore, a sub-category of survival precepts and are related to, and will be seen to resemble, the other survival precepts, breach of which does not risk disruption. Thus, whereas, at first, a community will have a mixed bag of survival precepts, some of which will lead to disputes if transgressed and others of which will not, with effective dispute solution, those precepts which need to be hardened into legal rules will become separated from the others. Thus, the earliest compilations of survival precepts are a mixed bag of religious, moral and, what will be, legal precepts. Among such compilations may be mentioned the Bible, the Qur'an and the Hindu Vedas. With the emergence of legal rules, separate compilations of such precepts may be found. Thus, it has been suggested that the Twelve Tables did the Roman people the great service of separating its legal rules from its religious precepts.[45] Again, there is widespread evidence that the earliest legal codes were composed of customs, moral precepts and the like, which had hardened into legal rules but still bear the traces of their origins. The Hittite Code of 1300-1250 B.C. is a collection of judgements which have been assembled to form a code of laws,[46] and the law codes of early mediaeval Europe are also, by and large, collections of customs, often, as with the Anglo-Saxon laws, liberally sprinkled with laws which are clearly hardened versions of Christian precepts of good living.[47] The role of the courts or the legislature in enunciating legal rules is, then, to convert survival precepts into a form in which they can be used to solve disputes while preserving the peace. Thus, the law-enunciating organs may well retain the right to convert any survival principle into a legal rule should the need arise. The Court of King's Bench in England has had claimed for it both in the time of Lord Mansfield and more recently the role of guardian of the public morals or *custos morum*.[48] Such a role is clearly a function of a law-enunciating organ of the community when one remembers that morals, too, are a form of survival precept, being guidelines on how to behave if society is to cohere and individuals to survive. It is instructive to realize that if the twin goods of cohesion and survival were thought to depend upon it, any survival principle could be hardened into a legal rule. Thus, a deliberate breach of a rule of grammar or a rule of mathematics or logic could be the subject of a legal rule if such a breach were to cause disputes likely to disrupt cohesion and survival.[49] Less unlikely examples are rules concerning manners, etiquette, dress, morality and religion, some of which are already the subject of legal rules. The conventions of the constitution, as discussed by Dicey, are an interesting example of a set of precepts in the process of being hardened gradually into legal rules. Professor Basil Mitchell has described the situation very well. He wrote: "Law and morality are two forms of social control aimed at preventing certain injurious consequences."[50] This, it is submitted, is true of all manner of survival precepts. It should be remembered, however, that all such precepts as articulations are approximations of what is required, and this is true of legal rules no less than of other types of survival principle. All such precepts may, therefore, be in need of correction or adjustment. In early mediaeval Europe, decisions in concrete cases were often inserted into an appropriate place in the governing code of law where they threw light upon or modified an existing, enunciated principle.[51]

Legal systems emerge as a result of this institutionalizing of dispute situations and their solution in a manner which attempts to preserve the peace of the community. Solving or avoiding disputes to maintain cohesion and survival is the function of law.[52] The first stage in the development of a legal system is the institutionalizing of disputes; the second the enunciation of legal rules which will solve the disputes in the required manner. That legal systems develop in these stages is shown by the evidence available. The subject of the first treatises on law is, therefore, procedure. Thus, the earliest treatises on Roman law concentrate on the law of actions, and, in the common law, the focus of attention is the writs which commence actions. The same is true of the early treatises on Hindu law, which focus on the court and sort of disputes which it will hear.[53] Only with the success of this institutionalization and the development of a judicial staff who regularly try the disputes, do legal rules as such emerge. Thus, in all systems, the law of procedure seems to antedate the development of substantive law. So Henry Maine must again be given the last word on this topic, for he summed up this situation in a famous sentence. He wrote: "So great is the ascendancy of the Law of Actions in the infancy of Courts of Justice, that substantive law has at first the look of being gradually secreted in the interstices of procedure; and the early lawyer can only see the law through the envelope of its technical forms."[54] The first peering of the common lawyers through that envelope can be seen in Book VII of Glanvill and in Bracton's treatise, where the first attempts to spell out legal rules from among the procedural requirements can clearly be seen.

III

In what has been said so far concerning the emergence of a legal system within a social group, it has been necessary to anticipate a little and to mention occasionally the existence of a best-suited method of settling disputes and enunciating the principles which will avoid or settle disputes. It is now time to consider in greater detail the emergence of a community's best-suited principle, as it marks an important stage in the group's legal, political and general social development.

Even when speaking of the development of the child within the family, the existence of a best-suited principle had to be acknowledged. There, it was the father who was recognized as the best-suited person whom the child should follow if he wished to survive, and hence it was that the parental image became the basis of the child's ego-ideal, the standard according to which, throughout his life, he would measure his behaviour or achievements by means of the superego. In chapter two, attention was drawn to the similarities which exist between the development of the individual and that of the social group, and in particular, it was suggested that the best-suited persons or procedures would be to the group what the superego was to the individual. Thus, the stage in social development marked by the recognition that a certain person or persons fulfil the role of judicial go-between very successfully, and accordingly ought to be accepted as being established in that role, or as judges, is the stage in social development equivalent to that in the development of the individual where the child sees the father as the person whose example he should follow if he wishes to survive. In other words, the go-between is accepted as the best-suited person to solve disputes and becomes, at that point, a judge. At that stage, his solutions will no longer be accepted solely because they successfully solve the disputes and restore order, they will now be accepted and ratified as solutions which ought to be obeyed because of the authority which the go-between now has as judge, that is, it will be believed that his solutions work not only because they actually do but also because he is the best-suited person to solve disputes. This authority will eventually be carried over from his isolated solutions or judgements to his principled decisions, and, in the enunciation of legal rules, his enunciations will make valid law because they will be accepted and ratified. Each correct solution he reaches thereafter will strengthen his authority and position as the best-suited person, and, only if his solutions cease to work, will that authority be eroded and his position forfeited.

The best-suited person to solve disputes in a community is often, as has been mentioned earlier, the chief, king or leader of the group. The functions of such chiefs sometimes include priestly duties and very often military leadership, but always, in the early stages of communal development, the chief is the person on whom the onus of finding a peaceful settlement to disputes falls, and he becomes the best-suited person to do so.[55] Only as the community develops do these functions adhere to separate persons. Thus, it can be seen that both legal and political power tend to centre at first and develop around the person who best preserves the peace and integrity of the community by overcoming threats to its cohesion and survival. The combination of judicial and military leadership in the person of the king or chief is extremely common and occurs, for example, in the Homeric world of Greece in the eighth century B.C.[56]

The fact that the judicially best-suited person is also the war-leader illustrates the fact that the chief is generally regarded as best-suited to protect the cohesion of the group and its survival, whether the risk of disruption is a small one from inside the group in the form of a dispute, or is a larger one which threatens to extinguish the group altogether as in the case of a hostile attack with that purpose in view either from within, civil war, or without. That the chiefly authority is often greater in times of war than in peace-time is borne out by the evidence. Thus Diamond noted that this was the case among the Plains Indians of North America, and modern communities also accept their governments' right to exercise special powers in times of war or great emergency. Violent attack is not the only thing which can threaten to extinguish a social group. The threat of disease, particularly an epidemic of a deadly disease, can lead to the best-suited persons having to exercise considerably more authority in directing the life of members of the community in an effort to save it from extinction. Thus, the government of England took stiff measures against the plague in 1665. All threats to survival have to be overcome if the community is to continue, whether they come from human beings or not, and it is at times such as these that the best-suited principle is really put to the test. If it can bring the group through the dangers of war or disease, then it proves itself to be the best-suited method. If it manages to ensure survival at such times, its position as best-suited method will be powerfully confirmed, and the acceptance and ratification of its measures thereafter further ensured. Failure at such times, of course, more than at any other, leads not only to its probable downfall but possibly to the extinction of the community. The role of acceptance and ratification at such times is particularly clear cut, as at such times the objectives of the best-suited persons and the other members of the community in question are particularly congruent. Both are painfully aware of the need to survive and the danger of extinction.

Moreover, it is not surprising that it is the persons who are able to direct the community onto the correct path for survival at such dangerous times who become recognized and accepted as the best-suited persons to enunciate the survival principles of the community after the danger has passed, and also perhaps actually to solve the lesser disputes which arise in peace-time as well as stating the principles which should be used in reaching such solutions. Thus, Maine noted that the Hebrew judges of Scripture were heroes raised up by the people at moments of national disaster, that is, the persons who saved the Jews from extinction in such catastrophic times. Such times are, of course, not only those in which customary survival precepts are particularly prone to become hardened into laws through enunciation, but are also the times at which completely new precepts may have to be found and enunciated as laws immediately. Such precepts which emerge as fully-blown legal rules, rather than developing gradually from infancy as survival precepts of a different kind, can be regarded as the type of legislation proper as opposed to judge-made law. At such times also, it may be necessary to depart from, or even ignore, established precepts already enunciated as laws. This can occur even where the precepts are regarded as having been revealed by God himself. Jewish law furnishes two interesting examples of this phenomenon.

"When dealing with certain biblical narratives and other traditions the rabbis came to notice their being at variance with established norms. Instead of assuming a violation of the law, they developed the idea of emergency powers existing beside the ordinary norms, so as to meet the needs of a grave situation. Thus Maimonides in his code describes the talmudic law of evidence, declaring confessions to be inadmissible. He then cites two biblical cases where the accused was found guilty on his admission and was consequently executed. These cases, he explains, reflect a royal privilege of disregarding normal rules, a privilege granted in order to prevent High Treason.

"Similar privileges were conferred on the courts of later generations for the purpose of securing the maintenance of the law. At the beginning of the second century B.C. a Hasmonean tribunal inflicted severe punishments against Hellenistic transgressors of the law. The rabbis did not justify these hard sentences under the ordinary rules, but referred to 'the needs of the hour.' According to this idea, a court may punish, at its discretion, any act harmful to the community, though such an act was not expressly dealt with by the law. The judges thus, serve as a kind of legislators in retrospect."[57]

Similarly, the freedom of speech guaranteed to the people of the United States by their Bill of Rights has had to be waived occasionally in time of war, and the traditional rights of the British people are also interfered with in times of emergency under Emergency Powers Acts. Illegalities committed during times of emergency in the interests of survival are, on occasion, subsequently ratified and declared _ex post_ *facto* legal by Parliament, by means of Acts of Indemnity.[58] The fact that sudden changes and needs produce legal rules by means of legislation rather than by gradual development by solving disputes is also apparent from the early history of law in Scandinavia, particularly in Iceland. There, although laws had existed in the form of custom coupled with survival precepts of other sorts, the need for legislation arose through the changes involved in setting up agrarian and religious communities, the change in the religion of the people to Christianity, the settlement and organization of conquered territory and subjection to foreign power and taxation.[59] The last mentioned marks, of course, a clear failure of a best-suited method and its replacement by a new one.

Thus, it can be seen that it is generally the case that the best-suited principle of a community emerges at times when the cohesion and possibly even the survival of the group is in jeopardy. When the risk is of disruption to the cohesion of the community by internal disputes, the best-suited principle develops by noticing who are those persons who are best able to solve such disputes without threatening the stability of the community as a whole. In such circumstances, the best-suited persons are judges, and the enunciations of legal rules will come in the form of the principles which have helped them solve disputes in the required manner. Where, on the other hand, the threat is greater, as where the community is attacked by a hostile neighbour or sub-group, or is threatened by disease, the luxury of developing legal rules gradually from the customary suvival principles will have to be forgone and the precepts will have to be enunciated promptly as the need arises in the form of legal rules. Those best able to do this will be regarded as the best-suited persons, and the law of an attacked community will be legislative in character rather than judicially made. It is noticeable that communities which are less susceptible to attack, such as island communities like Great Britain, are more likely to develop case-law than communities that are situated on a large, land mass where other groups may attack them. The latter tend to incorporate their laws into codes as a result of the needs of dangerous hours. Where the best-suited principle has emerged in a wartime context, the military leaders may be called upon to adjudicate the lesser dangers of internal disputes in later times. Where the best-suited principle has emerged in peace-time, the judges may be called upon to legislate in times of war, but this is less likely. Where a different, legislative best-suited principle has emerged in a community with an already established dispute-solving best-suited principle, the established method is likely to hold its place with regard to dispute solving, but the judges will probably accept the enunciations of the legislature as valid laws. Thus, a metagame of the judges having to decide which body is best-suited to enunciate the dispute-solving precepts comes into being, of the kind described in chapter two. In all cases, however, the best-suited principle of a community emerges as a response to the group's cohesion and survival being threatened and some person or procedure being able to overcome the danger. The precepts for survival which are then enunciated according to the emergent best-suited principle will be accepted by the community as its legal rules, and accepted and ratified by the group. Such acceptance and ratification will continue while the enunciations obtained according to the principle appear to work the double oracle of furthering cohesion and survival. This will lead to the acceptance and ratification of the best-suited principle itself. It is upon such acceptance and ratification of both kinds that legal systems are based, and it is with their advent that laws first emerge from among the survival precepts of a community.[60]

IV

Having looked at the process by which the best-suited principle of a community emerges, it is now necessary to examine the various forms of best-suited method which are in existence, and to consider the factors which mould the methods into those forms. It is interesting to note that quite often the names given by the community to a best-suited person or procedure reflect the community judgement of his particular gift. Among the Eskimo tribes, the name used by the Baffin Islanders is particularly interesting; it is <u>pimain</u>, meaning 'he who knows everything best'. Names meaning father or elder or wise man are particularly predominant.[61]

As has been noted, the first best-suited person accepted by most individuals on a personal level are their fathers, and this was due to the fact that the father had succeeded in surviving to manhood. Just as his superior years signified his greater and successful experience, so did the age of the old men of a given community imply that their knowledge and example were particularly worth following.[62] The old men or elders of a group, therefore, are frequently the first persons accepted by the group as being the best-suited to enunciate the group's survival precepts, customs and laws. Thus, the customs of German communities in the early Middle Ages, particularly those of rural communities, were declared by the elders or aldermen of the villages and called Weistumer, and represent observed practices. Similarly, amongst the Cheyenne Indians of North America, only the council of old men is entrusted with making peace, pronouncing the ultimate sentence of banishment and commuting any sentence passed on a delinquent.[63] It has been noticed by Freud, amongst others, that among the Aboriginals of Australia, such assemblies antedate the existence of any individual leader.[64] Sometimes, variations occur so that such assemblies are not limited to the old, but are extended to include all weapon-bearing men, as among the rural cantons of Switzerland in the Middle Ages,[65] or those who carry out the priestly functions of the group, although the latter are frequently synonymous with the old men of the community in question.

The emergence of one leader, chief or king is frequently the first development which occurs in such a community, and this man will then probably be accepted as the best-suited person to settle disputes and enunciate the legal rules of the group. He may just be the eldest,[66] and thus be taken as having the greatest experience, but he may also have been the one noticed in times of emergency as the best enunciator of the precepts which led to survival. Hence, the remark of the Comanche that the chief was chief because he just got that way.[67] The influence of such a person increases with his reputation for good decisions.[68] Again, he may be the religious or ritual expert of the group, as with the leopard-skin chief who solves disputes among the Nuer.[69] Examples of such leaders include all chiefs, kings, and even the Pope, who has this role within the Roman Catholic Church.

The problem arises of what is to happen where a person who has held such a position dies or loses the qualities which earned him the role of leader or best-suited person to enunciate. It is possible that such a position will not be regarded as established, so that the group will revert to treating the council of elders as best-suited or whatever unit it relied on prior to the emergence of the leader. If, however, a successor is desired, one may emerge, as did the last, spontaneously, just by getting that way, or one may be deliberately chosen as the wisest, strongest or eldest. Such election took place for the office of king in Anglo-Saxon England, the election being made by the Witan. Another alternative would be for the previous best-suited person to nominate his successor, or it might be accepted that one of his relatives was likely to inherit his qualities particularly the eldest son, as being the most experienced descendant of the last leader. Succession by inheritance could also arise as a result of noticing that descendants tend to possess the qualities of their ancestors. Succession by inheritance hits a problem when the heir is of tender years, and this can give rise to the problem of who is best-suited to govern until the heir comes of age, the problem of who is best-suited to be regent.[70] Different societies answer such problems according to what they deem best for cohesion and survival, and rules may be accepted as giving the best solution to such questions.

One of the features of the best-suited principle in its early stages is that it does not distinguish between the questions of who is best-suited to solve disputes and who is best-suited to enunciate the legal rules by which the disputes are solved. Thus, the judicial and legislative functions are not usually divided in early societies. Indeed, it was not until the thirteenth-century in Europe that government was thought of as being a separate function from legislation.[71] Often, the first forms of legislation come directly from the decision of lawsuits. The Lombard enactments of Liutprand in large measure came into existence through judgements given in deciding litigation.[72] The Norweigian law-things delegated both judicial and legislative functions to a committee of thirty-six members, the Lagretten, and the link between the role of legislator and judge in early societies is clearly illustrated in the saga of the "Case of Sigurd Ranessön", where to clarify the rule of law which applied, the judges abruptly stopped the judicial proceedings and commenced a judicial debate as to what the law should be. When this had been determined and enacted, the trial resumed.[73] The Cheyenne Indians also provide an illustration of this phenomenon. Hoebel records how in the case of Wolf Lies Down, having settled the issue, the judges immediately went on to declare a new rule, that is, to act as legislators.[74] The fact that the English House of Lords is part of the legislature and the highest court of appeal in the land, albeit with different personnel, provides evidence that such a stage was passed through in this country as well.

In time, however, the task of settling disputes came to be separated from that of enunciating the legal rules.[75] The leader then retains the role of governor and enunciator of legal rules, but passes the judicial function to an officer or deputy. Thus, in mediaeval England, the king delegated the hearing of disputes to sheriffs in the localities, and in Germany the local Graf received the same task.[76] Among the Hebrews of the old Testament, the sarim were the judicial officers who so emerged.[77] Such developments were particularly common where a new governor was imposed from outside, as in England after the Norman Conquest. In Islamic law, an instance of this development also exists. When under the Umayyad dynasty (A.D. 661-750), local governors were appointed to supervise conquered territories, the judicial powers of such governors were regularly delegated to spokesmen of the local customs, called qadis.[78] With this division of judicial from legislative power, it also became necessary for the judges to know whose enunciations to accept as the rules to solve disputes, and thus a metagame development occurs at this stage.

Whether the leader solves disputes himself or whether this task has been delegated to a judicial officer, the person who solves the disputes will only continue to be regarded as the best-suited person to do so while the other members of the community accept and ratify his enunciations as promoting cohesion and survival. Without such regular acceptance and ratification, the best-suited principle will not continue long to be accepted and ratified itself and the enunciations obtained via it will lose the force of valid law. As the acceptance and ratification of the best-suited principle lies with the members of the group as a whole, there is clearly a great deal of truth in statements of the sort made by Fleury that there is no true law unless it is accepted by custom.[79] At first, therefore, the best-suited person to enunciate the precepts for survival, whether king or chief or whatever, did no more than enunciate the customs of the group, and made no attempt to change the community's customary rules. Thus, in early mediaeval Europe, kings had to consult the nobility of the group before a change in the folk-laws could occur.[80] Change in the customs or laws required consent, so that acceptance and ratification of changes was a very real process. The baronial rebellion against King John in early thirteenth-century England was due, to a large extent, to his tampering with traditional rights without first consulting his nobles. Arrangements for such consent to be given frequently existed; thus in Lombardy and Burgundy, principles formulated by the elders of the community were submitted to the local assembly for approval,[81] and in Scandinavia it was understood that the Things were to approve laws given by the kings before they attained validity.[82] In the Jewish communities of the Middle Ages also, consent to changes in the traditional law was required, and the ordinances so made were known as _haskamah_ (conventions).[83]

The Roman writer, Tacitus, noted that on minor matters the chiefs of the ancient German people were able to decide principles amongst themselves, so that their authority to make changes to that extent was accepted, but that more important matters had to be discussed with the whole tribe.[84] These more important matters were, it is submitted, the fundamental rights referred to in chapter three. Likewise, at a later stage, when the authority of leaders to make changes autonomously had become accepted, as in Northern Europe in the twelfth century, some interests were still regarded as being immune to change, and Magna Carta marks an enunciation of such interests for the English people.[85] It is at this stage, when the enunciations of the best-suited person or procedures are regarded as being acceptable and ratifiable because of their genesis rather than their content, although the content, as was shown in chapter two, remains of importance, that rules are becoming independent of their subjects and a strong best-suited principle can be said to have developed. From here on, the best-suited method will clearly be trusted unless it errs seriously or regularly.

There is always, of course, the danger of the best-suied principle failing to provide the correct enunciations for cohesion and survival. The best-suited principle has to be constantly ratified through continued acceptance of its enunciations. Thus it is that mechanisms and procedures are to be found built into the operation of the principle to prevent unacceptable formulations and the demise of the method. It has already been noted that Umayyad governors allowed qadis to judge disputes as they had a knowledge of local customs, a clear attempt to ensure acceptance and ratification of dispute solutions. A frequent device, even when the actual consent of the governed is no longer required, is to give them the chance to dissent from enunciations. Social groups, therefore, often promulgate their laws to the people, to give them the opportunity to dissent. Thus, in ancient Rome, each magistrate had to announce to the assembled people the policies he intended to pursue at the start of his term of office, and the magistrate who most interfered with the law, the praetor, issued an edict at the start of his annual term. Similarly, in Scandinavia, in early times, new laws were promulgated at the Thing or law-gatherings and among the Tswana tribe of Africa, new laws are considered and enacted at an assembly of all the adult males, called a pitso.[86] Even in the case of judicially-made law in Europe in the early mediaeval period, the chance of dissent was present with the people being in the courts when decisions were reached.[87] Another feature of these courts was that the people were frequently represented on the tribunal in the forms of lay judges called in their respective countries, scabini, schöffen, and so on.[88]

The idea of ensuring acceptance and ratification of enunciations made according to the best-suited principle by having among the persons who operate under the principle representatives of the group who must endorse its findings is one which occurs over a wide area. The courts which the British set up in India incorporated, at first, experts in local law so as to ensure that their findings were correct, the so-called moolvies or pandits.[89] Even in England today, judges who sit in Admiralty cases are assisted in reaching their decisions on seafaring matters by brethren of Trinity House. The idea of having a representative legislature is based upon the same principle of ensuring its best-suitedness to enunciate. Societies with a marked cosmopolitan membership often make considerable efforts to ensure that the personnel operating their best-suited procedures are representatives of the various elements which go to make up the group. Some conventions of the Canadian constitution illustrate this feature very clearly.

"In Canada some rules can be laid down with complete assurance and the first and most binding of all is that there must be French- and English-speaking

Canadians in the Canadian Cabinet and that Quebec must be represented. Secondly each of the Canadian provinces must, if at all possible, have at least one representative in the Cabinet. Then there is a usage, probably a convention, that Quebec and Ontario must have approximately equal representation; and that the Protestant minority in Quebec should be represented in the Cabinet; that English-speaking Catholics, probably outside Quebec, should be represented, and that the French Canadians outside Quebec shall not be overlooked. Obviously these arrangements are not always all possible at the same time, but there are strong pressures which tend to make them obligatory."[90]

The best-suitedness of the government may also be guaranteed by demanding a large proportion of unity on matters of considerable importance, such as fundamental rights. Indeed, the demand for unanimity is not unknown.[91]

Even where the enunciations are those of persons who like Confucius or Napoleon were living embodiments of their people's virtues, the enunciations have constantly to be ratified by the members of the group, and just how precarious the position of a given best-suited person or procedure is, is a question of fact in each case. The best-suited method must provide the precepts which will aid cohesion and survival, and the dangers of failure are, therefore, as serious as they are obvious. The matter is effectively brought home by John Stuart Mill's illustration of the Locrians, among whom the proposer of a new law was obliged to stand in the public assembly with a halter about his neck, and if his proposal was not accepted, the halter would instantly be tightened.[92] The best-suited principle is constantly tested after this fashion. Amongst the Jews, the problem of dispute solving according to precepts is regarded as difficult and dangerous. "The judge is to consider himself 'as if a sharp sword is lying upon his neck', which is a form of describing his responsibility."[93] Rabbis tended, therefore, to prefer to see disputes settled by extra-judicial compromise, as they realized and feared the danger of judicial error.[94] A successful best-suited method, on the other hand, means that the law of a community is based squarely on the authority of the enunciations made by that principle, and that virtually any enunciation so made will be accepted and ratified as being the best thing for cohesion and survival. The law of ancient Rome attained this prestige.[95]

Indeed, the Roman emperor came to be regarded as _lex animata_, the embodiment of law.[96] Even in Rome, however, devices were used to ensure that the best-suited principle would meet with success. Thus, successive praetors regularly issued as their edicts facsimiles of those which had been issued by their predecessors with such additions and subtractions as thought fit, so that in time the edict became a fixed body of rules constantly re-iterated, and was indeed eventually put into a standard form in A.D. 130 as the Edictum Perpetuum.[97] The doctrine of precedent in the common law, based on the notion that like cases should be decided alike, is a similar manifestation of this tendency. Another technique used by the common law to ensure ability in deciding disputes is to demand that those who are deciding disputes should have served a term of apprenticeship in the activity before being let loose upon the demanding public. Thus, common law judges in England and Wales have to have practised for at least a decade at the Bar, witnessing dispute solving by experienced judges, before they become eligible to sit upon the bench.[98] In ancient Rome, juristic experts were accepted by the magistracy and later by the emperors as being best-suited to expound the technicalities of the law. Such men, too, learnt the techniques of enunciation by apprenticeship in the service of established jurists.[99] Such scholarship was the key ingredient in Jewish law.[100]

The opinions of jurists in Roman law became finalized eventually around the opinions of those jurists whose opinions were regarded as being of the greatest authority, the very best enunciators for all time. Thus, the so-called Law of Citations of A.D. 426 gave prominence to the works of Papinian, Paul, Gaius, Ulpian and Modestinus. If they differed as to a point, the majority was to prevail. If there were a tie, Papinian's view was to be taken, and if he were silent, only then was the judge to be given the task of deciding the issue for himself.[101] This again is clearly a device to ensure that judicial enunciations and decisions should be acceptable. Recourse to the opinions of jurists, in effect to their enunciations of what the law is, is in itself a metagame acceptance of where is the best place for judges to turn to find the correct survival precepts. The role of constitutions and statutes in this function has already been discussed.[102] Other societies, as well as ancient Rome, provide examples of the phenomenon. Thus, the _qadis_ of Islamic law were eventually advised on doctrinal matters of law by legal scholars called *fuqaha*, who formulated the law which the *qadis* merely applied.[103] Islam also provides a parallel to the Law of Citations in that a universal consensus among the legal scholars of a generation on a point of law, so-called *ijma*, was deemed infallible.[104] Where it is feared that a best-suited person to solve disputes may err from time to time, one mechanism for preventing such errors leading to a weakening in, or possible breakdown of, the best-suited principle is to establish a procedure of appeals, so that decisions can be reviewed. Ultimately, of course, a final arbiter must be reached, as with the House of Lords in England and Wales, or the Emperor in ancient Rome. Where an established rule cannot work the oracle of settling disputes, fictions may be used to adapt it so that satisfactory settlements can be reached. The development of the common law is particularly rich in such occurrences. Thus, wrongs, or trespasses, which did not really fall within the jurisdiction of the King's courts, were sneaked in at the close of the thirteenth century and after by fictitiously alleging that they had been committed *vi et armis et contra pacem domini Regis*.[105]

A very important recognition that enunciated rules may sometimes have fallen short of the mark is the readiness of the leaders of communities to retain the right to dispense justice in cases where the enunciated principles signally fail to do this for some reason. Thus, the praetorian edict mentioned earlier was meant to overcome defects in the civil law of Rome, and formed eventually a secondary system of precepts to correct these deficiencies and was called *ius honorarium*. Similarly, in England, the King retained the right to dispense justice when the rules of common law failed to achieve this, and this right was eventually delegated to the Chancellor who, in the Court of Chancery, in time developed the secondary line of precepts called Equity.[106] Thus, by these means, inefficiencies in the best-suited principle can be overcome without disturbing it unduly, although the development of a secondary set of precepts clearly does involve a change in the best-suited principle of a group.[107] Such developments do, however, prevent outright rejection of the best-suited principle through failure to enunciate the correct, that is acceptable, principles. Such rejections do occur. Thus, among the Ashanti, chiefs or kings who fail to reach the required level of enunciating are destooled.

When a best-suited principle ceases to provide the enunciations which can be accepted as correct for cohesion and survival, changes do occur. Frequently, also, dissatisfaction may arise from the fact that it is noticed that better enunciations are available. Thus, as the common law developed in England during the Middle Ages, there was a gradual but perceptible movement of litigation away from the local courts in the direction of the King's courts, where it had become known, partly as a result of the fact that the King's justices had toured the localities periodically in the twelfth and thirteenth centuries on general Eyres, that the royal courts provided better and more efficient remedies.[108] Likewise, royal officials were accepted as chairmen in the local courts in the shire courts of England and in the gouw assemblies of the Netherlands.[109] Mediaeval Germany probably provides the best illustration of such a change in the best-suited principle with the phenomenon of the Reception of Roman Law. The Reception occurred to a certain extent in many parts of continental Europe, but it is perhaps most distinct in Germany. There, towards the end of the Middle Ages, under the influence of counsel learned in Roman law, litigants moved their disputes from the Schöffen courts to those of the administrative officers of their territorial sovereign to be determined according to Roman Law. The temptation of having one's disputes settled according to Roman law was increased by allowing appeal from the Schöffen to the Imperial Kammergericht, where the case would be finally determined according to the Roman system.[110] Thus, a new best-suited principle emerged in Germany as the old withered. What must, however, be noted is that such changes can occur, as here, gradually, within the structure of the legal system so that continuity is not broken. Changes in the best-suited principle of a group do not mark the formation either of a new group or necessarily of a new legal system. At the base, the function of the group and of its legal system remains unaltered - to promote social cohesion and survival. Many of the same precepts will, then, be found before and after the change, only some precepts will have been replaced by what are regarded as better, and a better best-suited principle for enunciating such precepts will be said to have been discovered. The problems of continuity in such circumstances has already been discussed.[111]

V

The emergence of the best-suited principle and its development is only one facet, however, of the development of a legal system. The other facet is the process by which the legal rules which are enunciated according to it obtain their validity and are enforced. It is now time to focus attention upon the methods used to promote the cohesion and survival of the group by means of its legal system.

As has already been shown, the community in order to protect itself from disruption and extinction evolved a system of institutionalizing dispute situations, and that from such institutions emerged the idea of a court in which disputes could be settled peacefully and according to principle. In these circumstances, the courts would direct the parties as to what should be done both to settle the dispute and at the same time maintain the cohesion of the group. The problem has to be faced, however, that although the other members of the group may be satisfied that what the court says should be done is what will promote cohesion and survival, the parties to the dispute, or one of them, may not be satisfied that their interests have been satisfactorily protected. In that situation, the dissatisfied party may ignore the court's ruling and this may lead either to his taking private vengeance, as where restitution has not been made, or to his being attacked, where he himself has failed to make reparation. It is likely that in the earliest stages of legal development, the courts were unable to enforce their decisions because the group as a whole could not turn on its members, which it should be recalled were families rather than individuals, without endangering its cohesion more than by tolerating the existing rift. Thus, the earliest legal rules were not enforced by way of sanction, but undoubtedly the group would disapprove of its members refusing to follow the decisions of its best-suited procedure for settling quarrels. Resort to self-help would, however, be the only way of carrying out the verdict of the courts. This was the view held by Sir Henry Maine.[112]

As well as the risks of disruption to the community which existed in such arrangements, or more accurately the lack of them, a further danger lay hidden in this situation. The person who flounted the enunciations of the best-suited persons, having broken a survival precept, could in such circumstances be seen to take the benefits of social existence without submitting to its burdens. That such a person should survive was clearly a contradiction of the precepts which held that the opposite of his conduct was what should be done if survival was to be achieved. Such a person embodied, therefore, an ideal contrary to that of the community and presented to the other members a bad example, which, as he had been successful, the other members might be tempted to emulate. If the community was correct in its original beliefs, the taking of such an example as a survival standard would lead to ruin. This consideration, it is submitted, coupled with the risk of immediate disruption through the other party to the dispute's need for vengeance, was what caused the community, once strong enough to do so, to expel such recalcitrant members from membership of the group. As only members of the group were aided by the group's legal rules, the excluded member was no longer within the ambit of the law's protection; he was outlawed. The thinking behind this is that a person who enjoys the benefits of group membership, that is the increased chances of survival, must submit to the burdens which the group places upon him to achieve the goals of cohesion and survival, and a rejection of the burdens must mean a loss of the benefits. This is implicit in the Scandinavian concept of the outlaw, or utlagar.[113]

However, if an excluded person were to continue to survive without the group's protection, then he would be clearly showing that survival was not dependent upon submitting to the burdens imposed by membership of the group, and would stand as a competing survival standard before others, representing standards conflicting with those of the community. For this reason, therefore, the other members of the group visit what they consider to be the consequences of failing to obey the survival precepts upon the delinquent, that is, they hunt him down and kill him. Thus, his example is seen to be one which, if followed, leads to extinction, and will accordingly not be emulated. His fate is seen as a symbol of what will occur if the survival precepts of the group, together with the enunciations of its best-suited persons or procedures, are not followed. If private vengeance were the reason for destroying the delinquent, one would expect only the wronged person and his family and friends to pursue the outlaw, but, on the contrary, one finds that every member of the community is, at this stage of the group's development, under an obligation to raise the hue and cry, and to pursue the outlaw like a wild animal until he is hunted down and slain.[114] The actions of the community smack of a political motive,[115] and the need to remove bad examples by visiting what the group believes to be the consequences of his actions upon the delinquent appears the explanation which best fits the facts.[116] A community needs, of course, to be strong to effect such sanctions, for the recalcitrant would otherwise be able to resist with the aid of family and friends. In the early stages of such developments, therefore, the consent of the group members, including such relatives and friends, for the execution may be obtained before carrying it out. Such consent is sought, for example, amongst the Eskimo.[117]

A strong community will also begin to exact punishments when the breaking of a survival precept is not merely a likely cause of dispute but where, in itself, the breach constitutes a serious threat to cohesion and survival. Here, too, the idea will probably be present that, if the group does not rid itself of the offender, it will not survive, and this may be coupled to the notion that groups which do not punish such delinquents will themselves be punished by their gods.[118] Such a notion is present among the Ashanti, for example.[119] Such wrongs hit at survival in that they are thought to harm the community's chances of cohesion and survival directly, and not indirectly by harming an individual member or members and hence giving rise to dispute situations to the detriment of the group. One of the earliest wrongs seen to harm a community in this way was incest, defined in this context as sexual relations with a person whom one cannot marry. In _Totem and Taboo_, Freud noted that among Australian aboriginals such wrongs necessarily incurred their believed consequences through human rather than natural agency.

> "The violation of the prohibition is not left to what might be called the 'automatic' punishment of the guilty parties, as in the case of other totem prohibitions, such as that against killing the totem animal. It is arranged in the most energetic fashion by the whole clan, as though it were a question of averting some danger that threatened the whole community or some guilt that was pressing upon it."[120]

Diamond also noted that incest was usually the earliest of these serious crimes to be recognized.[121] In Australia, the other early crimes were murder by magic and various sacral offences,[122] clearly involving divine wrath on the offender and on the group if it did not punish the offender. Those seem to be the basic wrongs to the community in most early societies, for only the most serious wrongs in Anglo-Saxon England were treated as crimes, and these were sacrilege, treason and witchcraft.[123] The question of what will be so treated is, of course, one which requires a separate answer from group to group, and will depend on the beliefs of the community in question. Thus, among the Eskimo, lying falls within the same category as sorcery and recidivist killing,[124] and the killing of a horse constitutes a capital offence among the Comanche Indians of North America.[125]

As a society becomes even stronger, it is able to begin prohibiting and punishing a wider range of activities which it regards as harmful to cohesion and survival. Thus, many wrongs, such as homicide generally, which were at first only regarded as private dispute causers and regulated only as such to avoid private vengeance causing disruption, eventually come to be treated as wrongs against the community, or crimes. Homicide becomes a capital offence in most groups at this stage.[126] Such extra strength, however, also indicates that isolated wrongs against the community are less likely to bring it down now than was previously the case, and that the possibility that the delinquent can be punished so as to destroy his bad example without actually destroying the man himself is also realized. If allowed to live, there is also the chance that the individual in question may in future contribute to cohesion and survival. Thus, as communities strengthen, their punishments become more varied, so that outlawry and capital punishment are resorted to less often, and lesser penalties are created. The offender may, instead of being outlawed, be reduced to slavery, or even suffer civil death, the state of living in a community but having no right to sue on a contract, inherit property and the like.[127] The punishment is still a symbol, however, of what could happen if members of the group were to follow the offender's example, only here the reminder is not confined to the moment of despatch but is extended to cover the remainder of the natural life of the delinquent. Imprisonment, a punishment which only appears upon the scene when a society is economically viable enough to afford the luxury of keeping citizens locked up, also involves a loss of some of the rights which non-delinquent members of the community enjoy, and is also a modified version of outlawry and a symbol of the consequences of breaking survival precepts. Corporal punishments tend to be used by groups before the stage of imprisonment is reached as a rule. Such penalties are often fixed so as to be approximately equal to the wrong committed, and are referred to as retaliation or lex talio. To such categories belong the notion that if a man causes another to lose an eye, he must suffer an equivalent loss, and so on. It is the law of an eye for an eye and a tooth for a tooth. Similar to retaliatory punishments are the so-called sympathetic punishments, which deprive the delinquent of the limb or member used to commit the offence, Hence, thieves lose hands, rapists are castrated, and so on. Such punishments also serve to remind other members of the community of what will occur if the precepts of the group are not followed.[128]

In punishing delinquents, the community turns the aggression of the group members, which could work to destroy the group, back upon itself, as it were, to maintain the group's cohesion. Punishment marks an internalization of force.[129] In this, it is a mechanism similar to that of the psyche wherein the force generated by the impulses arising in the id of an individual is transferred to the superego and used to repress the very impulses in which it originated. It is important, however, that the punishment is sufficient to assuage the impulse to give vent to aggression in response to a crime. Thus, criminals caught in the act were frequently allowed to be killed in early law, and even in more advanced systems were punished more severely than those merely proved on judicial evidence to have thieved.[130] Thus, Gaius records how in classical Roman law, the manifest thief had to pay fourfold damages, while the non-manifest thief only paid double. Later on in the development of a legal system, moral turpitude is regarded as being the factor which should go to increase the penalty, but it is worthy of note that when diminished responsibility was introduced as a defence to murder in England and Wales in 1957, one of the arguments for so doing was that it would reduce the crime of killing a spouse or lover caught in the act of adultery from murder to manslaughter,[131] a clear concession to aggressive instincts. Maine regarded such concessions as evidence of a low morality.[132] Failure to rechannel the aggression will, of course, allow it to cause disruption, and the object of the exercise will not have been achieved.

Discretion within limits is often given today to the judiciary, or to juries,[133] to fix the sentence for a crime, recognizing the organ in question as best-suited to gauge the degree of punishment needed to rechannel the aggression of the group. Not for nothing did Sir James Fitzjames Stephen describe the role of a High Court judge as being that of the organ of the moral indignation of mankind. The community must also rely upon its best-suited method to declare which acts are sufficiently serious to merit criminal punishment. This task was also frequently left to the judges, although in recent times the legislature has become the normal body for deciding what constitutes criminality. The judges occasionally, however, still exercise their role in this area.[134] That the object of the exercise is to protect the group emerges clearly from the vast discretion given on occasions to the judges of a group in performing this role. In 1721, the Faculty of Helmstadt was faced with a case in which a man charged with manslaughter had pleaded self-defence, and the records of the proceedings were in another state and could not be obtained;

"the decision was that "in order to protect the community from this dangerous individual", he should be confined in a penitentiary or some other well-guarded place at moderate labor <u>for the rest of his natural life</u>".[135]

In pre-Revolutionary France, where the judge had a discretion in sentencing, he was able to sentence to death if he so determined.[136] Provided such powers are accepted and ratified, they are clearly valid in the communities in question and are believed to be the best thing for cohesion and survival.

Just as the individual who has forfeited his right to the benefits of a group by rejecting the burdens may lose some of the benefits by way of punishment and then be able to contribute thereafter to the community's cohesion and survival, so some persons may be saved from a penalty by being adjudged worthy in some way to survive. An odd example of this comes from mediaeval Germany where it was a custom to spare a condemned man if a woman was prepared to marry him.[137] More generally, some classes of people were regarded as too precious to the community's cohesion and survival to be killed in any eventuality. Thus, in Hindu law, Brahmans are not subject to capital punishment, and the rule of benefit of clergy once conferred the same privilege upon clerics and those who could read generally under the criminal laws of England.[138] The modern practice of granting foreign heads of state and diplomats immunity from criminal prosecution in the courts of a state they are visiting is a similar phenomenon, illustrating that to punish them would cause more trouble than it is worth, that is, that to inflict punishment upon such persons would hinder rather than aid the welfare and survival of the group. Where the group is so small as not to be able to afford the loss of one member but yet has criminal laws, it may disapprove strongly of informing on a delinquent. This is so among the Trobriand islanders.[139]

One particular method of hindering or endangering the cohesion and survival of a group is worthy of mention. If the best-suited principle is regarded as enunciating the precepts which will ensure cohesion and survival, clearly to interfere with its work either by criticizing it or tampering with its operation may be regarded as an extremely serious, if not the most serious, form of wrong. Thus, to question the authority of the best-suited person or to kill him is to undermine the group's chances of cohesion and survival. That the best-suited persons are regarded as being at a premium within the community is clear from the development of laws relating to treason. In ancient Rome, any criticism of the magistracy was regarded as the crime of _majestas_,[140] and similarly, in mediaeval France, a large number of acts constituted _lèse majesté_.[141] In England, treason was defined by the Statute of Treasons of 1352 and includes interfering with the best-suited principle by killing the king, his consort or his eldest son, violating his consort, eldest unmarried daughter or the wife of his eldest son, and levying war against the king in his realm. It can be seen that the English definition places considerable importance upon succession to the office of best-suited person. Such a wrong can be found in various forms in societies which value their best-suited principle.[142] The earliest best-suited person an individual learns from is, as has been said, the child's father. Parricide, therefore, is also regarded as a particularly heinous crime, as in some societies is any insult delivered by a child to its father. The person of the husband is often similarly protected. Indeed, masters of servants and lords of vassals are protected by the law in much the same way as local best-suited persons, and for them to be slain by their charges is termed in England, _petit_ treason.[143] The act which constitutes interference with the best-suited principle will again vary with the beliefs of the community. The touchiness of the Trobriand islanders concerning the authority of their best-suited person is witnessed by the conduct they regard as treasonous. Hoebel lists the following as capital offences against the person of their paramount chief.

"1) being too successful as a gardener, 2) possessing too many goods, 3) wearing personal ornaments reserved only for chiefs, or overdecorating a house, 4) boasting about one's wealth in the presence of a person of higher rank, 5) failure to do proper obeisance, 6) use of improper language directed towards a chief".[144]

Hoebel also notes[145] that between commoner and chief there may be no disputes. Until the Crown Proceedings Act, 1948, much the same was true in England and Wales.

A particular protection is sometimes given to judges who enunciate the legal rules of the community as best-suited persons. Thus, to slay one of the King's justices while sitting in his seat of office is treason in England under the 1352 statute. In the mediaeval German town of Brünn, it was regarded as highly improper even to criticize the judgements of the schöffen or lay-judges. A person who did so according to the Brünner Schöffenbuch, was to be punished by being nailed to a stake by his tongue, and given a knife with which to effect his release.[146] Clearly, no further hindrance to the community's goals could emanate from his mouth. As late as 1866, it was reported that in Germany an eminent professor, Zachariae, was in danger of being prosecuted for contempt as a result of critical comment made on a Supreme Court decision.[147]

The above analysis demonstrates the growth of the criminal law of a community according to the theory that the law of the group is produced to aid its cohesion and survival via its best-suited principle. The starting point, however, was the visiting of outlawry upon those who would not observe dispute solutions. The point was chosen as a convenient way into the topic of the content of legal systems because the subject of disputes had previously been discussed. However, outlawry for refusing to carry out the decisions of the courts marks the beginnings of the enforcement of civil law rather than criminal law, and the development of civil law must now be examined.

It will be remembered that disputes arose because, as a result of a survival precept, possibly as yet unenunciated, having been broken, the conduct of one member of a group had in some way lessened another's chances of survival. This might either be by inflicting an injury upon, or by taking an advantage of, the other person. In any event, the conduct in question was likely to provoke a dispute between the parties which could lead to disruption within the community. The dispute solution is meant to avoid this. If the person has been injured, he is likely to seek vengeance for his injury; if he has lost an advantage or good, he is likely to attempt to recover his loss by means of self-help. Both situations are inherently dangerous to social existence. At first, therefore, the law will attempt to solve the first type of difficulty by suggesting compensation, and will eventually enforce its awards. In both situations, it will be necessary, of course, to establish that a recognized harm has been suffered, that is, that a survival precept has indeed been broken. The compensation is meant to placate the injured party and buy off his aggression. Inasmuch as it does so, it represents, that is, symbolises, restitution or what has been lost. Thus, if a man lost a hand through another's conduct, one could describe the developments as follows. To begin with the man had his hand and was devoid of aggression against the tortfeasor. When he lost his hand owing to the tortfeasor's conduct, his aggressive impulse to avenge his loss appears. Then when he receives his compensation, the impulse again disappears, so that the compensation, as it were, replaces the hand and restores the _status quo_, aggression-wise, between the parties.[148] This is what is meant by the compensation being restitution at a different level for the wrong which caused the dispute. If, however, no compensation can repair the harmony or no such compensation is available or forthcoming, it may be necessary to allow private vengeance to work its will, but even then some attempt may be made to institutionalize the disruption, as with the mediaeval German _Landfrieden_. Where compensation is available and forthcoming, the amount which had to be paid originally varied from case to case depending upon how much was actually necessary to buy off the aggressive impulse, but as the community strengthened it was able to impose fixed tariffs for such injures.[149] Indeed, early codes of law tend to consist of statements of the amounts needed to make compensation for such private wrongs. Where actual restitution of some object or right was required, Maine's suggestion[150] that distress was taken to force the opposing party to go to the courts is very interesting, as such a taking would indeed indicate that a dispute situation was indeed in existence.

As the earliest societies were composed of families rather than individuals,[151] so it was up to the family of the wrongdoer to compensate the family which had suffered the injury. The price for serious wrongs was very great and if it could not be met, then recourse would be had to private vengeance with its attendant dangers. One consequence of the price was that if the family of the wrongdoer did not value him highly, and this might well be the case if his offences were frequent, they might not be prepared to pay up, and would prefer to hand him over to the injured parties to wreak their vengeance upon him. Such occurrences are to be found amongst the Ashanti,[152] and in many other contexts.[153] As even private wrongs involved a risk of disruption, a payment of atonement to the community was also demanded as the group grew stronger.[154] Maine believed that such payments were made to meet the cost of adjudicating the dispute.[155] They are exemplified by the _wite_ payable to the king in Anglo-Saxon England by a wrongdoer in addition to the _bot_ payable to the injured party. Once the community became strong enough to enforce its judgements, then outlawry for failure to comply with the verdict and recourse to private vengeance disappear and methods of enforcing civil judgements are developed. Fixed compensations also give way to determinations of the loss to the injured party by a body deemed suitable to make such assessments. An interesting example of payments made to buy off wrath are the penances imposed in the Middle Ages under canon law for sins, meant to restore the _status quo ante_ between the sinner and God.[156]

A feature of the modern law of compensation for private wrong is the concept of no liability without fault. According to the theory presented here, the notion of fault would only be relevant if it made a dispute more or less likely.[157] Thus, if an injury were likely to lead to a dispute regardless of whether the wrongdoer was at fault, then the community in the interests of cohesion is likely to impose strict liability. If, however, the lack of moral blame reduces the likelihood of disruption, or the imposition of strict liability increases it, then the notion of fault is likely to play a part in deciding in which cases compensation must be paid. However, in recent times, the danger of allowing the loss to lie where it falls in cases where fault has not been established has been recognized as a potential dispute causer if not a factor weakening the authority of the law in this area, and it has been suggested that an insurance scheme to cover all personal injuries might solve issues more effectively, that is, in a fashion better able to promote cohesion and survival by avoiding disputes and disrespect for the legal system. The insurance solution would be enunciated according to the best-suited principle thus increasing its authority through acceptance and ratification.

When the community has reached the stage of being able to order effectively compensation for wrongs committed, it may be strong enough to prohibit acts which are seen as likely to cause private disputes to arise, just as it can prohibit acts which harm the community directly, or crimes. Thus, injunctions are issued under English law to prevent the commission of torts in certain instances, and breach of such orders gives rise to punishment for contempt of court.

VI

Some disputes within a community arise as the result of members breaking faith in agreements and transactions into which they have entered with other members. In such cases, the agreements can be between individuals or families. The dispute-solving mechanisms of the community are faced with a difficulty in attempting to solve such disputes according to principle because proof of the terms of such transactions may not be available. The legal system of the community could choose to ignore such disputes as being beyond its capabilities to solve satisfactorily, but this would be dangerous as the disputes are, of course, potential causers of disruption. The traditional Chinese, however, did leave the regulation of commercial transactions to the individuals concerned.[158] Most communities, on the other hand, recognize the rights of individuals or of family groups to act as the persons best-suited to choose what to do with their property and to enter into transactions, subject to certain regulations, and attempt to find satisfactory solutions to disputes which occur as a result of recognizing that members should enjoy these powers.

One method of coping with the problem is to take the evidence of witnesses as to the terms of agreements and transactions which have given rise to disputes. Some communites submit the issue to divine judgement, but this does not always provide a satisfactory answer. One sure way of ensuring that witnesses should be available is to insist that there are witnesses to such agreements who will be able to supply the wherewithal to solve any disputes that may arise. Thus, it may be insisted that a go-between is used to make the transaction, as with the monbaga of the Ifugao. A more formal method of obtaining witnesses is to insist that the transaction be completed publicly so as to ensure the existence of witnesses. Such a development can be regarded as the first sign of the requirement that formalities must be observed to evidence or even to effect or authenticate certain transactions. Such formalities normally attach to those forms of property to which the group attaches considerable importance, and, therefore, in relation to which the maximum risk of supervening discord attaches. Thus, in ancient Rome, res mancipi - slaves, Italic land and beasts of draught and burden[159] had to be transferred by the ceremony of mancipatio; in mediaeval England, freehold land had to be conveyed with livery of seisin, also involving a ceremony, and among the Ifugao, property is divided into ibuy property and property adi-ma-ibuy, the former being rice fields, heirlooms and forest lands,[160] transfer of which must be accompanied by a ritual feast at the buyer's house. Important changes of status, such as marriage, coming of age, freedom from slavery, and the like, are also normally effected by ceremonies and formal words, which can in such contexts acquire the aura of magical, transformatory power.[161] Even amongst the Chinese, it was demanded that certain formalities should attach to marriage and succession, as here, it was believed, the natural order of things, which these institutions mirrored, could not be contravened on any account if the community was to prosper.[162]

With the advent of literacy in the community, writing becomes the witness needed to show that an agreement was reached or a transaction carried out. The law of the community will, therefore, insist less on ceremonies and more on the reduction of contracts to writing, particularly, again, in relation to the more important forms of property, that is, those highly valued and therefore more likely to give rise to disputes. Thus, transactions relating to land in English law have usually at least to be evidenced by writing. Unlike the ceremony, however, the writing may only be known to the parties to the transaction, so that third parties may be at a disadvantage in dealing with the subject-matter of the agreement, a fact which could lead to disputes. This problem is sometimes overcome by making the written witness available for public inspection or by a form of registration of interests. The latter method is widely used in modern English law in relation to real property transactions and interests.[163]

In the same way as disputes over what individuals, as the best-suited persons to govern their personal affairs, have decided to do with their property or even themselves may lead to disputes, so the decisions of the community's best-suited mechanism as to what is best for the community may give rise to disputes if the exact content of its enunciations is not known. It is, therefore, also the case that the decisions or enactments of such best-suited bodies are subject to formalities. Thus, laws are frequently declared to people ceremonially in pre-literate socities, as with the Scandinavian Things and the presence of the Roman centuries, and, in literate societies, laws are frequently published in solemn, written form to avoid disputes as to their content or existence.[164]

VII

As the legal system of the community deals with the task of preventing disruptions whether those threatened directly, by conduct likely to harm the community itself, or those threatened indirectly, by disputes arising between members of the group, the question will arise as to whether it is in the interest of cohesion and survival to seek out likely disruptions and disputes in order to avoid or solve them, or whether it is enough to deal with them as they come to the surface, as it were. The Chinese, of course, did not believe in dealing with any disputes unless they were actually threatening disruption, holding that allowing and forcing members to reach their own solutions was a better method or promoting the twin social goals. The accusatorial system of litigation also leans in that direction, although nowhere nearly so far, for it still bears the marks of an institutionalized dispute, of a contest between the disputing parties. The inquisitorial method, on the other hand, involves the community officials in getting to the bottom of a dispute situation or disruption in the belief that such delving will lead perhaps to a better, more lasting solution. In the area of criminal law, most communities eventually come to believe in the need for vigilance in such areas. A public prosecutor was instituted in the Italian towns, therefore, as early as the later thirteenth century.[165] Ancient Rome never got around to this step, however, not even in its criminal administration, and most societies remain content to solve private disputes, that is, civil litigation, as they arise. Each community decides which method it considers preferable according to what it believes to be best for its cohesion and survival, while the question of which is actually the best is also an empirical one which requires an answer for each community in turn.

VIII

Just as individuals or families decide to form larger groups in the belief that it is necessary to do so to survive, and then maintain the cohesion of the new group at all costs, so in turn these groups may decide that cohesion with other similar bodies is necessary for survival. They will, in such instances, conclude that disputes with the other groups or disruption of the cohesion between them will harm the chances of survival. If such a belief is really held, then the principles for achieving that aim will be accepted and ratified as survival principles, and will go to make up the morality of the groups, and when used to solve disputes or overcome disruptions, will be a law unto the groups in question as well as a survival principle. It is on the hope that such a development can occur on a world-wide basis that the International Law movement is based.

When such groups dispute among themselves, the question of whether they have survival precepts must be answered according to how they conduct themselves. The crux of deciding whether they have laws is similarly based on what they do in such dispute situations. If, when a risk of disruption occurs, the dispute is solved on a higher level than that which threatens disruption, so that cohesion and survival are maintained, then clearly the dispute has been institutionalized and a form of legal system can be claimed to exist. Hoebel has shown how the Murngin people of Australia have institutionalized disputes with other groups, at least to a certain extent.

"In the Murngin way, the injured group is restrained by its elders until it has cooled down. Then it sends a messenger to the offenders with an invitation to formal "combat." If the invitation is accepted, the warriors of both parties arrive at the designated dueling ground on the given day. They come dancing and singing - for this is a ritual affair. Once there, they line up facing each other beyond the range of a hurled spear just to play it safe. The ceremony proper opens with the injured group approaching the offenders while doing its chief totemic dance. The dancing approach done, they turn and walk back to their places. Now the offenders dance and approach likewise, and then return to their places. The fight is now ready to being.

"The men who were accessories to the homicide, called "pushers," come forth to be thrown at. Headless spears are hurled by the warriors of the offended group, while the pushers dodge back and forth, shielded by two protectors who are close relatives of the throwers. Everyone throws at least one spear, while those who are not engaged in throwing spears hurl imprecations at the offending group who by usage cannot reply.

"When there has been enough of this the actual killers come forth to be thrown at with headed spears. Yet they must not be hit, for such an accident will lead to a general fight in hot blood. So while all in the offended group are throwing spears to their heart's content, their elders are exhorting them not to hit anyone. On the other side the old men are urging their young men not to lose their heads and become angry.

"At last, when the offended party has spent its energy for spear throwing, the killers stand quietly while all the warriors of the offended group dance up to them. Now comes the crucial moment. If a spear is jabbed through the thigh of one of the killers, it means that all is over. If only a slight wound is given, it means that the aggrieved group is not wholly satisfied and, after allowing a temporary truce, it will come for vengeance. No wound means immediate vengeance and may lead to a general fight on the spot.

"After all, there is no superior restraining

power; it all depends on the self-control of each group and the strength of the desire to raise the interest of mutuality above the emotions of group antagonism. The significant thing to recognize is that even on the very primitive level a distinct effort is made to regularize and resolve disputes and conflicts that endanger social well-being even when the local groups involved are sovereign and there is no superior force to hold them in check. In such instances as these they create the restraint (such as it is) themselves."[166]

The Murngin way, Hoebel described, is not dispute solving by war. Some writers regard war as the sanction of International Law. This view is mistaken. A dispute solution must solve the dispute on a higher level or else it is not a dispute solution but just a dispute. War is, thus, the disruption which it was sought to avoid, and not a solution to the threat of disruption.

One way of seeking to avoid disputes, as has been seen, was to use a go-between to arrange dispute-solving terms between the parties. This marks an attempt to regulate disputes, and when a dispute-solving mechanism, a court, has come into regular operation, a legal system can be said to have been developed. The international scene at the time of writing, shows signs of such unofficial go-betweens being used, but no sufficiently accepted method of solving disputes has yet emerged. For this reason, it appears to be premature to speak of an International Law.[167] An instance of an accepted procedure for solving inter-group disputes coming into existence is the arbitral procedure of solving disputes within the Swiss Confederation. By the mid-fifteenth century, disputes between the cantons were settled at a higher level than that which threatened disruption so that the cohesion of the Confederation and the survival of its members was ensured.[168] Until nations do so accept and ratify precepts for international cohesion and survival, no true international morality can be said to exist, and no International Law until precepts for resolving disputes without risking the cohesion of the group are accepted and ratified. One sign of such a development would be the idea that it was a crime or possibly a treason to perform an act which would damage the cohesion of the group. Even the Swiss cantons found it difficult to acknowledge this development.[169]

When inter-state law develops, it may only be

between certain countries who believe that they must cohere to survive and act on this belief. Such beliefs may already exist between some states; certainly, in wartime, allies do band together. On a fully international level, however, such a phenomenon can hardly be said to exist as yet.[170]

IX

The theory of law presented in this work describes law as the mechanism which promotes the cohesion and survival of a group by preventing and overcoming disruptions and disputes. Law achieves this by means of precepts aimed at achieving these ends, which precepts are in part gained from experience and in part are enunciated according to the best-suited principle. All such precepts, including the best-suited principle itself, are valid inasmuch as they are accepted and ratified by the group as the correct course to promote cohesion and survival. In this chapter, an attempt has been made to show how, in its development, a legal system is tailored according to the need to achieve these goals. The questions of how to avoid disputes, or how to overcome those that have arisen, whether to enforce the dispute-solving principles, whether to punish acts which are judged to threaten directly the community aims, that is, crimes, which acts are to be treated as crimes and which as private wrongs, how severe the penalties should be, whether to tolerate self-help in private disputes, and so on, are all answered according to the belief of the group as to what is best for cohesion and survival, and it is the answers to questions such as these that dictate how the legal system of the group will develop. The method believed to be best for cohesion and survival will be that adopted. Thus, if enforcing judgements is believed to cure disruptions more than it may cause them, judgements will be enforced. Similarly with inflicting punishments, discouraging self-help, and the rest. Every development which the legal system undergoes marks a belief that the course taken is better than the available alternatives for achieving cohesion and survival. Therefore, inasmuch as the legal system reflects the beliefs of the community it serves, it is indeed, as one author has described it, a cultural fact.[171] Whether the community's choices are in fact the best for cohesion and survival is always an empirical question which has to be answered in relation to each community at any given moment of time. The theory here presented merely purports to explain the factors which govern the development of legal systems, and, therefore, their nature.

Now that the nature of legal rules, legal validity, legal concepts and legal systems have, according to the new theory, been explained, the construction of the theory in itself is complete. It is now proposed to use the completed theory to show how it can reduce some of the traditional problems concerning law into questions the answers to which are to be obtained empirically, thus illustrating the merits of the theory as an explanation of the nature of law. In the last three chapters of this work, three such problems will be so treated, namely the problem of whether laws have to be moral to be law at all; the problem of whether law should enforce morality, and the problems caused by the phenomenon of civil disobedience. Some conclusions on jurisprudence generally will then be offered.

****

1. Contra, vide _LMS_, 247 (J.M. Finnis).
2. _PFL_ II, 98-9; cf. A Ross _On Law and Justice_, 365-7.
3. Cf. Lucas, _PP_, vii-viii.
4. Hart, _CL_, 187-95.
5. Lucas, _PP_, 1-5.
6. Maine, _AL_, 141-2; _ELC_, 199.
7. Maine, _AL_, 141.
8. _Ibid_., 144-8.
9. Contra, vide e.g. Hoebel, 258-9.
10. Freud, _CW_, XVIII, 116.
11. _Oxford Essays (2)_, 3 (A.M. Honoré).
12. Cf. Wittgenstein's family resemblances and the fictions introduced into royal writs during the Middle Ages to gain entry into the King's courts.
13. Maine, _ELC_, 243.
14. _ILS_, 116 (H. McAleavy).
15. _Ibid_., 106 (H. McAleavy).
16. Hart, _CL_, 85.
17. _PFL_, II 110-1.
18. Freud, _CW_, XXI 95.
19. _ILS_, 96 (J.D.M. Derrett).
20. Freud, _CW_, XXI 122.

21. ELO, 116.
22. Hoebel, 143 - Postulate IV.
23. ILS, 107 (H. McAleavy).
24. Ibid., 115.
25. Ibid., 123.
26. Ibid., 125.
27. Hoebel, 197-8.
28. Ibid., 92.
29. Ibid., 98-9.
30. ELO, 23-4; PL 168-9.
31. Maine, ELC, 170-1.
32. ELO, 62-3, 110, 113; Hoebel, 145, 172.
33. Hoebel, 158.
34. ELO, 43.
35. ILS, 140, 145-6 (A.N. Allott).
36. CLH VI, 98-9.
37. ELO, 63-4.
38. Hoebel, 114.
39. Maine, AL, 397.
40. On Ethiopia, vide, ELO, 276 and PL 392; on Scandinavia, CLH VI, 121. The same is true of the muthamaki among the Kikuyu of Kenya, who with experience could become muthamaki wa chira (leader in law), and the olaigwenani among the Arusha of Tanzania; vide, ILS, 134 (A.N. Allott).
41. PL, 320.
42. Maine, AL, 4, 8.
43. Ibid., 4-5.
44. Vide, T.G. Watkin "The Significance of 'In Consimili Casu" in the American Journal of Legal History.
45. ILS, 3 (J.A.C. Thomas).
46. PL, 71-2.
47. W. Ullmann, Law and Politics in the Middle Ages, 194-5, 197-8.
48. Shaw v. D.P.P. [1962] A.C. 223.
49. Cf. Thomas S. Szasz, The Myth of Mental Illness, 165-8.
50. B. Mitchell, Law, Morality and Religion in a Secular Society, 74.
51. CLH I, 32-3.
52. Cf. A. Watson, The Nature of Law, 13-5, 29.
53. Maine, ELC, 380-92.
54. Ibid., 389.
55. Ibid., 160.
56. A. Ross, op.cit., 229.
57. ILS, 41 (Ze'ev W. Falk).
58. A.V. Dicey, An Introduction to the Study of the Law of the Constitution, 49-50.

59. CLH I, 533-4.
60. Cf. Hart, CL, 94 on the connection between the rules of adjudication and recognition.
61. Hoebel, 82.
62. Maine, ELC, 24-5.
63. Hoebel, 145.
64. Freud, CW, XIII 2.
65. CLH I, 507.
66. Maine, ELC, 198.
67. Hoebel, 132.
68. ELO, 115-6.
69. PL, 238.
70. Maine, AL, 262-5.
71. W. Ullmann, op.cit., 33-4.
72. CLH I, 35.
73. Ibid., 540.
74. Hoebel, 24.
75. PL, 284-5.
76. Maine, ELC, 171-2.
77. PL, 132-3.
78. ILS, 58 (N.J. Coulson).
79. CLH I, 707-8.
80. W. Ullmann, op.cit., 204. Cf. Oxford Essays (2), 4-5 (A.M. Honoré); A. Ross, op.cit., 230-1.
81. CLH I, 47.
82. Ibid., 541.
83. ILS, 36 (Z.W. Falk).
84. ELO, 134.
85. W. Ullmann, op.cit., 219.
86. ILS, 135 (A.N. Allott).
87. CLH I, 77-8.
88. Ibid.
89. Maine, ELC, 2; ILS, 82 (J.D.M. Derrett).
90. K.C. Wheare, Modern Constitutions, 131.
91. As was once true in the Swiss Diet; vide, CLH I, 495-6.
92. Mill, 89.
93. ILS, 42-3 (Z.W. Falk).
94. Ibid., 38.
95. Ibid., 4 (J.A.C. Thomas).
96. Vide, d'Entrèves, NL, 67.
97. Maine, AL, 68-9.
98. Oxford Essays (2), 95 (A.W.B. Simpson).
99. ILS, 6 (J.A.C. Thomas).
100. Ibid., 30 (Z.W. Falk).
101. R.W. Lee, Elements of Roman Law (4th Ed. London 1956), 19-20.
102. The role of constitutions and statutes in relation to this function has already been discussed; vide, supra, chapter 2.

103. ILS, 59-60 (N.J. Coulson).
104. Ibid., 63.
105. Vide, S.F.C. Milsom "Trespass from Henry III to Edward III", (1958) 74 L.Q.R. 195, 407 and 561.
106. Vide, Maine, ELC, 164-6.
107. Vide, Maine, AL, 33-5 on the stages in this development.
108. Vide, Radcliffe and Cross, The English Legal System (6th Ed. by G.J. Hand and D.J. Bentley) (London, 1977), 47, 93-4; S.F.C. Milsom, Historical Foundations of the Common Law (London, 1969), 16 ff.
109. CLH I, 456-7.
110. Ibid., I, 338, 363-6.
111. Vide, supra, chapter 2.
112. Maine, ELC, 387.
113. CLH VI, 134.
114. Vide, Pollock and Maitland, A History of English Law before the time of Edward I (2nd Ed.) (Cambridge, 1968), ii, 449.
115. PL, 63.
116. Cf. Freud, CW, XIII, 33.
117. Hoebel, 89.
118. PL, 260-3; Hoebel, 260.
119. Hoebel, 253 - Postulate IV.
120. Freud, CW, XIII, 4.
121. ELO, 20.
122. Ibid., 21.
123. ILS, 179 (A.K.R. Kiralfy).
124. Hoebel, 90.
125. Ibid., 140.
126. PL, 395-6.
127. CLH VI, 272.
128. ELO, 192, 291-300; PL, 98, 398-400.
129. Cf. H. Kelsen, General Theory of Law and State, 21-2.
130. Maine, AL, 399-401.
131. Homicide Act, 1957 s.2.
132. Maine, AL, 401.
133. E.g. in France.
134. E.g. Shaw v. D.P.P., op.cit.
135. CLH VI, 240-1.
136. Ibid., 264.
137. Ibid., 117.
138. Vide, on brahmans PL, 111, and on benefit of clergy ELO, 286-7; PL 96.
139. Hoebel, 186. Cf. H. Kelsen, op.cit., 234.
140. H.F. Jolowicz, Historical Introduction to the Study of Roman Law (2nd Ed.)(Cambridge, 1952), 327.

141. *CLH* VI, 281-5.
142. *ELO*, 192-3, 210; *PL*, 345.
143. *ELO*, 253.
144. Hoebel, 196-7.
145. *Ibid*.
146. *CLH* VI, 106.
147. *Ibid*., 374.
148. *PL*, 64; *ELO*, 35.
149. *ELO*, 110.
150. Maine, *ELC*, 374-5.
151. Vide, Freud, *CW*, XIII, 6.
152. Hoebel, 219.
153. *ELO*, 110-1; PL, 264-5; *ILS*, 151 (A.N. Allott).
154. *PL*, 293-5.
155. Maine, *AL*, 397.
156. *CLH* VI, 9; *CLH* I, 722.
157. The same would be true of the notion of intention and recklessness.
158. *ILS*, 110 (H. McAleavy).
159. Vide, *supra*, Introduction.
160. Hoebel, 105.
161. K. Olivecrona, *Law as Fact*, 241-2.
162. *ILS*, 110 (H. McAleavy).
163. Vide generally, Maine, *AL*, 349-61; *ELO*, 259-62.
164. Cf. Hart, *CL*, 75.
165. *CLH* I, 723.
166. Hoebel, 308-9.
167. *Ibid*., 125-6.
168. *CLH* I, 491.
169. *CLH* VI, 355.
170. Cf. Hoebel, 331-3.
171. A. Ross, *op.cit*., 375.

CHAPTER FIVE

LAW AND MORALITY

In this chapter, the question of whether a precept in order to be a valid law must also be moral will be discussed. As the question of what constitutes legal validity has already been dealt with,[1] the topic for discussion can, therefore, be reformulated in the light of the conclusions reached concerning legal validity. As the validity or invalidity of a purported law has been said to depend upon whether it is accepted and ratified by the members of the group as a whole, the question to be dealt with here is to what extent the morality of a purported law affects its acceptance and ratification. This is the basis upon which the question will be discussed here.

In its original form, the question is one of the traditional problems for discussion in jurisprudence, a hallowed old chestnut. That is not to say that it is one which arises only in academic contexts. It is from time to time relevant, often painfully so, to reality. Wherever an individual or group is faced with a statute which commands immoral conduct or forbids behaviour considered to be morally obligatory, the question poses a dilemma. Often, the dilemma is faced where a tyrannical government holds sway, as with the Nazi regime in Germany in the nineteen-thirties and -forties, and the issues at stake are matters of life and death. In such circumstances, the question is posed in an acute form. The answers given to the questions reflect, on occasion, the answerer's background; those which are purely academic are reasoned responses, coolly delivered, while those of people who have been caught in the dilemma are often emotional and purposive.

The school of thought which propounds the idea that laws must be moral to be laws at all, is known generally as the Natural law school. The phrase,

Natural law, has meant different things to different groups, but all are united in the belief that morality is an essential feature of law. Without a quantum of morality, there can be no legality. On the opposing side, there are ranged the legal positivists who hold that a law is still law even if it is immoral, and that the dilemma is really whether to obey a bad law and not whether it is law at all. The proponents of Natural law include Aristotle, Cicero, St. Thomas Aquinas; the legal positivists have in their camp, Bentham, Austin and Professor Hart. In recent years, the last mentioned has had a stimulating debate with Professor Lon L. Fuller, who propounds the idea that there is a procedural or inner morality of law which must not be transgressed if legaility is to be preserved, a position which Professor Hart does not concede. It is proposed therefore, to examine these issues - Natural Law v. Legal Positivism and Hart v. Fuller - according to the theory of law put forward in these pages. The question will, therefore, be analysed rather than answered, although it is hoped that an answer will in fact emerge.

It is best to begin by defining, or at least describing the nature of, the two concepts. The nature of law has already been described. As individuals form groups in order to increase their survival chances, so thay accept certain precepts to ensure cohesion and survival. However, the impulse for individual survival may at times conflict with that for cohesion, and disputes and disruption can occur. If the community feels that it is better for cohesion and survival to solve such disputes and overcome such disruptions, then the precepts which it accepts to meet those needs will be its laws. The morality of the group is also conditioned by its aims of cohesion and survival. Those precepts which it regards as important for cohesion and survival, so that their breach will be at least disapproved, are its moral precepts. Thus, both the laws and morals of the group are engendered by the same needs and serve the same function. Laws, however, deal with an attempt to solve disputes and overcome disruptions by institutionalizing them, while survival precepts if regarded as sufficiently important for cohesion and survival are, in themselves, moral rules; they only become legal rules if the community is prepared to use them in solving actual disputes and overcoming actual disruptions or the threat thereof. It is clear from this, of course, that law and morality are bound to share a certain content, both being based on the group's survival precepts. The morality of the group will include some precepts which the law does not, that is, those the breaches of which are not considered to endanger and to merit solutions, and the law will cover some areas which morality does not, as with requirements peripheral to dispute situations such as formalities and regulations, such as which side of the road moving motor-traffic is to occupy.

Formalities and regulations, of course, are not rules which can be enunciated from the experience of the group, but can only emanate from the best-suited persons or procedures. The best-suited principle is, indeed, central to the whole question of the morality of law, for if no precepts were enunciated according to this principle, the whole of the community's law would be derived from accepted practices and could not be different from its morality. The question concerning law and morality is, in effect, whether a precept which has been enunciated according to the best-suited principle of a group can be accepted and ratified, and so become a legal rule, if it is contrary to the morality of the group in question. Clearly, the answer to this question must be related to two factors, namely the degree of strength which the best-suited principle enjoys in the group and the degree to which the precept in question offends against the community's idea of what is necessary for cohesion and survival, that is, the degree of immorality involved. If the best-suited principle is strong, certain incursions upon the group morality may be accepted; if it is weak, a slight transgression may lead to non-acceptance and even to rejection of the best-suited principle itself.

It should also be clear that no fixed line can be drawn between law and morality other than for a given group at a given moment of time. The question of whether a precept is only a legal rule or only a moral or both or neither must always be answered by asking firstly whether it is thought necessary for cohesion and survival, and secondly whether it is so necessary that its breach will necessitate the group's institutionalizing any disputes or disruptions that may arise. That content cannot provide the answer is clear from the fact that a precept can be both a legal rule and a moral rule. Thus, it is common for deliberate homicide to be regarded as both immoral and illegal. However, as the morality of the group will normally be derived from accepted practice and not enunciation, while with the law of the group the reverse is more likely, clearly, the question of whether enunciated precepts must be moral to be laws turns on whether the best-suited principle is regarded as a safer means of discovering the best survival principles than accepted practices. As such, the question is similar to that posed in the second chapter in the case of conflicts between precepts enunciated by different bodies, such as the constitution enunciated by the founding fathers, and statutes enunciated by the legislature. If the best-suited principle is preferred to accepted practices, the fact that a rule offends against the practices of the group may not affect its validity, whereas if the best-suited principle is not so strong, it may well do so, always remembering that the strength of the principle may diminish if it repeatedly offends the notions of the group. In England, for example, the position has altered over the centuries. Early in the seventeenth century, it appears that the courts would not accept every Act of Parliament as valid. This is clear from Coke's judgement in Dr. Bonham's Case:

"it appears in our books, that in many cases, the common law will construe Acts of Parliament, and sometimes adjudge them to be utterly void: for when an Act of Parliament is against common right and reason, or repugnant, or impossible to be performed, the common law will construe it, and adjudge such Act to be void."[2]

Similarly, about a hundred and fifty years later, Blackstone refused to consider statutes contrary to the law of God, or "impossible to be performed", or with "absurd consequences manifestly contradictory to common reason" as valid laws.[3] At that time, at any rate, the courts would appear to have realized that such statutes would not be accepted and ratified by the community and, in order to protect their own position as best-suited to solve disputes, would not utilize such precepts in dispute solving. By today, however, the strength of the presumption in favour of Parliament's enunciations is so great that such opinions appear quaint, but the underlying basis is still the same, the precepts most likely to aid cohesion and survival are those applied by the courts according to the best-suited principle in their dispute-solving metagame. The group can still, of course, reject the courts as best-suited to enunciate, or merely one of their enunciations. An example of the Coke-Blackstone type rejection is the Hindu view, referred to in chapter three, that unseen rules are of greater importance than seen rules and cannot be contradicted by them or by administrative directions.[4] An example of rejection at the hands of the group rather than its courts is the destooling of an Ashanti chief whose decisions are contrary to the laws of nature and the will of the ancestors.[5]

The question to be asked of each society at any moment of time is how great a departure, if any, from its morality will be tolerated before the offending enunciation, made according to its best-suited principle, will fail to be accepted and ratified, and, as has been said, two factors of importance are the strength of the best-suited principle and the extent of the departure. While King Herod might be able to order the deaths of all male children in Bethlehem under the age of two years, and Pharoah that all Jewish males be killed at birth, the English Parliament might not succeed in getting a precept that all blue-eyed babies be killed accepted and ratified.

It is according to this approach to the question of must law be moral to be law that the Natural Law debate and the Hart *v*. Fuller encounter will now be examined to see what light the new theory can cast upon the arguments which have been presented.

II

To the Greeks, everything had its proper end or purpose, that is, they took a teleological view of their world. The end of a stone was to fall to the ground and rest there, and this aim was prescribed by a law. They confused prescriptive and descriptive laws, and believed that human beings also had their proper end or purpose and that human laws, to accord with the law of nature, had to advance that end or purpose. If human laws did not so conform, then they were not really laws at all.

The Romans adopted their view of natural law from the Greeks but advanced in that they noticed how certain rules were to be found in all societies known to them. They therefore considered that where a consensus as to a particular rule existed in all groups, this showed what nature intended humans to do. From this, they developed their concepts of *ius gentium* and *ius naturale*, what nature teaches all creatures.

The idea that human beings were subject to natural laws, which they could discover through reasoning but which they could also disobey, was adopted and perhaps taken to its intellectual zenith by the scholastic philosophers of the mediaeval Catholic Church. The Schoolmen used the concept of Natural law for two purposes. Firstly, it was the law which God had given to all things, including mankind, and which could be discovered by mankind either through it being revealed by God or though the right exercise of the faculty of reason with which mankind was endowed by God. Revelation naturally took precedence over reason. Secondly, Natural law as well as being a standard of conduct was also a standard by which other standards of conduct, of human origin, could be measured and criticized. Thus, the laws which were enunciated by human agency were to be judged as satisfactory or unsatisfactory according to the standard of the law given by the divine agency, and if found wanting, such human enunciations were not laws at all. This scholastic view of Natural law is exemplified in the writings of St. Thomas Aquinas.

"St. Augustine says: 'There is no law unless it be just.' So the validity of law depends upon its justice. But in human affairs a thing is said to be just when it accords aright with the rule of reason: and, as we have already seen, the first rule of reason is the Natural law. Thus all humanly enacted laws are in accord with reason to the extent that they derive from the Natural law. And if a human law is at variance in any particular with the Natural law, it is no longer legal, but rather a corruption of law."[6]

As Professor d'Entrèves has written:

"This is no academic statement devoid of any practical significance. The words must be taken literally. They mean that allegiance to the State - even though it be the highest embodiment of natural morality - can be only conditional. Unjust laws are not properly laws. 'They do not, in consequence, oblige in conscience.'"[7]

Post-mediaeval exponents of Natural law theory took the same line as St. Thomas, but were prepared to admit that no difference would be made if God were left out of the picture. Thus, Grotius and Pufendorf were to declare that human laws were only worthy of obedience inasmuch as they accorded with the law of nature discovered by man through his faculty to reason correctly. The modern view, therefore, while still relying on the capacity to discover by reasoning, did not rely on the law of nature being a divine *fiat*, although this was still held to be the case even if it was not a necessary part of the theory.[8]

There are obvious similarities between the Natural law position and the theory of law presented in these pages. The main difference is that the new theory presents law as being an enunciation of precepts for the cohesion of a social group and the survival of its members, and postulates that the validity of laws depends upon the acceptance and ratification of the precepts by the members of the group. Clearly, therefore, what human reason strives to discover under the new theory is the correct strategy for cohesion and survival, and not a law posited by a divinity or by nature.[9] Another important difference stems from this. Natural lawyers would assume that the correct answer can be found through right reason. According to the new theory, while the group may also believe that a correct answer can be found to the question concerning its goals, it is not the case that such an answer will actually exist. Just as in a game of chess, a point may arise at which it is clear that one player cannot win, so too in social affairs, a point may be reached where a group can no longer cohere, so that no solution to their difficulties can exist. The Schoolmen would certainly not have accepted this. According to the new theory, it is certainly the case that not all enunciations will be valid laws, but the reason for this is not that they contravene an actual natural order of things, but rather because they are not accepted as being the course which will promote cohesion and survival. The most that can be taken to detract from the validity of laws enunciated according to the best-suited principle of the group under the new theory, therefore, is that they do not conform to the community's belief of what is necessary for cohesion and survival. Only those beliefs can be regarded as the natural law of that community, and its precepts cannot be extended beyond that social group other than as critical judgements by one group of the precepts and survival chances of another community. Cohesion and survival only shape such hidden systems of beliefs.[10] In other words, no right answers as to what is best for cohesion and survival are available by which to judge the enunciations, only group opinions as to what are the right answers. Such views are totally contrary to Natural law thinking.[11] The new theory accords with the Natural law outlook in that it regards the content of an enunciation as being very relevant indeed to the question of its validity, but does not agree that there are any absolute standards by which the content is to be judged. It could, of course, be said that, for the good of the community, God's will should be done and that enunciations should be judged by this standard, but this would be to abandon legal theory for legal politics.

One of the hallmarks of Natural law theory is the idea that law enshrines values and that it is these values which give laws their validity.[12] The new theory agrees with this inasmuch as it is prepared to accept that it is a value which gives law its validity, namely the value of the rule in providing cohesion and survival. Thus, when Professor d'Entrèves writes that for his part he believes that

"in every human society, in fact in 'human nature' itself, there are certain standards or values which determine approval or disapproval, assent or dissent; and .... that it is these same values that determine our judgment as to whether a law is 'just' or 'unjust': in other words - to use a very ancient language that seems perfectly appropriate at this point - whether we are bound in conscience to obey it or not",[13]

the new theory dictates that the statement can be accepted provided that the "ultimate standards" mentioned are taken as being those of the cohesion and survival of the group in question. These are the values with which human judgements are shot through, according to the new theory.

The same modification leads the new theory to accept also the natural lawyers' idea that as valid laws are binding in conscience, only the wicked have to obey the law because it is imposed upon them, for the good are able to accept the law as being in tune with their conscience. The new theory would present this as saying that the good agree that the enunciations are the best course for cohesion and survival, and follow them because they wish to see these goals achieved, while the wicked only obey because they are forced to do so, their own inclination being to pursue their own selfish ends, even at the cost of disrupting the cohesion of the community and thus endangering survival. Of course, it is the very same criteria which lead to laws being accepted or rejected which are used to determine whether a person is wicked or good, a good person being the one who seeks cohesion and survival, a wicked person, one who is prepared to put his own goals above those of the group. The same, however, would be true if the will of God were put in the place of cohesion and survival as the basis of the law's validity.

Thus, the new theory is able to accept the Natural law idea that the content of a law is material to its validity, subject to the modification that to be valid the content of the rule has to be accepted and ratified as being in the interests of the cohesion and survival of the group in question. If this is not the case, then the enunciation will not be accepted as a law by the group. The acceptance may, of course, stem from the content of the best-suited principle as much as from that of a particular enunciation, but the content has still to be acceptable.[14] However, the Natural law position has been subjected to severe attacks, and as the theory here presented coincides to a certain extent with Natural law thinking, the basis of those attacks must now be examined.

III

The attack on Natural law thinking has come in the main from the school of jurisprudential thought known as legal positivism. Positivism maintains that laws are posited in some manner, for example according to certain rules, and obtain their validity from the manner of their creation. The school has had many adherents and variants so that it is as infeasible to attempt to describe it as a whole as it was to try to give an overall picture of Natural law thinking. Attention will, therefore, be concentrated on Professor Hart's defence of the positivist position in relation to the question of the morality of law in his article _Positivism and the Separation of Law and Morals_.[15]

Positivism, according to its exposition in the works of Bentham and Austin, considered law to be the commands made by one sovereign person or body, which habitually obeyed no one, to its subjects who were in the habit of constantly obeying the sovereign, such commands obtaining their binding force by being backed up by sanctions for disobedience, the threat of which generally produced obedience. This command theory has been systematically demolished by Professor Hart in _The Concept of Law_. However, according to it, any command issued by such a sovereign was law in the community in question regardless of its content, moral or immoral. Two points followed from this for the question of law and morality as Professor Hart pointed out.

"What both Bentham and Austin were anxious to assert were the following two simple things: first, in the absence of an expressed constitutional or legal provision, it could not follow from the mere fact that a rule violated standards of morality that it was not a rule of law; and conversely, it could not follow from the mere fact that a rule was morally desirable that it was a rule of law."[16]

According to the new theory of the nature of law presented here, neither of those principles can be entirely accepted or entirely rejected. It has already been stated that where there is a sufficiently strong best-suited principle, an enunciation which offends against the group's morality may be accepted owing to the trust placed in the best-suited principle. This would suggest that the first point made is correct, but that is due to one of the weaknesses of positivism. The legal positivists developed their theory around institutions like the British Parliament which were the subject of a very strong best-suited principle. Under a weaker best-suited method, an enunciation which goes against the grain of group morality will not be accepted and ratified, but rejected. Thus, in Hindu law, administrative directions cannot go against unseen rules, nor in Ashanti law can the legal organs go against nature or the ancestors. Similarly, the second point, that a rule does not become law by being morally desirable, fails to take into account the growth of customary law because of positivism's focus on mature legal systems with formal methods of enunciating legal rules. It is true that some precepts which are regarded as important for cohesion and survival are a part of group morality yet no part of its law because they are not regarded as so important as to cause serious disruptions or disputes if transgressed, but it is also true that other moral precepts will harden into laws when sufficiently serious transgressions occur, and such hardening may occur through group experience as well as through enunciation by the best-suited principle. Thus, although there is some truth in the two simple points, their positivistic basis is ill-founded as law is not the product of a command structure but of acceptance and ratification by the community, and this is the key which will open the casements to let in the light on the fallacies of legal positivism.

The main force of Professor Hart's attack in his Harvard lecture was against the notion that it was morality which, as it were, filled the gaps in the law when laws came to be applied and interpreted. Hart considered that such a notion was obfuscatory and confusing.[17] He examined the criticism that to fail to take into account moral and social values when applying and interpreting laws led to automatic or mechanical jurisprudence, the vices of formalism, but refused to accept them on the basis that no one who stigmatized such automatic decisions would deny that they were law, or that the system in which they were made was a legal system. Here, however, one is again faced with the positivists' awkward, focal imbalance, whereby it can only see mature legal systems with a well-developed strong best-suited principle. If an automatic decision goes against group morality, it can only be accepted because it is the enunciation of a strong best-suited method which is given more credence than group experience. If the best-suited principle were not so strong, the decision might well be rejected.[18] Automatic or mechanical jurisprudence is, in other words, a luxury which a developing best-suited method cannot afford; a developing dispute-solving organ has to be in tune with the community's values if its dispute solutions are going to be accepted. The positivist position is based on too much theory and too little fact, the cause of its weakness.

Hart then criticizes the notion that it is morality which shapes the law when its exact interpretation is in doubt by pointing out that just because, in such penumbral areas, the courts may say what the law ought to be, although it has not been enunciated, it is wrong to equate the presence of 'ought' with morality as <u>the</u> standard of criticism rather than just with <u>a</u> standard of criticism. He states that an 'ought' can be entirely immoral as in the baffled poisoner's remark: "I ought to have given her a second dose",[19] which is hardly a moral judgement. Again, however, these remarks lose sight of the reality of law amid the clouds of theory, a rare occurrence in Hart's writing. The facts simply are that law and morality are related functions, and they are related in that they are both meant to promote cohesion and survival. If the members of the group were united by the need to poison some individual, then perhaps to effect that end might be describable as morality, but such notions are widely separated from social life as it is known. Hart himself has acknowledged how differently composed men and groups might have very different legal and moral ideas.[20] Thus, he wrote, if men were clad in impenetrable carapaces like giant land crabs and could extract food from the air by some internal chemical process, freedom from violence and minimum property rights might not be features of their precepts. However, his poisoning example is of the same type. It is possible that the poisoner's remark could be taken as a moral judgement, but a very different social milieu would be required for it to be accepted as such. One does not, however, have to look all that far to find moral rules concerning the infliction of mortal injury. Undoubtedly, the Nazis saw nothing wrong in exterminating millions of Jews as they believed that such a course aided the Reich's cohesion and the survival of 'the master race', and therefore accepted and ratified precepts which promoted that purpose.[21] The rules relating to the conduct of warfare present another example of a morality or etiquette for human destruction. All that is required for the poisoner's judgement to be a moral one is an appropriate context. It appears nonsensical to call it a moral judgement because it is so at odds with what is generally regarded as needed for cohesion and survival - poisoning disrupts society rather than cements it. Unfortunately, the same can be said for the tenets of positivism if one examines a variety of social organizations in their light rather than merely the developed societies of the Western world. Both legal and moral precepts in the known societies of the world are meant to promote cohesion and survival, but legal precepts differ from morality in that they are engendered by the need to solve disputes caused by transgressions. To ignore the common basis of law and morality in these social aims is to lose sight of the reality which legal theory seeks to describe.

Holding that law is a system of commands, norms or rules, the positivists have been forced to concede that the rules enunciated by the Nazi Government of Germany in the nineteen-thirties and -forties were valid laws. This view is not held by Natural law thinkers who despise the Nazi precepts for their, to them, immoral content. The positivist position is somewhat strained as they too despise the content of what they are forced by their theory to recognize as valid laws. The positivists find their _deus ex_ *machina* by stating that although such immoral precepts are valid laws, there remains the moral question of whether they ought to be obeyed. Some positivists, including Professor Hart, do not seem to realize that there is an important difference between holding a precept to be invalid for immorality and holding it to be law but nevertheless immoral. If the third century B.C. Babylonian scholar in Jewish law, Mar Samuel's view be taken as general that Jews should obey the laws of the state in which they settle as well as their own Jewish law, the difference becomes painfully apparent.

One theorist who rejected positivism as a result of his experience of the Nazi regime was Gustav Radbruch. Hart's comments on Radbruch's apostasy, or perhaps conversion, are very illuminating.

Of Radbruch, Hart wrote:

"His considered reflection led him to the doctrine that the fundamental principles of humanitarian morality were part of the very concept of *Recht* or Legality and that no positive enactment or statute, however clearly it was expressed and however clearly it conformed with the formal criteria of validity of a given legal system, could be valid if it contravened basic principles of morality. This doctrine can be appreciated fully only if the nuances imparted by the German word *Recht* are grasped. But it is clear that the doctrine meant that every lawyer and judge should denounce statutes that transgressed the fundamental principles not as merely immoral or wrong but as having no legal character, and enactments which on this ground lack the quality of law should not be taken into account in working out the legal position of any given individual in particular circumstances."[22]

If one casts this passage into the terms of the new theory, its accuracy is evident. Basically, what Radbruch says is that if an enunciation made by the best-suited method is so contrary to what the group thinks is necessary for cohesion and survival, it will not be accepted and ratified by the group. Where the courts as dispute solvers, according to their dispute-solving, metagame, best-suited principle, are confronted with a harmful enunciation, they should reject it and not use it in solving disputes. Radbruch's views clearly anticipate the new theory to this extent. However, he fails to perceive that acceptance and ratification take place according to the standards of the community and not according to any absolute moral standards. The bitter truth was that the Nazi community did give the degree of acceptance and ratification to the enunciations of its best-suited mechanism to make those enunciations law, even if Radbruch could not bring himself to accept such precepts. Only if the judges or the group had been persuaded that the precepts were harmful for cohesion and survival would acceptance and ratification, and thus legal validity, have been withheld from them. Unfortunately, Radbruch's view did not command such support. However, when the war was lost, it became clear that the Nazi precepts were not the best course for cohesion and survival, so the best-suited principle changed accordingly, and acceptance and ratification of the harmful enunciations ceased as they were recognized as harfum to the aims of the community. Indeed, in some instances their rejection was so total that their validity at any time was abrogated, a particularly striking example of desuetude.

One example of this occurrence is given by Hart in the text of his Harvard lecture. A wife denounced her husband to the authorities for criticizing the government, an act proscribed by a statute of 1934. After the war, she was brought to trial for illegality depriving her husband of his freedom, a crime under the German Criminal Code of 1871. She pleaded the 1934 Statute by way of defence, but the validity of the statute was rejected. The Natural lawyers claimed a victory against positivism as the statute was rejected due to its content. Hart could not share their enthusiasm.[23] If, however, the new theory is applied, it is clear that the change in the best-suited principle was sufficient to lead to the rejection of prior enunciations as harmful to cohesion and survival, and their acceptance and ratification was accordingly out of the question. Hart, and Radbruch, would prefer to have seen a retrospective repeal of the statute, but this misses the point. If the best-suited principle had changed, but prior enunciations were not considered harmful, then there would have been an accepted precept to repeal, but here the enunciations were themselves so harmful as to be rejected absolutely with the old best-suited principle so that there was nothing left to be repealed. This is nothing more than an admittedly striking example of desuetude of the kind mentioned above. The new theory explains the occurrence without endangering the basis of legality because it can account for the phenomenon as a result of its being itself based upon the social realities which lie behind law. Each enunciation is a valid law only so long as it is accepted and ratified by the group in question, and is law while it is so treated. When it is no longer so treated, whether it will be accepted and ratified as having been a law also depends upon whether such acceptance is conducive to cohesion and survival. This answers both Hart and Radbruch.

The positivist would say that precepts are never too evil to be law but merely too evil to be obeyed. However, when dealing with the rules of other legal systems, even the English courts refuse to apply rules which are contrary to public policy.[24] Thus, the English courts will refuse to enforce a contract relating to prostitution even if the proper law of the contract recognizes such transactions as legal.[25] This does not undermine legality. In any event, the purpose of law is to promote cohesion and survival not the legality of systems, particularly not defunct systems like that of the Nazis. The legality of contracts for prostitution under the other system will not be affected while the other group accepts and ratifies the rule in the belief that it furthers rather than hinders the group's cohesion and survival. Unfortunately, that is the test of legality in all circumstances. If a sufficient number of the group accepts and ratifies the enunciation, it is valid law even though it is repugnant to other members and possibly to other groups. It is deception to pretend that the Nazi laws were not legally valid to the Nazi community and did not enshrine their morality, despite their repugnance to others, whether contemporaries or successors. Legal validity and, indeed, moral value must be determined from group to group, from time to time. Merely because a precept appears grossly immoral to one group does not mean that it cannot be perfectly moral to another and obtain legal validity. The eating of meat may be acceptable to one group, for example, but be as repulsive as cannibalism to another. Similarly, a group can change its mind as to the morality of certain conduct and even the legal validity of certain precepts. It is doubtful whether Bentham, Austin, or even Professor Hart would consider it necessary for Christian missionaries to repeal an edict of a native chief making human sacrifice a group obligation after the tribe's reconversion to Christianity had rendered the precept nugatory, and would treat murders during the interregnum accordingly. The change in the best-suited principle in this example is the same as that in the Nazi situation, and the new theory suffices to explain the occurrence. Where what to some is an immoral precept has obtained legal validity, the choice of whether to obey of course remains, as does the dilemma facing followers of Mar Samuel.

IV

Professor Hart's defence of positivism provoked a reply from Professor Lon L. Fuller,[26] in which he criticized positivism for pushing its doctrine of the separation of laws and morals so far that it becomes unreal in outlook, divorced from the extralegal needs of human life.[27] Fuller in his reply postulates the notion of an inner morality of law, a morality that makes law possible. This takes the form of a procedural rather than a substantive form of Natural law,[28] and in his later work, The Morality of Law, he developed this notion considerably. In the later work, he spoke of eight ways of failing to make law, thus asserting that if his inner morality of law was not observed by law-makers, their enunciations would not be valid laws. Clearly, if this were to be described in the language of the new theory, one would say that Fuller was asserting a metagame for the best-suited persons or procedures, the rules of which, if broken, would lead to their enunciations not being accepted and ratified by the group in question. Fuller, however, fails to incorporate the best-suited principle into his theory, and this, as will be seen, leads to his theory being inaccurate and itself somewhat out of tune with the realities of human life. It is also responsible for what will be shown to be the less than useful distinction between procedural and substantive Natural law. The damage to Fuller's theory caused by the absence of the best-suited principle from it is signalled in two examples which he uses in his reply to Professor Hart. In both of the examples, Fuller postulates dilemmas to which, he argues, positivism can provide no answers. The first he called the judge's dilemma.

"Let us suppose the case of a trial judge who has had an extensive experience in commercial matters and before whom a great many commercial disputes are tried. As a subordinate in a judicial hierarchy, our judge has of course the duty to follow the law laid down by his supreme court. Our imaginary Scrutton has the misfortune, however, to live under a supreme court which he considers woefully ignorant of the ways and needs of commerce. To his mind, many of the court's decisions in the field of commercial law simply do not make sense."[29]

Fuller then demonstrates that positivism cannot help his imaginary Scrutton by giving him any advice worth having.[30] However, Fuller does not provide a solution either. The new theory, however, can pinpoint the difficulties by using the best-suited principle. The judge's difficulty is that according to the best-suited principle which guides the court as to what law to apply, the decision of the supreme court should be applied. However, the judge's own decisions will only be accepted and ratified if they solve disputes satisfactorily and peaceably for the community. The metagame of which law to apply is meant to ensure such acceptance and ratification. If he feels that acceptance and ratification of his decisions will only be achieved by departing from the metagame best-suited principle, altering it in other words, his own position of best-suited to solve disputes for the community will be strengthened if he is correct. If he is incorrect, it is the authority of his role which will be weakened. This is the judge's dilemma, and it neatly illustrates that the best-suited principle is constantly being tested. At every decision point, the principle is either strengthened or weakened by the decision reached.

Fuller's second example is of the same sort of situation. It can be termed the absinthe example.

"One can imagine a course of reasoning that might run as follows: This statute says absinthe shall not be sold. What is its purpose? To promote health. Now, as everyone knows, absinthe is a sound, wholesome, and beneficial beverage. Therefore, interpreting the statute in the light of its purpose, I construe it to direct a general sale and consumption of that most healthful of beverages, absinthe."[31]

To prevent this sort of reasoning, Fuller falls back on what he admits are the rather hazy notions of structure and structural integrity.[32] He does not, however, examine these notions in any detail, but it is submitted that he may have been attempting to get at what is called under the new theory the best-suited principle. For what the absinthe example amounts to is an acceptance by the court that promoting health is important for cohesion and survival but a denial that the enunciation banning absinthe furthers those ends.

The statute is not, therefore, accepted and ratified by the courts. It remains to be seen whether the courts' view will be accepted and ratified by the group. If it is, the court has fulfilled its best-suited role to decide between legal sources, in other words reached the correct decision by the standards of the community it serves. If it is not, then its position as best-suited decider is weakened if not destroyed and in future the position of the legislature as best-suited enunciator is likely to be stronger, even with reference to the courts

In both examples, the relevant questions centred on the best-suited principle; the central question was whose enunciations would be accepted and ratified. The courts in both instances have to decide whether to accept or reject the enunciations of the best-suited enunciators according to the metagame, in order to protect their position in the group as best-suited enunciators and dispute deciders. Fuller fails to give a satisfactory account of the two dilemmas because the best-suited principle does not feature in his approach to legal theory. This same defect mars the development of his thesis in The <u>Morality of Law</u>.

Fuller, as has been said, in his developed thesis speaks of eight ways of failing to make law, and each of these will be looked at in turn. He begins his presentation with an allegory of these eight ways to fail which takes the form of the tale of a king called Rex who is the law-giver of the group in question. The new theory instantly recognizes that the community has a best-suited principle, namely that Rex is best-suited to enunciate. The best-suited principle forms the hub of the critical examination which follows.

Rex' first failure is to generalize sufficiently to make rules of law. He set himself up as a judge to decide disputes, but "After he had handed down literally hundreds of decisions neither he nor his subjects could detect in those decisions any pattern whatsoever."[33] Thus, thinks Fuller, Rex failed to make law. The evidence, however, goes against this view. Law, as has been shown, emerges with the solving of disputes at a level that avoids disruption. At first, all the effort goes into solving disputes individually and not into making rules to solve disputes. Thus, Rex succeeds in making law in that disputes are brought to him for decision and are decided. Although his position as a dispute decider depends on his being accepted as a satisfactory dispute decider, whether his failure to generalize will affect that position is a question of fact in each case. Merely because the earliest treatises on law concentrate on procedure not substantive law does not make them any the less legal treatises. The question is simply will Rex' decisions continue to be accepted and ratified if they are merely individual decisions. The question is empirical, and Rex cannot be said to fail to make law while he manages to get his decisions accepted and ratified even in individual cases.

Rex' second failure comes when he decides to lay down general rules for solving disputes but not to publish them to his subjects. Fuller asserts that a failure to promulgate precepts is a failure to make law.[34] At first blush, this may appear true as it may be thought that what is not known to the group cannot be accepted and ratified by it. However, even this question involves the best-suited principle, for if the group really has a vast confidence in Rex as enunciator, it may be prepared to accept and ratify his enunciation that the laws are best kept secret. Such a view will be strengthened if, in dispute solving, such rules prove successful. It is, of course, more likely that such an enunciation would meet rejection, but the question is nevertheless an empirical one and turns on the strength of the group's best-suited principle.

Rex then decides that in future he will decide all disputes after the event and not lay down any rules in advance, but retrospectively. Fuller maintains that to attempt to make precepts retroactively is the third failure to make law.[35] However, the issue is again one of whether the group will accept and ratify such precepts, which is again an empirical question. It is true that there is a risk that retroactive precepts will cause more disruption than they cure[36] and will thus be rejected, but even if this is a likelihood, it does not alter the empirical nature of the question any more than the existence of an odds-on favourite decides the outcome of a horse race.

Fuller's fourth method of failing to make law is by failing to be clear. However, it has been emphasized that all precepts are approximations and, therefore, the matter of clarity is one of degree not of kind.[37] While it is acknowledged that unclarity can lead to rejection of an enunciation and a persistent lack of clarity to possible rejection of the enunciator as best-suited, whether either of these will occur is always a question of fact in each case. The same is true of Fuller's fifth method of failure, contradiction.[38] If the best-suited persons contradict themselves, their enunciations or even their positions may be rejected, but whether this will occur is still an empirical question and an exceptionally strong best-suited principle will survive such storms.

Rex' sixth failure is of particular importance. Fuller asserts that if an enunciation is impossible of fulfilment, then it will not be law.[39] This is clearly sensible, but it must again be objected that no general answer can be given to the question of whether impossible enunciations will be accepted or rejected. If the impossible is asked of the community generally, the enunciation may well be rejected, but if it is only asked of some, there may be no objection. The content, therefore, of the enunciation is valid in this instance, indeed the whole notion of impossibility turns on the content of the enunciation so that Fuller has slid unnoticingly from procedural to substantive questions. In the early law of India, Brahman's who contravened the law were punished with impossible fines to emphasize the seriousness of their crime.[40] Similarly, in contemporary France, drugs offences are often punished with massive fines which express the condemnation of the community even though the fines are so large as to be unpayable by the convict. Thus, impossibility is not a general bar to acceptance of a precept. Fuller rightly linked to impossibility the notion of rejection because a precept was too difficult to accept.[41] Again, content enters into the picture and Fuller comes his closest to discovering the true nature of the limitation of law by morality, that is, that the enunciations made according to the best-suited principle have to be accepted and ratified by the group to be valid laws and that each enunciation has to be treated separately. In other words, Fuller's point here is not materially different from that of Blackstone when he spoke of statutes contrary to the law of God or impossible to be performed or with absurd consequences manifestly contradictory to common reason, or Coke's statutes contrary to natural justice. Both men regarded such precepts as too difficult or impossible to accept as valid law. The difficulty of acceptance can be as fatal as the difficulty of performance to legal validity, and the former is what really matters. Everything depends on what the group will accept, and it is the group's morality which is relevant to determining whether an immoral precept will be law. If their morality is low, immoral laws may be accepted.[42] Thus,

Hart's remark that procedural morality is commensurate with great iniquity[43] is fully justified. Unfortunately, as only the group's morality can be significant, substantive morality is no safeguard against a minority of the group[44] or the totality of outsiders holding the group's laws to be iniquitous.

Rex' penultimate method of failure is by not achieving constancy in his precepts. Fuller believes that by constantly chopping and changing the rules of the social group, Rex fails to make law.[45] Again, while it is acknowledged that such fluctuations can weaken the best-suited principle and destroy it or its enunciations, whether this will actually occur is still an empirical question depending upon the strength of the best-suited principle in question and the extent of the transgression of group needs involved. Fuller's last way not to make law, through failure of congruence between the rule as enunciated and as administered, harks back to the absinthe example and requires a determination as to whether to accept the enunciations of the legislature or those implicit in the decisions of the precept-applying organs.[46] In other words, a choice of best-suited methods is involved, as where a legislature purports to be following the constitution but contravenes a basic freedom of the people, a situation discussed in chapter two.

At the end of this examination, it can be seen that there is no difference between the basis of the procedural Natural law outlined by Fuller and the more traditional, substantive concept of Natural law, or between the external and internal moralities of law. The underlying question is always whether, enunciations made according to the best-suited principle will be accepted and ratified by the group in question. This question is always a question of fact, the answer to which will depend upon the group of which it is asked and the time at which it is asked. However, two factors will always be relevant, namely the strength of the group's best-suited principle and the extent to which the enunciation departs from the group's understanding of what is required to meet its needs. Towards the end of <u>The Morality of Law</u>, Professor Fuller again comes near to reaching the conclusion arrived at here. Speaking of the connection between efficacy and inner morality, he wrote:

"The case then becomes like that of a man who tells me a reckless falsehood, but leaves me uninjured because before I act on what he told me I happen to learn the truth for myself. In such a case though I may not have suffered any immediate injury, damage has certainly been done to my relations with the man who told me the falsehood and my trust for him in any future dealings will have been impaired.

"If we view the law as providing guideposts for human interaction, we shall be able to see that any infringement of the demands of legality tends to undermine men's confidence in, and their respect for, law generally. It is worth recalling in this connection that there is an ancient crime of disturbing boundary markers and a very modern crime of moving, destroying, or defacing official highway signs. Neither of these crimes requires that the perpetrator's action inflict any direct injury on anyone. Part of the basis of such laws is that if the physical pointers by which men guide their actions toward one another are sufficiently tampered with, those that remain intact will lose their meaning and men will no longer feel secure in relying on them. If this is true when men tamper with well-placed markers, what shall we say of the engineer who puts the signs up in the wrong places to start with, or of the legislator who bungles the job of laying out the vital written paragraphs by which men's rights and duties toward one another are defined?"[47]

The seeds of the best-suited principle are clearly present in these remarks, but Professor Fuller fails to gather the harvest.

V

In classical and scholastic theories of Natural law, in legal positivism and in more modern attempts to link law with morality, there are inevitably elements of truth. However, all these attempts are flawed in that they lose sight of law as a social phenomenon and just do not fit the facts about law which are known. The new theory, based as it is upon law as a social phenomenon, and armed as it is with the best-suited principle to explain legal validity, is able to provide a more accurate explanation of the nature of the problem. To begin with, it recognizes that law and morality are both systems which aim to achieve the same basic end, namely to promote cohesion and survival. The difference between them lies in the fact that law seeks to achieve this by solving disputes and overcoming disruptions and emerges as a

Figure 3. Criteria and Process for deciding whether Precepts are Valid Laws.

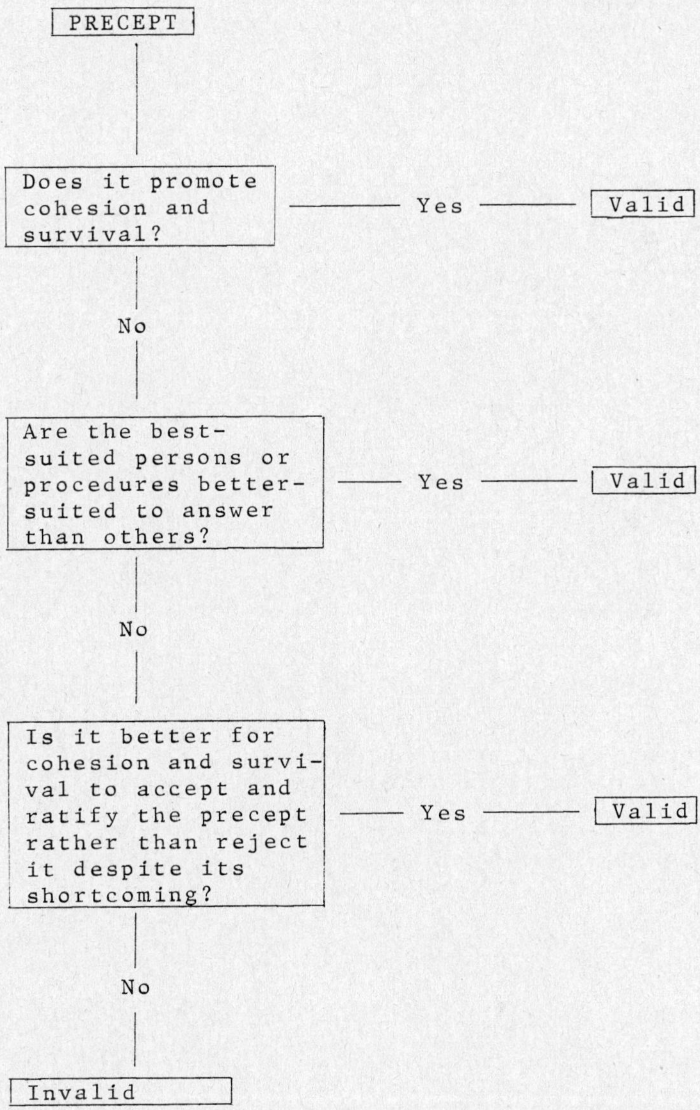

consequence of such activities, while moral precepts merely guide people as to how to maintain cohesion and survival and avoid such disputes and disruptions. Law takes over when disputes and breaches of precepts threaten disruption, and institutionalizes the breakdown so as to avoid the risk of a breakdown in social cohesion. Legal precepts, that is, precepts which aim to promote cohesion and survival by solving disputes and overcoming disruptions, have to be accepted and ratified by the group in question before they are valid laws. This is true whether the precepts emerge from the experience of the group or are enunciated according to its best-suited principle. If the precepts arise from experience, they will clearly mirror the morality of the group, which is normally based on experience, although a moral teacher or best-suited person or institution can exist. If the legal precepts are enunciations, there is then a risk that they will offend against the group's morality. If this occurs, then whether such precepts will be accepted and ratified depends on whether the community trusts its best-suited principle more or less than its own judgement in deciding what is best for cohesion and survival. In each case of conflict, whether the enunciation will be accepted depends on the relative strength of the best-suited principle and the extent to which the enunciation offends against the morality of the community. Whether such an enunciation will be accepted is an empirical question which must be answered for each individual case as it arises, but the relevant factors are the same in each case, namely those set out above. To this extent, therefore, the law of a social group must mirror its morality. However, whether the morality of the group is regarded as moral by other groups or indeed by all the members of the group in question is not a relevant factor. Provided a sufficient number are satisfied with the morality of the enunciation, it will be accepted. Law need not, according to the new theory, be moral in any other sense than that of what the group considers moral, for there can be no absolute moral standards but only group values for cohesion and survival.[48]

****

1. Vide, <u>supra</u>, chapter 2.
2. (1610) 8 Co. Rep. 118a.

3. W. Blackstone, *Commentaries*, I pp. 91, 160.
4. Vide, *supra*, chapter 3, n.16.
5. Vide, *supra*, chapter 4, p.140.
6. Vide, St. Thomas Aquinas, *Summa Theologica*, 1a 2ae 95, 2., quoted in d'Entrèves, *NL*, 46.
7. d'Entrèves, *NL*, 46.
8. *CLH* I, 180.
9. This is, of course, only submitted as being the case as a result of the Fall of mankind.
10. Cf. Hart's minimum content of natural law, *CL*, 187-95.
11. Vide, d'Entrèves, *NL*, 79.
12. *Ibid*., 161-2.
13. *Ibid*., 164-5.
14. Vide, *Ibid*., 46, quotation from Aquinas, *Summa Theologica*, 2a 2ae 104, 6.
15. (1958) 71 *Harvard Law Review*, 593.
16. *Ibid*., 599.
17. *Ibid*., 614.
18. *Ibid*., 612.
19. *Ibid*., 613.
20. *Ibid*., 622-3.
21. *Ibid*., 613-4; it was only immoral to outsiders - in a physical and ideological sense.
22. *Ibid*., 617.
23. *Ibid*., 619.
24. *Ibid*., 620.
25. Vide, G.C. Cheshire, *Private International Law* (9th Ed., by P.M. North) (London, 1974), 229-36.
26. *Positivism and Fidelity to Law* (1958) 71 *Harvard Law Review*, 630.
27. *Ibid*., 656.
28. *Ibid*., 644-5.
29. *Ibid*., 646.
30. *Ibid*., 646-7.
31. *Ibid*., 670.
32. *Ibid*.
33. Fuller, *ML*, 33-4, 46-9.
34. *Ibid*., 34, 49-51.
35. *Ibid*., 34-5, 51-63.
36. Cf. A. Watson, *The Nature of Law*, 69.
37. Fuller *ML*, 35-6, 63-5.
38. *Ibid*., 36, 65-70.
39. *Ibid*., 36-7, 70-8.
40. *PL*, 112.
41. Fuller, *ML*, 79.
42. Vide, A. Watson, *The Nature of Law*, 125.
43. Hart, *CL*, 202.
44. Or even a majority, provided a sufficient number of the others ratify the rule.

45. Fuller, *ML*, 37, 79-81.
46. *Ibid*., 37-8, 81-91.
47. *Ibid*., 222-3.
48. For a diagrammatic representation, vide Fig. 3.

CHAPTER SIX

MORALITY AND LAW

I

In the last chapter, the question under discussion was whether law had to be moral in order to be law. In this chapter, another question concerning law and morality will be treated, namely whether the law ought to enforce morality. This can be reformulated as a question concerning upon what criteria a group should decide to transform its moral precepts into legal rules. It is the purpose of this chapter to examine this question, and some of the answers which have been given to it, in the light of the theory of the nature of law which this book presents.

The essential background to the examination is again, therefore, that individuals, motivated by their need to survive, form groups in order to achieve that purpose, and that as a consequence the maintenance of the cohesion of such groups is viewed as important to achieving the end of survival. Acts which weaken the cohesion of the social bond, or actually threaten to destroy it, are therefore thought to be dangerous both to the continuation of the community and the survival of the individuals who compose it. The group, therefore, must recognize what sort of behaviour produces such results, and such behaviour will be adjudged wrong or harmful. At the outset, it is probably as well to re-emphasize that behaviour may be adjudged harmful to the group either because it directly threatens the cohesion of the group, or because it harms cohesion indirectly by provoking a dispute with another group member, and that dispute may lead to disruption. Thus, if a group regards the favour of a certain god as being necessary for its welfare, a person who desecrates the shrine of that god may find that his conduct is adjudged harmful because it draws down divine vengeance upon the group which will threaten cohesion and survival. On the other hand, if the same person were to destroy a crop belonging to a farmer, the community might only consider that act harmful because it provoked a dispute between the farmer and the vandal, which dispute threatens the good order and thus the cohesion of the community.

When the group has decided which conduct is bad for cohesion and survival, it is still however faced with deciding what to do if the precepts forbidding such conduct are broken. The same would be true of precepts enjoining conduct thought necessary for those goals. In the case of the desecration, for example, the group has to decide whether cohesion and survival would be better aided by taking action against the vandal or whether such action would provoke more disruption that it cured. Similarly, in the crop-destruction example, the group has to face the question of whether attempting to solve the dispute would provoke a greater threat to cohesion than merely allowing the disputants to settle the affair between them. Thus, in relation to any act or conduct, a group has to ask whether it aids or hinders cohesion and survival, and, if the latter, it is adjudged wrong, harmful or immoral. It then has to decide whether cohesion and survival are aided or hindered by attempting to prevent or punish the act or solve the dispute it has caused; if the goals are hindered, the group will leave the conduct as being immoral and subject it to disapproval, but if enforcement would aid cohesion and survival, then the immorality will become the subject of institutionalized group action and become illegal as well. Thus, in some groups entering a church with a hat on one's head may not be deemed harmful to the group, while in others it may be thought wrong. If it is thought wrong, it may nevertheless only be disapproved of if it is thought that attempting to interfere would cause more disruption than leaving the wearer alone, but if the damage done by the transgression is considered more detrimental than the disruption interference might bring in its wake, the group will act against the transgressor.

This last example may appear trivial but it is important to realize that everything depends upon what the group holds to be its interests, and the fact that outsiders or even some members of the group may think it ridiculous to answer the questions in the way the group does, will not affect the group answers if the group beliefs so dictate. The Ashanti, for example, believe that if they do not punish certain transgressions, the ancestors will punish the group as a whole. In other words, they believe that the consequences of not acting against certain transgressions will always be worse than those of so doing. Everything turns upon their convictions. Thus, as they believe that incest destroys the universe, any disruption which punishing a transgressor of the incest prohibition may cause can never be as bad as failing to do so.[1] If one really believes that homosexual acts cause earthquakes, they clearly ought to be punished according to these criteria. It was pointed out in chapter four[2] that a sound reason for punishing offenders was the idea that they constituted bad examples of what was needed for survival and must be seen to suffer the consequences lest they should be followed and the group led along the path to destruction. Such considerations as these also weigh heavily in deciding whether the consequences of punishment in the way of disruption are more or less serious than those of disapproval.

It must also be clear from what has gone before that different groups will answer the questions differently albeit that the questions remain the same, namely whether the conduct injures survival and, if so, whether interference will cause more harm than good. The fact that different answers will be given means that different groups will require a greater or lesser degree of conformity with their survival precepts. Some may hold only few things to be harmful, others many. Some may consider that only a few harms are so serious as to outweigh the harm consequent upon interfering, while others strike a different balance. The questions will always, however, fall for the group to determine, and its answers will emerge either directly from its experience or indirectly by acceptance and ratification of the answers provided according to its best-suited principle of enunciation. It is when an act is committed that it will normally have to be decided whether it is good or bad according to whether it hinders cohesion and survival or not, and, similarly, it is when disruption is threatened or caused that the decision will have to be taken whether to intercede will hinder cohesion and survival more or less than allowing the disruption to play itself out.

In this context it is difficult to avoid the notion of justice. Many will say that to consider it wrong when one person performs an act but not wrong when another does, or to punish one person for a wrong but to allow another to get away with it is unfair or unjust. However, while it is not denied that such decisions may be instances of injustice, whether they are right or wrong decisions morally can only be decided against the background of the avoidance of disruption and the promotion of cohesion and survival. If deciding like cases alike is considered to be one way of ensuring that disruption is avoided, then the principle will be followed, but if inconsistency is deemed more beneficial, then the principle will be rejected. The notion of justice, therefore, is no more than one strategy for achieving cohesion and survival. Indeed, this is clear from the facts concerning legal systems. If a person is struck by two individuals successively in the market place, he may decide to sue one but not the other for the tort committed, and the community is normally prepared to countenance this as perfectly justifiable for there is only one dispute to be solved if only one action is brought. Similarly, in ancient Rome, the practice of Christianity, although prohibited generally, required a private complaint to be brought before it activated legal penalties. This can again be seen as an instance of the group only stepping in where actual disruption is threatening, where a person is actually aggrieved. When Christianity was regarded as itself threatening the group's cohesion, then the State, as under Marcus Aurelius, would step in periodically, that is, as required, to avoid the danger threatened. Thus, the evidence supports the notion that the principles of justice are only resorted to to avoid disruption, and if disruption is better avoided through injustice, then injustice is the order of the day for the group in question. The criteria are constant, namely is the conduct harmful to cohesion and survival or not, and if harmful, is interference by law more or less harmful to cohesion and survival than allowing the harmful conduct.

Different people will, not unexpectedly, provide different answers as to what is wrong and as to at is so wrong that group action is required. The fact that different answers will emerge demonstrates a diversity of belief as to what conduct is bad for cohesion and survival and as to what conduct is worse for these goals than the harm caused by group intervention, although the answers given may not be articulated in those terms. Some views may show direct criticism of the fact that certain conduct is met with a disruptive reaction and urge that it is the reaction not the conduct which is harmful. The fact that some of the views as well as prescribing what groups should do are critical of what groups actually do, has led to the standards being postulated in such arguments being referred to as a critical morality to distinguish them from the positive morality of the community's standards which are under fire. Different critical moralities lead to the different answers to the questions both as to of what the positive morality of a group should consist, and whether the group should enforce its positive morality and, if so, how much of it should be enforced. The questions have given rise to much controversy. Last century, there was a notable exchange between the philosopher, John Stuart Mill, and the judge and legal writer, Sir James Fitzjames Stephen. More recently there has been "a splendid encounter"[3] between another leading member of the judiciary, Lord Devlin, and the distinguished legal philosopher, Professor H.L.A. Hart. It is now proposed to examine some aspects of the views put forward in these contests not so much to establish which are worthy of support, but rather to demonstrate the way in which the criteria suggested by the new theory help to bring out the strengths and weaknesses of the arguments employed. Some conclusions may, nevertheless, not be out of place.

II

John Stuart Mill's essay On Liberty first appeared in 1859. In it, Mill vigorously propounds a principle which can hardly be better presented than in his own words. He wrote:

"The object of this Essay is to assert one very simple principle, as entitled to govern absolutely the dealings of society with the individual in the way of compulsion and control, whether the means used be physical force in the form of legal penalties, or the moral coercion of public opinion. That principle is, that the sole end for which mankind are (sic) warranted, individually or collectively, in interfering with the liberty of action of any of their number, is self protection. That the only purpose for which power can be rightfully exercised over any member of a civilized community, against his will, is to prevent harm to others".[4]

The principle which Mill puts forward for discussion is clearly one of critical morality, the principle which in Mill's opinion ought to be used by social groups in deciding what conduct is harmful and what conduct is so harmful that social intervention is justified. Now, this means that according to Mill, only the infliction of harm to members of the group is so bad as to be against cohesion and survival and this also is sufficiently harmful to justify group interference. Mill also believes that intervention or even moral coercion in other circumstances is wrong, that is it hinders cohesion and survival. To Mill, liberty was the greatest asset to society, that is, to achieving the two social goals already mentioned.

Mill, however, nowhere links his principle to the twin goals of cohesion and survival. He never looks at the reason why individuals form groups and have precepts governing their conduct in his examination of when precepts are needed. This is a weakness comparable to one mentioned in the last chapter. There, it was seen that Bentham and Austin's theory of law suffered from being overinfluenced by the laws and legal systems of the developed, western societies. Mill, the heir to Bentham's intellectual empire of utilitarianism, was afflicted with the same malaise. It is realistic not unkind to point out that Mill was a comfortably-placed gentlemen writing in a country which enjoyed prosperity and global supremacy. His theory only fits a society which does not really fear disintegration through external or internal attack or disease, and for whose citizens, at least those of Mill's status, the next meal is guaranteed as are the roofs over their heads. This is clear from Mill's attitude to freedom of speech. The criterion which societies use in relation to this freedom is clearly that it can be enjoyed so far as it does not cause or threaten disruption. Even in the United States, where freedom of speech is constitutionally guaranteed, in war-time particularly and in peace-time where aggressive words provoke a clear and present danger of disruption, the freedom is limited. Indeed, the awkwardness of the guarantee leads to such bizarre reckonings as that obscenity is not speech at all[5] in order to prevent disruption and respect the Bill of Rights simultaneously. The real meaning is clearly that obscenity is a greater threat to cohesion than its suppression, a clear example of the second criterion under the new theory. Similarly, in England and Wales, threatening, abusive or insulting words or behaviour are prohibited if they are likely to cause a breach of the peace,[6] that is, a disruption. Mill's theory assumes the existence of a strong society, that can withstand a great deal of criticism, and is not valid outside of such a context.

Many of his comments would, however, taken at their face value, let in a large number of group determinations which Mill would scarcely have welcomed. Discussing the limits of the authority of society over the individual, he describes just how much ought to be rendered to Caesar.

"What, then, is the rightful limit to the sovereignty of the individual over himself? Where does the authority of society begin? How much of human life should be assigned to individuality, and how much to society?

"Each will receive its proper share, if each has that which more particularly concerns it. To individuality should belong that part of life in which it is chiefly the individual that is interested; to society, the part which chiefly interests society.

"Though society is not founded on a contract, and though no good purpose is answered by inventing a contrace in order to deduce social obligations from it, everyone who receives the protection of society owes a return for the benefit, and the fact of living in society renders it indispensable for each should be bound to observe a certain line of conduct towards the rest. This conduct consists, first, in not injuring the interests of one another; or rather certain interests, which, either by express legal provision or by their tacit understanding, ought to be considered as rights; and secondly, in each person's bearing his share (to be fixed on some equitable principle) of the labours and sacrifices incurred for defending the society or its members from injury or molestation. These conditions society is justified in enforcing, at all costs to those who endeavour to withhold fulfilment. Nor is this all that society may do. The acts of an individual may be hurtful to others, or wanting in due consideration for their welfare, without going to the length of violating any of their constituted rights. The offender may then be justly punished by opinion, though not by law. As soon as any part of a person's conduct affects prejudicially the interests of others, society has jurisdiction over it, and the question of whether the general welfare will or will not be promoted by interfering with it, becomes open to discussion. But there is no room for entertaining any such question when a person's conduct affects the interests of no persons besides himself, or needs not affect them unless they like (all the persons concerned being of full age, and the ordinary amount of understanding). In all such cases, there should be perfect freedom, legal and social, to do the action and stand the consequences."[7]

Taken literally, these remarks are capable of fitting the new theory. They allow, for example, the Ashanti view that any act adjudged displeasing to the ancestors must be punished lest the ancestors destroy the group. Clearly, such conduct is other-regarding and not just self-regarding. Similarly, if one believes with Justinian that homosexuality causes earthquakes,[8] then again to commit a homosexual act is to endanger the security and welfare of the community and the community has a clear interest in prohibiting the activity. In such circumstances, the individual offender "has infringed the rules necessary for the protection of his fellow creatures, individually or collectively. The evil consequences of his acts do not then fall on himself, but on others; and society, as the protector of all its members, must retaliate on him; must inflict pain on him for the express purpose of punishment, and must take care that it be sufficiently severe."[9]

Mill's words fit the needs both of the Ashanti and Justinian, but he would hardly have rejoiced at this. Both, he would have thought, laboured under woeful ignorance and stood in need of education to bring them up to the level of intellect which would allow them to appreciate the virtues of liberty. The injuries here, to Mill, would have been contingent, constructive and would occasion perceptible hurt to no individual once the veil of ignorance was lifted. Mill, in such cases, would argue that the inconveniences involved were ones which society could afford to bear, "for the sake of the greater good of human freedom".[10] In other words, Mill's theory presupposes a certain level of intellect and freedom from superstition before it can hope to be accepted, so that its criteria cannot be applied to societies which fall short of this level of development. Mill may be correct that freedom is the greatest good, but before his principle can be accepted, it must be accepted that it is freedom which gives the best chance of cohesion and survival, and this is not apparently accepted in early societies nor even in developed countries as the earlier remarks concerning free speech illustrate. Everywhere, what is sought is the avoidance of disruptions which could injure cohesion, and the criteria of the new theory, based on this end, are not limited in their application to the upper-echelons of the ladder of social development, let alone hovering like Mill's theory somewhere beyond the highest known rung. Mill's theory depends entirely on the existence of a strong group, and any society which reaches such strength does so through the operation of group opinion as to its survival principles, a point which must now be examined as it sums up the weaknesses of this position.

Some groups might insist upon a very high degree of conformity in the belief that this was necessary for cohesion and survival. Mill regarded such principles as "monstrous"[11] and then made some very interesting remarks concerning civilization. Speaking of the ill-feeling directed by his society against the Mormon practice of polygamy, he refused to believe that if the practice is uncivilized it has to be the subject of prohibition rather that of reasoned persuasion. He concluded:

"If civilisation has got the better of barbarism when barbarism had the world to itself, it is too much to profess to be afraid lest barbarism, having been fairly got under, should revive and conquer civilization. A civilization that can thus succumb to its vanquished enemy, must first have become so degenerate, that neither its appointed priests and teachers, nor anybody else, has the capacity, nor will take the trouble, to stand up for it."[12]

Mill, in this passage, totally fails to take into account the fact that if a group has achieved civilization despite barbaric beginnings, it has done so through the acceptance of precepts for survival and their enforcement, when accepted as necessary for the group. If this has been achieved through group opinion, it is not self-evident that the group is wrong to claim that to fail to strike out at barbarism is to become degenerate and court disintegration. Mill cannot have it both ways; either the group precepts have always been wrong and the group success a fluke, or group opinion is not so obviously wrong if it is at odds with Mill. Mill's glorious liberty is a luxury which strong societies can indulge, but, when the chips are down and disruption threatens, the criteria which decide whether to enforce moral precepts are the same everywhere, namely whether the conduct is harmful in that it hinders cohesion and survival and, if so, whether it is more harmful than the harm involved in the group having to interfere.

III

Mill's theory has been criticized, therefore, not because it cannot be the correct principle to promote cohesion and survival. That is something only its application can decide. The reason it has been criticized is because it betrays a total indifference to the way survival principles are formed and adopted, and accordingly, if it were to be applied, the notion seems to be that it would be instituted by the muttering of a magic incantation. It is totally divorced from social reality and its applicability limited, as Mill admitted, to societies at a high level of development. In 1873, Sir James Fitzjames Stephen replied to Mill in his book Liberty Equality Fraternity, and Stephen's views are again of interest not for their intrinsic merit but rather because of the degree to which they are in touch with the mechanism of social development.

At the outset, it has to be admitted that Stephen may have failed to grasp the full implications of Mill's argument. If Mill's principle is cast into the terms of the new theory, it would be that cohesion and survival are best guaranteed by the existence of liberty and, if the principle of liberty were accepted by a group, it would greatly aid its cohesion and survival. Stephen never fully grasps that the principle of liberty would be the group's positive morality; the group would really accept that liberty was the best course for the achievement of its goals. Stephen seems to approach the principle on the basis that it has been imposed upon the group from outside so that there is no real acceptance. This is scarcely surprising seeing that Mill, in failing to connect his theory with the realities of social life, never explains this postulate with any degree of clarity. Stephen's misunderstanding is caused by the fact that he has the social realities constantly in view, and although this may have led to his failing to grasp Mill's point, it also leads to the strength of what he has to say about law and society in his criticisms of Mill.

To begin with, Stephen is quite clear on the fact that the group, if it is to cohere, must hold its survival precepts very tenaciously. Half-heartedness is clearly not something which can aid cohesion and survival. He concludes that any attack upon the survival precepts of the group is, by its very nature, going to be regarded as dangerous. He thought that:

"to publish opinions upon morals, politics, and religion is an act as important as any which any man can possibly do; that to attack opinions on which the framework of society rests is a proceeding which both is and ought to be dangerous. I do not say that it ought not to be done in many cases, but it should be done sword in hand, and a man who does it has no more right to be surprised at being fiercely resisted that a soldier who attacks a breach".[13]

Stephen clearly realises the importance which the precepts for survival must hold for the members of the group, and concomitantly suspects that a society in which general scepticism prevails about the content of such precepts is unlikely to flourish.[14] He has, of course, failed to understand that Mill's principle of liberty would be the precept which would be fiercely and tenaciously held in Mill's sort of society, but his words are nevertheless valuable for the understanding of the basis of human social existence which they reveal. Indeed, it is the distance at which Mill's principle stands from societies as Stephen knew them that caused the misunderstanding.

Although Stephen never acknowledges anything like the best-suited principle of the new theory, he does appear to understand that, to be valid, laws which are enunciations have to be accepted by the group. He sees that those whom the new theory calls the best-suited persons are placed in the position of having to enunciate the precepts, and what he says of the British in India could be adopted as of wider generality.

"Little by little they were forced to become the direct rulers of the whole country, and to provide it with a set of laws and institutions. They found, as everyone who has to do with legislation must find, that laws must be based upon principles, and that it is impossible to lay down any principles of legislation at all unless you are prepared to say, I am right, and you are wrong, and your view shall give way to mine, quietly, gradually, and peaceably; but one of us two must rule and the other must obey, and I mean to rule."[15]

This language unfortunately savours too much of the command theory of law and would tend to rule out acceptance of the legislators as best-suited to enunciate if it were not for the fact that elsewhere Stephen makes it clear that the enunciation of the best-suited persons must be acceptable to the group. "You cannot punish anything", he wrote, "which public opinion, as expressed in the common practice of society, does not strenuously and unequivocally condemn",[16] but as well as pointing out that public opinion need support condemnation and punishment, he made it clear that it was also necessary to support tolerance, stating that if the law of the land did not deal with what the community regarded as vice, lynch law infallibly would.[17]

Stephen, therefore, recognized that it was necessary to be clear about the point at which the survival precepts should be backed up by the law, and he described the point at which compulsion, as he termed it, should be resorted to in language reminiscent of the criteria set out according to the new theory. He believed that it was necessary before compulsion could be resorted to that it "could increase the happiness of the persons compelled to such an extent as to overbalance the pain of the compulsion itself".[18] If these words are taken in the context of the "pain of compulsion" resulting in disruption and that it was this phenomenon which the compulsion was meant to avoid, one is in much the same position as that of the new theory when it states that precepts should only be enforced when the breach is more dangerous than the interference. The same similarity emerges from the following paragraph.

"Compulsion is bad: (1) When the object aimed at is bad. (2) When the object aimed at is good, but the compulsion employed is not calculated to obtain it. (3) When the object aimed at is good, and the compulsion employed is calculated to obtain it, but at too great an expense".[19]

Here, again, if good and bad are interpreted as being judgements of what aid and hinder cohesion and survival respectively, and the too great expense a worse injury to the social goals, the third statement is a virtual translation of the second criterion of the new theory, and Stephen at this point came within an ace of grasping the full force of Mill's theory when he wrote that: "It can be justified only by showing as a fact that, self-protection apart, compulsion must always be a greater evil in itself than the absence of any object that can possibly be obtained by it."[20]

This statement, if adopted, would translate Mill's thesis into realistic social terms; it is the premiss which Mill failed to enunciate largely because of the distance by which he was removed from the reality of social living in his theorizing.

Stephen is also clear in his mind that there are areas in which the presence of compulsion would work more harm than good. He wrote:

"there is a sphere, none the less real because it is impossible to define its limits, within which law and public opinion are intruders likely to do more harm than good. To try and regulate the internal affairs of a family, the relations of love or friendship, or many other things of the same sort, by law or by the coercion of public opinion, is like trying to pull an eyelash out of a man's eye with a pair of tongs. They may put out the eye, but they will never get hold of the eyelash."[21]

Stephen has realized that compulsion is a means not an end, for the ultimate goal is social cohesion. Hence, it is not to be used when it threatens greater disruption than the conduct it is attacking. Moreover, he regards the limits as undefinable in clear obeisance to the fact that each society has to make its own judgement on such issues. Only the best-suited persons can go so far as to prescribe such limits and they gain their position through the experience of the group and retain it by their continued success in enunciating acceptable and successful precepts.

Stephen also anticipated the new theory in his remarks concerning the concepts of justice and equality. He maintained that such notions were only of value inasmuch as they were "generally useful".[22] If this is taken as meaning generally useful for cohesion and survival, and avoiding or solving disputes to achieve those goals, then Stephen is once again in harmony with the new theory. He clearly put forward the notion that the only reason for considering equality or justice to be good things was because they had been found to be expedient according to experience.[23] There is no need to reiterate the gloss which the new theory would give to Stephen's concept of expediency, nor probably to say that it would endorse fully his view that for each society the question of whether equality or justice were expedient would be an empirical one.

The whole of Stephen's argument against Mill

turns, therefore, on the one issue that to Stephen it was for a social group to mould its precepts, legal or otherwise, so as to fit its purpose,[24] and to specify that a group should conform to notions such as liberty, equality or justice was to misunderstand the genesis of these concepts. To Stephen, each group would make up its mind what was best for cohesion and survival according to its experience, and to produce theories which did not reflect social development in these terms was, in some way to him, beyond comprehension. His belief that concepts such as justice, liberty, right and so on had no meaning other than as expedients for social living is clearly shown by the answer which he gives to the question of whether Pilate was right to crucify Christ. To that question, the evangelical Christian Stephen was forced by his appreciation of social life to reply:

"Pilate's paramount duty was to preserve the peace in Palestine, to form the best judgment he could as to the means required for that purpose, and to act upon it when it was formed. Therefore, if and in so far as he believed, in good faith and on reasonable grounds, that what he did was necessary for the preservation of the peace in Palestine, he was right".[25]

If one compares this realistic assertion, in which Stephen could not possibly have taken any pleasure, with the tergivisations which more recent scholars have performed in a graceless effort to avoid accepting the awkward fact that to certain groups even genocide can be accounted not only legal but moral, the extent of his appreciation of the foundations of social and legal development cannot fail but to provoke a profound respect and a deserved admiration.

IV

Mill died shortly after the publication of Stephen's criticisms so that their debate was abruptly ended. Towards the end of the nineteen-fifties, however, the Report of the Wolfenden Committee on the law relating to homosexuality and prostitution sparked off a similar controversy between Lord Devlin and Professor Hart. In its report, the Wolfenden Committee did what Stephen declined to do and attempted to spell out the limits which the criminal law should not exceed, and their formulation echoed strongly the sentiments of Mill in the, by now, famous phrase: "there must remain a realm of private morality and immorality which is, in brief and crude terms, not the law's business".[26] It was this view which eventually attracted the criticisms of the then Sir Patrick Devlin in the 1959 Maccabaean Lecture to the British Academy, criticisms similar to, and grounded in the same perceptiveness of social development as, those of Sir James Fitzjames Stephen.[27] Lord Devlin has since repeated and expanded his remarks on that occasion.[28]

Devlin begins from a position which is identical to that of the new theory by holding that the criminal law, which was the original topic of debate, exists to protect society rather than the individual.[29] Likewise, the new theory holds this belief by saying that law interferes to avoid or overcome disruptions which would threaten the cohesion of the group and, as a consequence of this, the survival interests of the individuals. He is close to the new theory's position also inasmuch as he conceives of popular or public morality as being the shared moral values of the community and esteems these as being of great importance inasmuch as they are the cement which keeps society in one piece.[30] He does not, however, as does the new theory, base the group's judgement of right and wrong, good and evil, morality and immorality upon ideas of what respectively aids and hinders cohesion and survival, but this background can be read into his views credibly and without affecting their substance or force. Following from this view of a shared morality as a social necessity, he deduces that breaches of this morality cannot be lightly tolerated. He likens immorality to treason and sedition in that it is an attack upon an institution which helps to hold society together and, if tolerated, could lead to its disintegration. He refused to accept that there can be such a thing as private immorality any more than there can be an entity of private subversive activity.[31] In this, too, he is on all fours with the new theory and his views can be explained in its terms. It will be recalled that under the new theory, a group has to determine whether conduct hinders its goals or not. Conduct which hinders is forbidden by the survival precepts and stigmatized immoral. Immoral conduct is accordingly conduct which is harmful in that it hinders cohesion and survival. Such a definition does not allow of a concept of private immorality which is not the group's concern.

Devlin is also strong in his examples. He supposes that a man gets drunk every night and acknowledges that by doing so he is not really as effective a member of society as he would be if he practised sobriety. If everyone behaved this way, the group would be weakened considerably, and also seeing such behaviour go unchecked might well weaken the efficacy of the precepts regarding drunkeness.[32] Devlin is here close to what has been said earlier about the need to punish transgressors lest their example be followed and, in particular, the need to illustrate or symbolize the consequences of failing to uphold the survival precepts either upon individuals or upon the group as a whole. Here as elsewhere, Devlin shows that, like Stephen, he is close to the social realities, but here, too, again like Stephen, he shows that he has not fully grasped Mill's point, for Mill's principle would be the guiding precept of the shared morality in his utilitarian utopia, the precept which would be most highly prized as that which had to be observed if cohesion and survival were to be achieved.

The next question which faces Devlin, having postulated the importance of maintaining the shared morality, is just when that morality ought to be backed up by the law. Devlin's answer to this comes in two, somewhat unclear, stages.[33] The law, he considers, is entitled to interfere when the group disapproval of conduct considered immoral reaches the level of intolerance, indignation and disgust.[34] These words, as Devlin himself has acknowledged,[35] have given rise to much controversy - indeed, almost to intolerance, indignation and disgust. Professor Hart, in his criticisms, referred to them as the "concert pitch" of public condemnation.[36] However, if one examines what the new theory has to say about the moment when the law should interfere in immorality, their native common sense can be recognized. The new theory would set the threshold for legal intervention at the point where harmful conduct threatened or actually disrupted social cohesion. Immorality of the sort Devlin is discussing, namely sexual immorality, is unlikely to disrupt cohesion in itself but rather to provoke a disruptive dispute. If one then asks what are the likely early warning signals that disruption may ensue, the arousal of intolerance, indignation and disgust is far from being a bad answer. Devlin again comes close to the new theory because again he takes the reality of social life and dispute situations as he experienced them in legal and judicial practice as his starting point.

The second stage is marked by the question of whether the law should intervene in such situations. It has to be admitted that, as Professor Dworkin has noted,[37] although Devlin speaks of a balancing process and various other devices, he never really gets beyond saying that the law should intervene where intolerance, indignation and disgust are present. The same criterion is, therefore, apparently used twice at different stages, and Dworkin calls this Devlin's intellectual sleight of hand. All Devlin manages to say is that the "limits of tolerance shift",[38] and that the "boundary between the criminal law and the moral law is fixed by balancing in the case of each particular crime the pros and cons of legal enforcement".[39] These remarks clearly mirror the new theory's view that the question of what will be a crime must be answered from society to society, from time to time, and it is this view which leads Devlin to deny the possibility of a theoretical limit such as that provided by the Wolfenden Committee.[40] However, the new theory would accommodate a theoretical limit in a given society, accepted there according to the best-suited principle and subsequently ratified by the group's practice. Further than this, it agrees with Devlin on the impossibility of placing theoretical limitations upon legal development. The new theory is, however, able to provide a criterion to answer the question of when the law should actually enforce, and it is submitted that the criterion provided would not be unacceptable within the terms of Lord Devlin's argument. Devlin refers in his essay on Mill[41] to Professor Hart's comment that with regard to the crimes concerning abortion, homosexuality and euthanasia "the misery caused directly and indirectly by legal punishment outweighs any conceivable harm these practices may do".[42] "This", comments Devlin, "is the balancing process."[43] His meaning, which in all fairness is hardly clear, seems to be that the misery caused by punishment must be weighed against the harm to the social cements in deciding whether the law should punish practices which give rise to intolerance, indignation and disgust or not. If this is his meaning, then he is again on the verge of the new theory's criterion. The new theory states that the law only proscribes what the group regards as harmful conduct when the harm caused by intervening is less than that caused by allowing the behaviour to go unchecked. Thus, it is a question of whether the misery caused by the legal punishment will result in greater disruption, through protest, dissent and so on, than would result from allowing the intolerance, indignation and disgust felt at the vice to go uninstitutionalized. In other words, the possibility that the punishment might arouse those sentiments is not excluded. Where the punishment would cause more disruption, it should not be instituted; where its absence causes more, it must be imposed. Where either course causes disruption, there is clearly a bad division in the society which might lead to disintegration, for there is no consensus as to what is needed for cohesion and survival, no shared morality. Devlin's views on intolerance, indignation and disgust are not so maverick as they may at first blush appear, for these sentiments clearly show impending disruption. He gives religious persecution in past ages as an example of how this threshold has moved and aptly comments:

"Men could not tolerate a heretic so long as they believed that he and all those whom he perverted were doomed to an eternity of Hell".[44]

Add to this that they may have feared that they too would be punished if they failed to punish him, and one finds oneself in a world like that of the Ashanti.[45] Devlin's theory, like Stephen's and unlike Mill's because of its roots in social realities, is not limited to one category of group but covers the whole gamut of communal development.

As the point at which it is better for society to intervene than to tolerate the hindrance is one for each to determine for itself, the question remains to be answered of how that determination is to be made. The new theory would answer that this is something the group must either learn from experience or accept as a good enunciation by means of its best-suited principle. Devlin is content with the enunciation being made by the courts according to a split function. It is for the judges as <u>custos morum</u> to declare that conduct which is harmful is also criminal, and it is open for them to leave it to a jury as being representative of the members of the group to decide from case to case what is so harmful.[46] Provided that two things are remembered, this view is perfectly in tune with the new theory. These are, firstly, that this is just <u>a</u> solution and not <u>the</u> solution, and secondly, that the jury under this solution works, as it always does, as part of the best-suited procedure, but here not merely for solving disputes but also partly for enunciating. As part of the best-suited procedure, the jury's opinions, like those of the courts, have to be accepted and ratified by the group to be valid. Devlin is clearly aware of this. He thought the courts used the standard of the reasonable or right-minded man to state "principles which every right-minded person would accept as valid".[47] Thus, to Devlin's mind, the law-maker, whom the new theory regards as the best-suited persons or procedures, did not need the assistance of moral philosophers, but was rather concerned with "what is acceptable to the ordinary man, the man in the jury box, who might also be called the reasonable man or the right-minded man",[48] and far from searching for some advanced theory for an advanced society, the law-maker has to find an acceptable level for the society in which he operates. In Devlin's words: "What the lawmaker has to ascertain is not the true belief but the common belief." He goes as far as Stephen if not farther in recognizing that what one group considers proper, another may find abominable. He wrote:

"There are, have been, and will be bad laws, bad morals, and bad societies .... Unfortunately bad societies can live on bad morals as well as good societies on good ones."[49]

Here his closeness to the social reality which he is describing allows him to recognize the truth even when it is unpalatable, a task which more theoretical writers seem unable to perform. His is a clear recognition of the social fact that law has to be based on what is acceptable to the group, and that means the popular morality. "What is important is not the quality of the creed for the strength of the belief in it."[50] Devlin's criticisms of Mill, like Stephen's, are based largely on the great distance between the theory and what is needed to make it work. Without a knowledge of the necessary mechanisms, Mill's views are no more than wishful thinking and Devlin is not afraid to say so.[51] The notion of acceptance, a keystone in the new theory, is one of the realities which writers like Devlin cannot ignore in estimating theories of what law is and what it should be, and writers who sound this chord, whether they describe it as political feasibility[52] or external limits,[53] show a certain kinship with the new theory.[54]

V

Lord Devlin's Maccabaean Lecture provoked a reply from Professor Hart. Hart's critical morality is liberal in flavour and not unlike that espoused by John

Stuart Mill. The new theory would treat of Hart's critical morality by saying that he believed that the best point for cohesion and survival for law to enforce morals was where the immorality was other-regarding rather than self-regarding, with the exception of paternalistic intervention in relation to some self-regarding acts, such as using dangerous drugs. Hart, however, does not connect his critical morality with the underlying social goals described by the new theory, and accordingly, like Mill, his arguments fail to take into account the social mechanisms by which any changes along the lines he proposes would have to be put into operation. Here, no attempt will be made to describe Hart's criticisms or arguments or to assess them, other than so far as is necessary to show that they are alternatively weak or strong inasmuch as they deviate from or comply with the new theory.

Hart's failure to take into account the social realities when morals are enforced and to base his views upon them are clear from his first reply to Devlin made in a BBC Radio broadcast.[55] In it, he asked two questions, the terms of both of which illustrate the gap between theory and practice which weakens his views. The first of these asked "whether a practice which offends moral feeling is harmful, independently of its repercussions on the general moral code".[56] This question totally fails to appreciate that the judgement made by a group that a practice is immoral in itself means that it is regarded as harmful in that it is a hindrance to cohesion and survival, and that this is the sense in which the concept of harm has to be understood and measured in the context of deciding both whether a practice is immoral and whether the law should interfere. Hart is using 'harmful' to mean harmful according to his estimation, but this is unrealistic as a basis for judging whether the group should intervene. Hart fails to see that the group has to be persuaded to adopt his estimate of harm before his views can be accepted, but this stage is omitted because the social mechanisms are ignored. His second question of whether it is really true that failure to translate the item of general morality into criminal law will jeopardize the whole fabric of morality and so of society,[57] also fails to see that it doesn't have to be true for society to intervene, it only has to be believed by a sufficient section of the group to be true. Hart is again in the position of having to persuade the group that his belief is nearer the truth than theirs before his views can prosper, but this is, of course, omitted from the picture. The whole argument, therefore, turns upon Hart's inability to see that Devlin's ideas of what is so intolerable as to be the likely cause of disruption is closer to the true facts which determine social responses than Hart's intellectualist assertion that such criteria are "no adequate substitute for a reasoned estimate of the damage to the fabric of society likely to ensue".[58] The plain fact is that Devlin's trio of intolerance, indignation and disgust is closer to reality than Hart's "reasoned estimate", and until the former gives way to the latter, rational views as to when law should enforce morality are not so accurate as those which are acceptable to the reasonable or right-minded man, which mirror what actually occurs in societies at every stage of development and could include the rationalist view as one species of the genus. This is all due, of course, to the omission of the actual foundations for such developments from the liberal thesis.

Hart returned to the issue of the legal enforcement of morality in the Harry Camp Memorial Lectures which he gave at Stanford in 1962. There, Hart repeated the mistake mentioned above of saying that immorality can be other than harmful,[59] and also fell into an error concerning paternalism. He cited paternalism as a coherent policy for protecting people from themselves which was not due to the immorality of the act in question. As an example, he cited the sale of narcotics and spoke of it as being a strange description of the law forbidding their unrestricted sale to say of it that it checked the seller's immorality rather than it protected purchasers from making misguided choices.[60] If one accepts that a drug addict is a person who is unlikely to contribute to cohesion and survival and is also a bad example to the group, the immorality is then the harm in society's view done by the purchaser in opting to use narcotics, and the law has to decide whether preventing such use is more or less harmful than tolerating it. In other words, one is back with the same criteria. The liberal theory has to make an exception in these circumstances, as Hart acknowledged, again because it is one step away from the social realities. The new theory again fits the facts without adaptation largely because it takes the facts as its starting point. This same failing to take into account the basic needs of preserving cohesion by checking situations or conduct which will give rise to disruption or present a bad example to the group, that is, an example contradicting the survival precepts of the community, lies behind Hart's inability to make the most of a useful distinction he drew between immorality and indecency.[61] Whereas, as Hart says, sexual intercourse in public between husband and wife would be an affront to decency, in private it is not immoral. If Hart means to suggest that it would not be immoral even in public, it is submitted that he is mistaken about popular morality. However, homosexual conduct is immoral in private as well as indecent in public, notes Hart, but he argues that this is no reason to punish the private conduct as well as the public. In this, it is submitted, he fails to realize that the reason for the prohibitions are slightly different though judged by the same criteria, namely that in public such acts are so harmful as to be illegal because they would tend to disruption - as in the husband and wife case - while in private they are so harmful because the knowledge that they take place would set a bad example contrary to the group's survival precepts condemning such conduct as harmful, in both cases the harm being adjudged worse than that caused by legal intervention.[62] The same is true of Hart's blasphemy example. Blasphemy, he wrote, was once punishable _per se_, but is today only punishable if committed in an offensive or insulting manner. Clearly, it was earlier believed that divine favour would be lost to the group if the breach went unpunished, as with the Ashanti, while today this is not held and only the direct threat of disruption is thought sufficiently harmful to merit group interferences. The distinction between immorality and indecency has been useful then in showing up the confusion and does not affect the judgement which the group has to make; if conduct is immoral, the question is whether it is believed to be so dangerous that it is better for cohesion and survival to intervene, and in some cases the answer will depend on the manner in which the words are spoken or the context in which the conduct is performed. The questions, however, remain the same.

It is important to stress that the second question turns on what the group believes is sufficiently dangerous to warrant intervention and not on what is so dangerous. Everything turns upon the group belief. Hart misses this in some of his criticisms of Devlin. He says of Devlin that:

"it is not at all clear that for him the statement that

immorality jeopardizes or weakens society is a statement of empirical fact. It seems sometimes to be an *a priori* assumption, and sometimes a necessary truth and a very odd one."[63]

Later, Hart states categorically that:

"There is no evidence that the preservation of a society requires the enforcement of its morality as such."[64]

In both statements, Hart refers to what as a fact jeopardizes or preserves society, whereas the opinion on which morality and law are formed is what the group believes jeopardizes or preserves its cohesion. This again shows how Hart, unlike Devlin and Stephen whom he criticizes, does not take social reality as the corner-stone of his arguments. For Hart and Mill to prevail with a community, they must succeed in changing these beliefs. Until then, the positive morality of the group will be immune not so much to criticism[65] as to any significant change. It is to show how important belief is that Stephen and Devlin heaped up the examples of law enforcing morality. These examples illustrate the basis upon which a community acts, but Hart does not see this because he leaves the basis out of the picture. The basis is what is "not apparent to the rationalist philosopher."[66]

VI

It has been the purpose of this chapter to show that according to the new theory, the question of whether the law should enforce morality is always answerable in any society according to the beliefs of the group in answering the two questions.

(1) Is a particular conduct a hindrance to cohesion and survival? If it is, it is harmful and will be condemned by communal opinion as immoral.

(2) Is it so harmful that it is better for cohesion and survival to interfere to prevent it disrupting cohesion either directly or indirectly, or would intervention be more harmful than the conduct? If it is so harmful that intervention is the lesser of the two evils, the conduct will be forbidden by law, while otherwise it will be condemned as immoral only.

These are the criteria by which the issue is always judged.[67] The debates between Mill and Stephen, and Hart and Devlin have been examined solely to show how close to or far from the criteria of the new theory

Figure 4: Criteria and process for deciding whether conduct is unlawful.

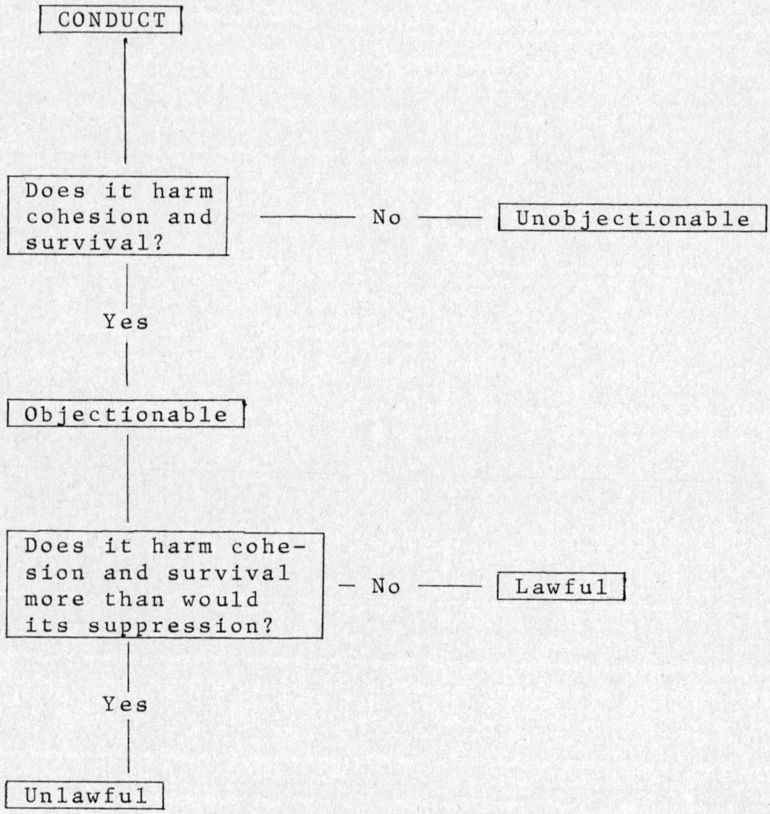

earlier writers have been. It is very interesting to note that Stephen and Devlin, both judges and as such part of a best-suited mechanism, were consistently nearer to the social realities on which the new theory and its criteria are based than Mill and Hart. Nevertheless, even the liberal theories of Mill and Hart can be accommodated within the terms of the new theory but require filling out to establish their undeclared bases. The new theory, therefore, again succeeds in establishing empirical criteria for establishing both the structure of social development and the shape of theories concerning it.

****

1. Hoebel, 253 - Postulate IV, 254 - Postulate XV.
2. Vide, *supra*, p.142-4.
3. B. Mitchell, *Law, Morality, and Religion in a Secular Society*, 1.
4. Mill, 72-3.
5. Vide, *Roth* v. *U.S.* (1957) 354 U.S. 476.
6. Public Order Act, 1936 s.5.
7. Mill, 131-2.
8. Vide, *Novels*, 77 Cap. 1 and 141.
9. Mill, 136.
10. *Ibid*., 138.
11. *Ibid*., 146.
12. *Ibid*., 149.
13. J.F. Stephen, *Liberty, Equality, Fraternity*, 103.
14. *Ibid*., 79, 105.
15. *Ibid*., 90.
16. *Ibid*., 159.
17. *Ibid*., 135.
18. *Ibid*., 68.
19. *Ibid*., 85.
20. *Ibid*., 86.
21. *Ibid*., 162. Cf. A. Watson, *The Nature of Law*, 97-8.
22. *Ibid*., 185.
23. *Ibid*., 186-7.
24. *Ibid*., 192.
25. *Ibid*., 110.
26. Report of the Committee on Homosexual Offences and Prostitution (Cmd. 247) (1957), para. 62.
27. As Hart recognized; vide, Hart, *LLM*, 16.
28. Vide, Devlin, passim.

29. Devlin, 6.
30. *Ibid*., 10.
31. *Ibid*., 13-4.
32. *Ibid*., 111.
33. Vide, R.M. Dworkin, *Taking Rights Seriously*, 244 on the issue of unclarity.
34. Devlin, 17.
35. Devlin, viii and 17 n.
36. Hart, "Immorality and Treason" in R.M. Dworkin (Ed.), *The Philosophy of Law*, 84.
37. R.M. Dworkin, *Taking Rights Seriously*, 244-6.
38. Devlin, 18.
39. *Ibid*., 22.
40. *Ibid*., 118.
41. *Ibid*., 117.
42. Hart, *LLM*, Preface.
43. Devlin, 117.
44. *Ibid*., 119.
45. Vide, *supra*, chapter 4.
46. On the jury and the death penalty, vide A. Bickel, *The Supreme Court and the Idea of Progress*, 74-5.
47. Devlin, 15.
48. *Ibid*., 90.
49. *Ibid*., 94.
50. *Ibid*., 114.
51. *Ibid*., 123 and 126.
52. Dworkin, *op.cit*., 245.
53. Vide, A.V. Dicey, *An Introduction to the Study of the Law of the Constitution*, 76-7.
54. Cf. the notion of *consensus universel*, vide, A. Giddens, *Durkheim*, 22 and 25-6.
55. "Immorality and Treason", *loc.cit*., n. 36 supra.
56. *Ibid*., 86.
57. *Ibid*., 85.
58. *Ibid*., 86.
59. Hart, *LLM*, 36.
60. *Ibid*., 31-3.
61. *Ibid*., 43-6.
62. *Ibid*., 48-9.
63. *Ibid*., 50.
64. *Ibid*., 82.
65. *Ibid*., 80.
66. *Ibid*., 28-9.
67. For a diagrammatic representation, vide Fig. 4.

CHAPTER SEVEN

THE NATURE OF CIVIL DISOBEDIENCE

I

The new theory considers that individuals form themselves into groups in order to survive, and that they thus consider it important that the groups so formed should cohere. As a result of these needs to cohere and survive, they cannot remain neutral to any conduct or events, but have to classify conduct and occurrences as either being a hindrance to the achievement of these goals or as not being a hindrance. If conduct is classified as being a hindrance, the group then has to make a further choice. It has to decide whether to condemn the conduct only, but not to interfere with it otherwise, is better for cohesion and survival than interfering by punishing, preventing or solving the dispute or disruption. In making these classifications and choices, the group will formulate precepts for cohesion and survival, and also rules for solving and avoiding disputes and dealing with disruptions. These precepts and rules will either emerge from the practice of the group in such situations or will be enunciated according to the group's best-suited principle, which itself will emerge from practice. In both cases, the precepts have to be accepted by the group and ratified by application. This is particularly the case with the best-suited principle's enunciations. For such precepts to be valid as laws of the group, they have to be accepted as valid by a sufficient number of the members of the group. What is a sufficient number is always an empirical question. Some members may accept an enunciation while others may not. The reason for rejection may be that the content of the precept is considered by them as being a hindrance rather than a help to cohesion and survival, or it may be that they disagree with the policy which the group has adopted in deciding what is a hindrance or what is the correct point at which to interfere with harmful behaviour. The first kind of rejection is exemplified by those who, like Radbruch, were unable to accept the precepts enunciated by the Nazi regime in Germany; the latter by the doubts expressed by Hart and Mill concerning the enforcement of morals. However, provided that a sufficient number of group members have accepted the precepts, the new theory does not withhold from those precepts the title of valid laws of the group.

This leaves the non-acceptors in a somewhat awkward position. Having become members of the group to ensure their survival, they now find that the precepts of the group, according to their judgement, do not advance that goal or perhaps its precursor, cohesion. Their awkward position also contains an awkward question, for they must clearly ask themselves what to do in such a situation.

There are several answers they could arrive at in this situation. Firstly, it is possible that whilst they believe themselves that the course indicated is not the best for cohesion and survival, they may have a stronger belief that the best-suited persons in the group's judgement are the best-suited persons in their judgement too to enunciate the correct survival principles and have a better judgement than they do. Accordingly they may be prepared to reject their own beliefs and accept the enunciations of the best-suited persons. This is really a form of acceptance. Secondly, it is possible that although they believe the precept to be bad for cohesion and survival, they consider it worse to attempt to reject or disobey an enunciation obtained according to the best-suited principle. Accordingly, they will accept the bad precept as valid while doing everything in their power to have it reversed if they consider that such moves are less harmful than just allowing the precept to stand. Again, this is a form of acceptance, but unlike the first it introduces an important element into the picture, namely, that of balance. It is one which has been met previously in other contexts. The dissenters have to decide two questions: whether to obey or disobey, and secondly, if to obey, whether to protest at the precept to get it changed. Both questions involve balancing the relative dangers to cohesion and survival involved in either course, and the answer will be the course deemed least harmful to the attainment of those goals. As individuals, survival issues will tend to predominate over cohesion issues if a clash should occur, unless a high degree of altruism is present in the person posing himself these admittedly difficulty questions.

The third solution to the problem is to decide to reject the enunciation as so bad that it is less harmful to cohesion and survival to disobey it than to obey it. This is the alternative answer to that given in the second solution. This would clearly present a challenge to the best-suited principle of the group stronger even than the criticism of it involved if mere protest were made at an accepted precept.[1] While protest at a precept indicates that the best-suited persons may not be producing the very best in survival precepts, it does not involve as does the third solution the judgement that the enunciation is more harmful than the disruption caused by disobedience.

The fourth solution may be regarded as an extreme form of the third. The dissenters may regard the enunciation as so harmful that they not only reject its validity but also the validity of the best-suited principle according to which it was produced. This solution contains the verdict that a process capable of producing such an harmful enunciation cannot be regarded as the best-suited method of obtaining the survival principles. This obviously is the most serious challenge to the group's best-suited principle. In all four solutions, two issues will influence the solutions which the dissenters adopt, namely the relative strength of the best-suited principle in question and the degree of harm to cohesion and survival which the bad enunciation is regarded as causing.[2] It will be seen that these were the issues which influenced the group acceptance of enunciations as described in chapter five. Thus, if the dissident has a high opinion of the best-suited method, he may respect its judgement more than his own, while if its status in his eyes is weaker he may obey it only because he judges this less harmful than disobeying, perhaps without even protesting. He may, however, decide to disobey, and if his opinion of the best-suited method is very low, he may reject it altogether. An example of free rejection of enunciations because of a low regard for the authority of best-suited methods as compared with individual judgement is the opinions of Henry David Thoreau.[3] According to Thoreau, dissidents worth their salt should not "wait until they constitute a majority of one before they suffer the right to prevail through them. I think it is enough if they have God on their side without waiting for that other one. Moreover any man more right than his neighbour constitutes a majority of one already."[4]

If the best-suited principle is weak in the eyes of the dissidents or the harm very great, they may decide to reject the best-suited mechanism. This is serious because the group still accepts the mechanism as being best-suited. There is, therefore, no possibility of a change in the best-suited principle other than by persuading the group to reject it or by actually attempting to replace it. Either way, a revolution of sorts has to be advocated or implemented, and its viability will depend upon the relative strengths of the orthodox members of the group who support the best-suited persons and the dissident body who do not. If, on the other hand, it is the third solution which is adopted, that of disobeying the particular enunciation while not rejecting the best-suited principle itself, precepts will still be broken. Thus, if the enunciation demands that black people be segregated from white people, but the dissidents regard this as so harmful that they cannot obey, they may still associate with people of the other colour group. Similarly, if a precept demands that a person enlists in the army, if that person regards this as sufficiently harmful, he may refuse to comply. The problem is somewhat more acute if the precept is not directed at the dissidents so that they could break it themselves. In such circumstances the most they can do is protest at the precept if they consider it harmful enough, but they may decide to break other precepts as part of their protest. Thus, those who dissented from Britain's policy of developing nuclear armaments protested by obstructing the highway. Such disobedience to group precepts is termed civil disobedience. Where the precept broken is the one to which objection is taken, the disobedience is said to be direct; when it is not that, but another precept which is broken, it is said to be indirect civil disobedience. Both kinds have this much in common. They both challenge the correctness of an enunciation made according to the group's best-suited principle and as such are a challenge to the authority of that principle.[5] The challenge may be intended to influence the best-suited persons or members of the group generally in their attitude to the enunciation, but there will always be a challenge and the fact that the best-suited principle is involved is key to understanding

Figure 5 : Criteria for determining upon Civil Disobedience and for whether it should be punished.

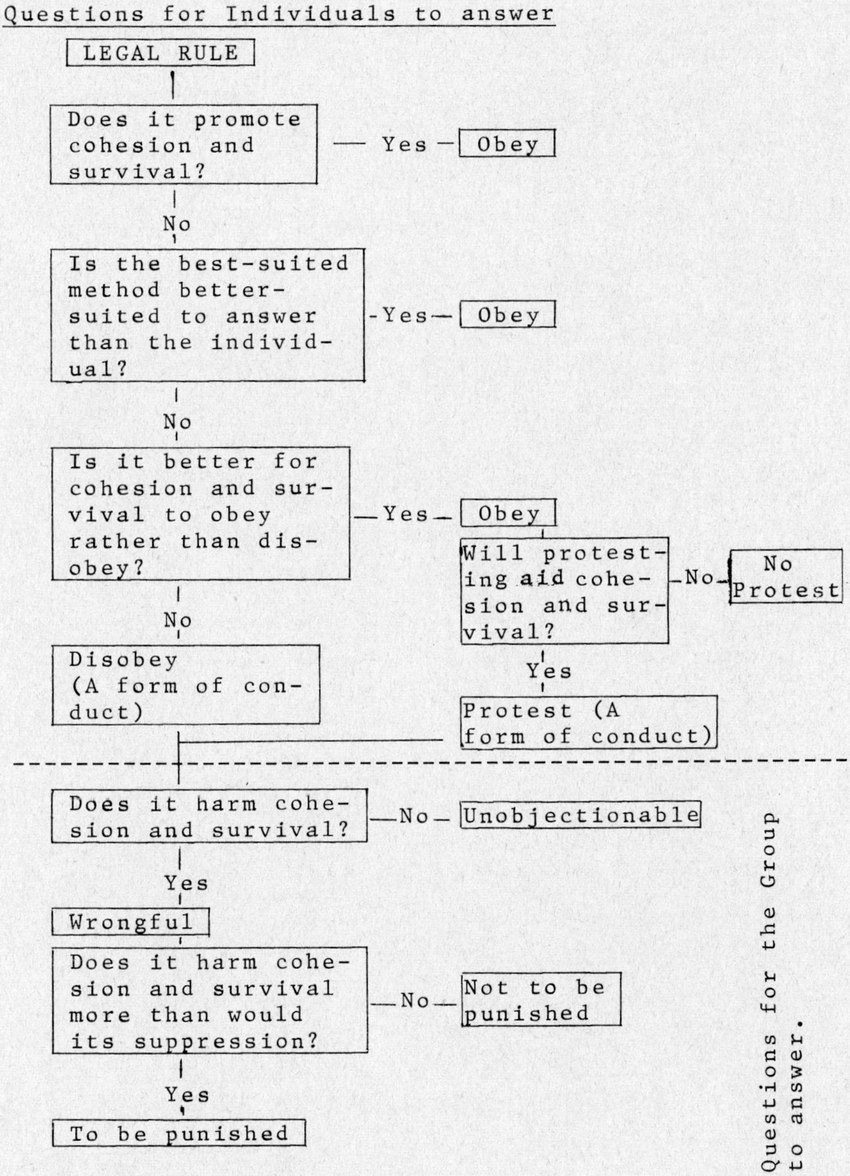

the response which civil disobedience may engender.

II

The seriousness with which any challenge to the best-suited principle of the group or its authority may be viewed is apparent if one recalls that the principle is meant to produce the precepts which will best lead the group along the path to cohesion and survival. To bring low the mechanism for producing such important information by criticism or attack can clearly be expected to give rise to resentment and possible retaliation. This fact has already been described in chapter four when it was recounted how in the early stages of social development almost every breach of a survival precept would lead to the transgressor losing all his rights in the group, being declared outlaw, and being hunted down and killed like a wild animal. In that chapter, it was recorded that severe penalties were inflicted too for interferences or criticisms of the best-suited principle of the group, or its personnel. Almost any act or word which would derogate from the authority of the best-suited person might be punished with death or severe mutilation. Thus, even to be a better gardener than the Trobriand chief was a capital offence,[6] and it was recorded how in the mediaeval township of Brünn, to criticize the lay judges or Schöffen was so serious that as a punishment the offender was nailed to a wooden stake by his tongue, and given a knife with which to release himself.[7] In the Bavarian Criminal Code of 1751, any contempt of the ruler, whether actual or apparent, was capital,[8] and even last century, a Professor Zachariae was almost punished for criticizing a supreme court decision.[9] All these acts challenge the authority of the group's best-suited persons and attract punishment accordingly, because the disruption caused by punishing is regarded as less harmful than the risk involved in the challenge of criticism. However, it is possible for a group to distinguish among such harmful acts and to reserve its strictest penalties only for the most harmful conduct. Thus, only those acts which are considered to threaten the existence of the best-suited person or principle will be classified as treason.

However, different societies at different times will vary in their judgement of what is so serious as to endanger the very existence of the best-suited mechanism. Thus, in ancient Rome virtually any criticism of the magistrates amounted to the crime of *majestas* and was punished accordingly. This attitude was to be found also in the laws of France under the *ancien régime*, where any undermining of the royal authority amounted to *lèse majesté* in the second degree.[10] Here, however, a distinction had been taken inasmuch as *lèse majesté* was divided into two degrees. The first degree comprised the more serious wrongs of attempts upon the life of the Prince, his children or those in succession to the throne, and attacks upon the State by leagues or associations. Similarly, in England, by the seventeenth century it was settled that only those matters mentioned in the Statute of Treasons of 1352 could amount to treasonable conduct, but criticism of the government might still be treated as seditious libel. Thus, in 1684, Sir Samuel Barnardiston was prosecuted for remarks passed in a private letter to a friend.[11] The question whether such distinctions can be taken by a group is one which has to be answered in relation to criteria which will be discussed shortly. The point which is made here is that the distinction turns upon the motive of the offenders. If they seek to overthrow the current best-suited principle of the group, they are involved in treason or sedition, while if all they reject is a portion of the enunciations made by the best-suited principle, then their conduct is better described as civil disobedience. Civil disobedience differs from ordinary crimes on the other hand in that ordinary crimes are committed so that an individual's chances of survival are increased regardless of the interests of the group, whereas the breach involved in an act of civil disobedience is meant to put the group back onto the path of cohesion and survival, while following the enunciated precept would not be so good at doing this. Civil disobedience then is a questioning of whether an enunciation or enunciations are the best course for cohesion and survival, and is different from ordinary crime in that it does not subjugate group interests to those of the offender, and from treason and sedition in that it does not necessarily threaten the authority or existence of the best-suited principle. It will be seen, however, that just how a particular piece of conduct is classified will vary according to the society and the times, and the important judgement will be that of the group, not an individual, a sub-group or that of outsiders. In this, the issue is again similar to that of whether a law is moral, discussed in chapter five.

III

If, having considered the various questions outlined earlier as to the harmfulness of the precept, an individual or group of individuals decides that the third solution, that of disobeying the precept, is required, then he or it embarks upon a course of civil disobedience. It is important to understand the significance of such conduct. If the disobedience is direct, that is, if the precept considered harmful is itself broken, then the individual concerned is taking it upon himself to state that the precept which the group accepts as being good for cohesion and survival and should be followed for that reason, is in his opinion so harmful to those ends that it should not be followed. He is saying in other words that disputes and disruptions are more likely to be caused by the precept's presence than by its absence. His breaking of the precept is, therefore, in the nature of a demonstration that disintegration or the threat of it will not follow from the breach, and that accordingly cohesion and survival do not depend upon this precept. His act of civil disobedience is, therefore a symbolic act, for if signs of disintegration do not follow from the breach, then his disobedience demonstrates what life would be like without the precept, and also its redundancy if no threat of disintegration follows its being transgressed. He also demonstrates, and this is a serious part of the issue, that the best-suited principle has, on this one occasion at least, not produced the correct survival precept.

A similar symbolism exists in the case of indirect civil disobedience, that is, where the precept objected to cannot itself be broken by the dissidents, so they break another as a protest against it. In this case, a precept is broken which is not thought superfluous so that a risk of disruption and disintegration is intended. However, the reason for this risk occurring is clearly the existence of the offensive precept, so that the existence of this precept, which should aid the twin social goals of cohesion and survival, has in fact provoked a disruption and the attendant risk of disintegration. Thus, the disobedience demonstrates that the precept is bad rather than good for survival, and again points to the best-suited principle having failed to deliver the correct goods on that particular occasion, that is, when it enunciated the offensive precept. In both cases, therefore, whether the civil disobedience is direct or indirect, the breaches can be seen to be symbols of the failure of the precept in question to fulfil its purpose of promoting cohesion and survival. The claim has in fact been made in court that disobedience is a form of speech, namely symbolic speech,[12] and it can be seen to be justified.

If the dissident is aiming to demonstrate that the best-suited person or procedure is wrong on this occasion, he is, however, equally asserting that on this occasion his own judgement is better than that of the best-suited mechanism. As to what the group will do about his disobedience, everything can be said to turn upon its reaction to this aspect of his conduct. The dissident is saying that the enunciation in question does not lead to cohesion and survival. It may be that there exist within the corpus of the group's survival precepts some standards by which the offensive enunciation can be measured to see if it is a hindrance rather than a help to the group's aims. If there is a Bill of Rights or some other source of fundamental rights which the precept is thought to offend against, then clearly the courts, using the metagame best-suited principle, will be able to determine the issue.[13] Even if there is no such 'strongbox', the courts may be prepared to listen to the plea that the precept in question is not valid as it does not further the purpose of the group. This would necessitate the court taking the line that Coke described in <u>Dr. Bonham's Case</u>,[14] and a particular metagame best-suited principle. However, the existence of widespread disobedience may, of course, be recognized as indicating that the external limits of the best-suited method's credibility are being reached, although while a sufficient number accept and ratify the enunciations, they will not be surpassed. Where the precept is upheld, it will be because the group accepts it as being the correct principle for cohesion and survival and this will give rise to the question of what is to be done to the well-meaning but misguided dissidents who believed they had a better course of action. All these judgements of misguidedness or wrongness are, of course, the group's; circumstances may yet prove the dissidents were correct.

To determine the attitude of the group to civil disobedience, two questions have to be asked. Firstly, it must be asked whether the group considers it harmful to cohesion and survival that individuals should disobey the enunciations of its best-suited persons or procedures. If the group were to accept that its best-suited method was not infallible and take a Mill-like view of criticism, even of a symbolic nature, it might not consider it harmful. If, on the other hand, it thought that such disobedience set a bad example, or weakened the authority of a best-suited principle which was worth preserving, then it would judge it harmful as a hindrance to cohesion and survival. If it is adjudged harmful, then the second question relates to whether it should be condemned but not punished, or punished as well. Again the question here is whether the harm to cohesion and survival caused by the disobedience is worse than that which will be done by inflicting punishment. The bad example issue will clearly be a matter of importance here, and is often cited in the form of asking what sort of society would result if everyone were allowed to break laws with which they disagreed. It can be seen that these two questions are the same as those described in chapter six in discussing when the morality of a group should be enforced by its law. They are likewise the criteria which determine the response of a group to the issue of what should be done about civil disobedience. This issue is again, then, one which cannot safely be divorced from the underlying social goals which the precepts in question are designed to serve.

IV

One of the problems that has been mentioned from time to time throughout this book is again attendant to this discussion. Individuals are not infallible and even though they think long and hard about the correctness of a precept, their ultimate decision concerning it may be erroneous. Inasmuch as civil disobedience involves acting upon such decisions, it involves the possibility of error. Indeed, error is the basis of the disobedience, for if the group was not believed to be wrong, no question of disobedience would arise. Clearly, however, the group may decide, through its deciding agencies, that the dissidents are wrong in their beliefs and this may mean that their disobedience is adjudged by the group as being harmful to cohesion and survival. This, of course, means that they can be treated as people who harm the group's aims, but this does not mean that the fact that they believed that they were furthering them has to be left out of account. In deciding whether the harm of disobedience is greater or less than the harm of punishing dissidents moved by loyalty to the group's aims, the sincerity and possibly the reasonableness of their motivations and opinions may be taken into account.

Whether they are taken into account, and what effect they have if they are, depends upon the same criterion, however. The question facing the group is always whether it is better for cohesion and survival to tolerate the civil disobedience than to punish it. Different groups and different times will assess the situation in different ways, but the criterion remains constant.

Two further issues are so frequently brought up in discussions concerning civil disobedience that the topic cannot be left without some reference being made to them in the light of the new theory. The first of these concerns the position of civil disobedience in a democratic society. Some believe that the form of government can influence the answer given to the question of whether civil disobedience is justifiable. The new theory makes no concessions to the form of government which exists in a society. Its criteria hold for all manner of groups and forms of governmental organization. When the individual is presented with the problem of being unable to accept a precept of his group, the form of government which the group enjoys will, of course, influence his answers to the questions he has to pose in determining his course of conduct, such as whether obedience will cause more harm than good, and whether protest will aid rather than hinder cohesion and survival. The form of government which the group enjoys will also influence the answer which the group provides to the question of whether it is more harmful to punish rather than tolerate dissent of this or any sort. However, the form of government only influences the answers which individuals and groups give to the questions. The questions themselves based upon the new theory are what are important to understanding the nature of civil disobedience and responses to it. The point is perhaps best answered by saying clearly that, according to the new theory, it is perfectly possible for an individual to believe that a democratically determined precept is so bad and so wrong that it has to be disobeyed, and also possible for a democratic group to tolerate such conduct. Everything depends upon the answers to the fixed questions.

The second issue which is of general concern to those who have pondered and discussed the topic is whether civil disobedience can ever justifiably involve violence. Some writers have proscribed violence absolutely, while others are less sure. Again, the new theory demands that the criteria for determining whether violent disobedience is called for should be the same as those generally employed. In deciding what form the disobedience should take, the question always involves balancing the harm to be avoided against the harm which the disobedience will cause. The conduct employed should always be believed to be less harmful than that against which it protests. If the harm which the dissidents seek to prevent is regarded as so severe that it outweighs the harm done to cohesion by violence to property or persons, or even through killing or maiming, they may decide to use such violence. The situation will stand comparison with that where individuals are permitted to use reasonable force in the prevention of crime, and allowed to kill in self-defence of their right to life. In the context of civil disobedience, the issue is one which individuals have to decide, and it is their judgements which will dictate the conduct and can be justified according to the same criteria, regardless of how wrong or repugnant their conclusions may seem to others. Likewise, of course, the group will decide whether violent disobedience of this sort can be justified according to the same criteria as it uses to consider non-violent disobedience. It will make its decisions according to its determination of whether the harm done by the dissidents is more or less severe than that which suppression would entail.

V

Many views and theories have been expressed concerning whether civil disobedience is ever justifiable and whether it should ever be tolerated.[15] It is not proposed to examine these theories as this would be a long and unnecessary process. It is expected that readers have by now come to understand the process by which theories are tested in the light of the criteria set out by the new theory, and it is assumed that having seen various views tested in the last two chapters, they can now safely be left to test such discussions for themselves. In testing theories of civil disobedience, it should be borne in mind that the question of whether an individual should indulge in civil disobedience is a separate question from what the group should do about such disobedience. The first is a question for the individual to answer, as was the question in chapter five, and depends upon whether he can accept a precept, and if not whether a contemplated course is regarded by him as being more or less harmful to the interests of the group than the injury he believes is done to them by the objectionable precept, the test here being very similar to that which determines whether a precept can be accepted by a sufficient number of group members to be law. The second is a question for the group, in this case the same as that posed in chapter six concerning the enforcement of morals, although it will be answered by its best-suited principle subject to acceptance and ratification, and depends on whether it believes disobedience of the sort involved to be harmful and, if so, whether it judges it more harmful than community intervention and perhaps punishment. It should be borne in mind, too, that this last decision, inasmuch as it is subject to acceptance and ratification, may be accepted by a sufficient number to be a valid precept but rejected by others so that further civil disobedience may result. This possibility may influence the group's answer to the question of what to do about civil disobedience. These then are the criteria which should be used in testing rival theories. They are dictated by the new theory and based on the social realities of the situations in which civil disobedience is contemplated. Other theories must stand or fall according to the social realities embodied in these standards.

****

1. Cf. T.H. Green, Lectures on the Principles of Political Obligation (1895), 120.
2. For a diagrammatic representation, vide Fig. 5.
3. Vide, H.D. Thoreau, "Civil Disobedience" in H.A. Bedau (Ed.) Civil Disobedience: Theory and Practice (1969).
4. Quoted in G. Marshall, Constitutional Theory, 206.
5. Cf. A. Watson, The Nature of Law, 128.
6. Hoebel, 196.
7. CLH VI, 106.
8. Ibid., 248.
9. Ibid., 373-4.
10. Ibid., 281.
11. Vide, J.F. Stephen, A History of the Criminal Law of England (1883), ii 313-4; and 9 State Trials 1334.
12. Vide, U.S. v. O'Brien (1968) 391 U.S. 367.
13. Cf. R.M. Dworkin, Taking Rights Seriously, 188-93 and 216.

14. (1610) 8 Co. Rep. 118a.
15. An example of approved tolerance is the provision for conscientious objection on conscription in wartime.

CONCLUSION

This work has been an attempt to explain the nature of law. The object of the book has been to produce a theory of law which explains the nature of the phenomenon, inasmuch as, although it is a theory, it is not divorced from, but is descriptive of, the social reality of law as it is experienced and has been experienced in the world. In order to achieve this end, the point chosen at which to start was the recognition of the fact that law is a phantasy, and that it is as a phantasy that law exists as a social reality, namely as a social phantasy system. From this primary observation of the nature of law, it was then possible to progress to an examination of legal rules to discover their nature. This was done using models which had been constructed to explain other phantasy systems which, being phantasy systems, had a certain kinship with law. The validity of this method was constantly checked by not allowing the discussion to stray from the reality of actual legal rules as they are found in actual legal systems. The theory and the facts were never allowed to become separated.

The function of legal rules also came to light in this way, being to solve disputes which threatened disruption at a level at which the disruption was avoided. This revealed the connection of law with the twin social goals of cohesion and survival. From this it was possible to explain the nature of legal validity in terms of acceptance and ratification, and from this in turn the very important best-suited principle was deduced by the theory and confirmed by the social facts. This vantage point was then used to examine certain problems concerning the operation of legal systems and the new theory was able to set out criteria which reduced these problems to a series of empirical questions to be answered by individual groups in particular circumstances. The vantage point was also used to discover the nature of legal concepts and the nature of legal systems. In particular, the development of legal systems could be seen to follow a certain pattern, again turning on the answers to certain questions set according to the criteria suggested by the new theory, so that the criteria for development obtained by organizing the rationally constructed theory around the known facts concerning legal systems could be used to describe and determine the progress of legal systems in any form of society whether primitive or complex. Once this stage was reached, the theory was complete and its merits were then tested by seeing how it dealt with three traditional problems of jurisprudence, namely those concerning the morality of law, the enforcement of morals, and civil disobedience. Again, the theory was able to produce criteria which reduced these problems to series of empirical questions for each society to answer at a given moment of time in the context of its beliefs and needs, or for individual members of such societies to answer by their lights. All through the work, therefore, the emphasis has been on producing a theory which is not only satisfying as a theory, but will also explain the nature of law as law is found in any and every society.

The point about keeping in touch with the social realities has been laboured because it is believed that too many theories fail to do this. It is a sad fact that some do not even try to do it, and one can almost sense a belief that historical and comparative evidence about legal systems is not really relevant and should be excluded at all costs. In large measure, this attitude accounts for the supremacy which legal philosophy now enjoys in the realm of jurisprudence. To some, jurisprudence is legal philosophy. It is the underlying conviction of this book, however, that legal philosophy is but one branch of jurisprudence and that the latter stands to the former as Pitt to Addington and London to Paddington.

When during last century, Sir Henry Maine held the chair in jurisprudence at Oxford, his official title was Corpus Christi Professor of Historical and Comparative Jurisprudence. This designation emphasizes that jurisprudence is devoted to the study and elucidation of legal institutions by means of more than just the techniques of philosophy, but that the disciplines of historical and comparative research also have a role to play. With regret, but without any great injustice, it must be reported that since the death of Sir Paul Vinogradoff in 1925, the historical and comparative aspects of the chair have been sadly neglected. Today, it is merely the Chair of Jurisprudence, and the philosophical technique holds sway. This is not to decry from the fact that the philosophical technique has contributed vastly to the understanding of law and legal institutions. One has only to mention Professor Hart's The Concept of Law to substantiate this fact. Hart's work is a masterpiece of philosophical jurisprudence to which all who subsequently write within the field must acknowledge a considerable debt. Much of the present work began as the result of studying closely certain aspects of Hart's theory. However, although Hart described his book as an essay in descriptive sociology, there is but little attempt in his work to link his theory to the corpus of known facts about law and legal systems, other than to those very close at hand. The sorry result is that, although a satisfying theory of law emerges, the values of the wider aspects of jurisprudence are lost. Such has been the emphasis of the philosophical aspect of the subject that some law schools have, perhaps unwittingly, acknowledged the demise of the comparative and historical technique by renaming their courses in jurisprudence as 'legal philosophy', which is as lamentably unfortunate as it is commendably accurate.

It is believed that, despite the value of the philosophical contributions, this shift has been to the detriment of jurisprudence and legal thinking generally, and that it should be checked. Only by taking into account the historical and comparative techniques can really accurate contributions to thinking about law and legal institutions be made. Jurisprudence involves all of the philosophical, the historical and the comparative techniques, each aspect complementing the others and enriching the overall picture presented. It is also believed that the failure to achieve this balance has been responsible for the growth of alternative methods of studying legal phenomena, to be found masquerading under a plethora of names, but all of which properly belong within the close of jurisprudence.

Sir Henry Maine clearly believed that a wide perspective was needed if legal theory was to be of value. He expressed this view in his classic work, Ancient Law, first published over a century ago in 1861. Many of the criticisms he made then concerning the failure of theorists to keep in touch with the social realities are still very much in point today, and he too seems to have believed that under superficial differences, the mechanisms of law were the same in all societies. The passage in which these things emerge is worth quoting in full.

"There is such wide-spread dissatisfaction with existing theories of jurisprudence, and so general a conviction that they do not really solve the questions they pretend to dispose of, as to justify the suspicion that some line of inquiry, necessary to a perfect result, has been incompletely followed or altogether omitted by their authors. And indeed there is one remarkable omission with which all these speculations are chargeable, except perhaps those of Montesquieu. They take no account of what law has actually been at epochs remote from the particular period at which they made their appearance. Their originators carefully observed the institutions of their own age and civilization, and those of other ages and civilizations with which they had some degree of intellectual sympathy, but, when they turned their attention to archaic states of society which exhibited much superficial difference from their own, they uniformly ceased to observe and began guessing. The mistake which they committed is therefore analogous to the error of one who, in investigating the laws of the material universe, should commence by contemplating the existing physical world as a whole, instead of beginning with the particles which are its simplest ingredients. One does not certainly see why such a scientific solecism should be more defensible in jurisprudence than in any other region of thought. It would seem antecedently that we ought to commence with the simplest social forms in a state as near as possible to their rudimentary condition. In other words, if we followed the course usual in such inquiries, we should penetrate as far up as we could in the history of primitive societies. The phenomena which early societies present us with are not easy at first to understand, but the difficulty of grappling with them bears no proportion to the perplexities which beset us in considering the baffling entanglement of modern social organisation. It is a difficulty arising from their strangeness and uncouthness, not from their number and complexity. One does not readily get over the surprise which they occasion when looked at from a modern point of view; but when that is surmounted they are few enough and simple enough. But, even if they gave more trouble than they do, no pains would be wasted in ascertaining the germs out of which has assuredly been unfolded every form of moral restraint which controls our actions and shapes our conduct at the present moment."[1]

No finer example of an exponent of the balance required between the philosophical, historical and comparative aspects of jurisprudence could be given than that of Sir Henry Maine. This work is intended to be a humble call for a return to this great tradition of jurisprudence, particularly in the light of the great advances in the study of human social life which have been made since Maine first wrote. If that call is answered, it is confidently believed that jurisprudence will be enriched, and the work here presented will not have been in vain.

****

1. Maine, AL, 136-7.

BIBLIOGRAPHY

Austin, J.L., Philosophical Papers (2nd Ed., Oxford, 1970).

Bickel, Alexander M., The Supreme Court and the Idea of Progress (New York, 1970).

Cardozo, Benjamin J., The Nature of the Judicial Process (New Haven, 1921).

Continental Legal History Series (New York, 1912).

Culler, Jonathan Saussure (Glasgow, 1976).

D'Entrèves, A.P., Natural Law (2nd Ed., London, 1970).

Derrett, J. Duncan M. (Ed.), An Introduction to Legal Systems (London, 1968).

Devlin, Patrick The Enforcement of Morals (Oxford, 1965).

Diamond, A.S., The Evolution of Law and Order.

Diamond, A.S., Primitive Law: Past and Present (3rd Ed.).

Dicey, A.V., An Introduction to the Study of the Law and the Constitution (10th Ed., London, 1967).

Dworkin, Ronald M., Taking Rights Seriously (London, 1977).

Friedenberg, Edgar Z., Laing (London, 1973).

Freud, Sigmund The Complete Psychological Works (J. Strachey Ed., London 1953-).

Freud, Sigmund The Pelican Freud Library (J. Strachey and A. Richards Ed., Harmondsworth, 1974-).

Fuller, Lon L., The Morality of Law (Revised Ed., New Haven, 1969).

Fuller, Lon L., "Positivism and Fidelity to Law - A Reply to Professor Hart" (1958) 71 Harvard Law Review, 630.

Giddens, Anthony Durkheim (Glasgow, 1978).

Gottlieb, Gidon The Logic of Choice (London, 1968).

Guest, A.G., (Ed.), Oxford Essays in Jurisprudence (Oxford, 1961).

Hacker P.M.S. and Raz, J. (Ed.), Law, Morality and Society: Essays in honour of H.L.A. Hart (Oxford, 1977).

Hare, R.M., Freedom and Reason (Oxford, 1963).
Hare, R.M., The Language of Morals (Oxford, 1952).
Hart, H.L.A., The Concept of Law (Oxford, 1961).
Hart, H.L.A., "Immorality and Treason" The Listener, 30 July 1959, pp. 162-3, reprinted in Dworkin, R.M. (Ed.), The Philosophy of Law (Oxford, 1977) pp. 83-8.
Hart, H.L.A., Law, Liberty and Morality (Oxford, 1963).
Hart, H.L.A., "Positivism and the Separation of Law and Morals" (1958) 71 Harvard Law Review, 593, reprinted in Dworkin, R.M. (Ed.), The Philosophy of Law (Oxford, 1977) pp. 17-37.
Hohfeld, W.W., Fundamental Legal Concepts (New Haven, 1923).
Hoebel, E. Adamson The Law of Primitive Man (Cambridge, Mass., 1954).
Jung, C.G., Collected Works (London, 1953-71).
Kelsen, H., General Theory of Law and State (New York, 1945).
Kelsen, H., The Pure Theory of Law (Berkeley, Calif., 1967).
Kenny, Anthony Wittgenstein (Harmondsworth, 1973).
Laing, R.D., The Divided Self (Harmondsworth, 1965).
Laing, R.D., Self and Others (Harmondsworth, 1971).
Leach, Edmund Culture and Communication (Cambridge, 1976).
Leach, Edmund Levi-Strauss (London, 1970).
Levi-Strauss, Claude "The Structural Study of Myth" in Levi-Strauss, Claude Structural Anthropology (Harmondsworth, 1968) pp. 206-31.
Lucas, J.R., The Principles of Politics (Oxford, 1966).
Lyons, John Chomsky (Glasgow, 1970).
Maine, Sir Henry Sumner Ancient Law (Pollock Ed., London, 1930).
Maine, Sir Henry Sumner Early Law and Custom (London, 1883).
Marshall, G., Constitutional Theory (Oxford, 1971).
Mill, J.S., On Liberty in Mill, J.S., Utilitarianism, Liberty and Representative Government (Everyman Library No. 482, London, 1910).
Mitchell, Basil Law, Morality and Religion in a Secular Society (Oxford, 1970).
O'Connor, D.J., Aquinas and Natural Law (London, 1967).
Olivecrona, Karl Law as Fact (2nd Ed., London, 1971).
Pears, David Wittgenstein (London, 1971).
Plamenatz, J.P., Consent, Freedom and Political Obligation (2nd Ed., Oxford, 1968).
Raz. J., The Concept of a Legal System (Oxford, 1970).
Ross, Alf On Law and Justice (London, 1958).

Ryle, Gilbert The Concept of Mind (Harmondsworth, 1963).

Simpson, A.W.B. (Ed.), Oxford Essays in Jurisprudence: Second Series (Oxford, 1973).

Singer, Peter Democracy and Disobedience (Oxford, 1973).

Stephen, Sir James Fitzjames Liberty Equality Fraternity (Cambridge, 1967).

Storr, Anthony Jung (London, 1973).

Summers, Robert S., (Ed.), Essays in Legal Philosophy (Oxford, 1968).

Summers, Robert S., (Ed.), More Essays in Legal Philosophy (Oxford, 1971).

Szasz, Thomas S., The Myth of Mental Illness (St. Albans, 1972).

Thomas, J.A.C., Textbook of Roman Law (Amsterdam, 1976).

Ullman, Walter Law and Politics in the Middle Ages (London, 1975).

Watson, Alan The Nature of Law (Edinburgh, 1977).

Wheare, K.C., Modern Constitutions (Oxford, 1960).

Wittgenstein, Ludwig The Blue and Brown Books (Oxford, 1953).

Wittgenstein, Ludwig Philosophical Investigations (2nd Ed., Oxford, 1958).

Wittgenstein, Lugwig Tractatus Logico - Philosophicus (trans. D.F. Pears and B.F. McGuinness, London, 1961).

Wollheim, Richard Freud (London, 1971).

INDEX

For cases and English statutes, see the tables on pp. x and xi.